Happiness, Growth

IZA Prize in Labor Economics Series

Since 2002, the Institute for the Study of Labor (IZA) has awarded the annual IZA Prize in Labor Economics for outstanding contributions to policy-relevant labor market research and methodological progress in this sub-discipline of economic science. The IZA Prize is the only international science prize awarded exclusively to labor economists. This special focus acknowledges the global significance of high-quality basic research in labor economics and sound policy advice based on these research findings. As issues of employment and unemployment are among the most urgent challenges of our time, labor economists have an important task and responsibility. The IZA Prize in Labor Economics is today considered one of the most prestigious international awards in the field. It aims to stimulate further research on topics that have enormous implications for our future. All prize-winners contribute a volume to the IZA Prize in Labor Economics Series published by Oxford University Press, which has been established to provide an overview of the laureates' most significant findings.

The IZA Prize in Labor Economics has become an integral part of the institute's manifold activities to promote progress in labor market research. Based on nominations submitted by the IZA Research Fellows, a high-ranking IZA Prize Committee selects the prize-winner. In conjunction with the Award Ceremony the IZA Prize Conference brings together a number of renowned experts to discuss topical labor market issues.

It is not by coincidence that the IZA Prize in Labor Economics Series is published by Oxford University Press. This well-reputed publishing house has shown a great interest in the project from the very beginning as this exclusive series perfectly complements their range of publications. We gratefully acknowledge their excellent cooperation.

Bonn, October 2009

1L. F. Jimmermann

Klaus F. Zimmermann, IZA Director

Winners of the IZA Prize in Labor Economics

2009   Richard A. Easterlin (University of Southern California)
2008   Richard Layard (London School of Economics)
        Stephen J. Nickell (Nuffield College)
2007   Richard B. Freeman (Harvard University)
2006   David Card (University of California, Berkeley)
        Alan B. Krueger (Princeton University)
2005   Dale T. Mortensen (Northwestern University)
        Christopher A. Pissarides (London School of Economics)
2004   Edward P. Lazear (Stanford University)
2003   Orley C. Ashenfelter (Princeton University)
2002   Jacob Mincer (Columbia University)

Richard A. Easterlin
2009 IZA Prize Laureate

Happiness, Growth, and the Life Cycle

Richard A. Easterlin

Edited by
Holger Hinte
Klaus F. Zimmermann

OXFORD
UNIVERSITY PRESS

OXFORD
UNIVERSITY PRESS

Great Clarendon Street, Oxford, OX2 6DP,
United Kingdom

Oxford University Press is a department of the University of Oxford.
It furthers the University's objective of excellence in research, scholarship,
and education by publishing worldwide. Oxford is a registered trade mark of
Oxford University Press in the UK and in certain other countries

Published in the United States of America by Oxford University Press
198 Madison Avenue, New York, NY 10016, United States of America

British Library Cataloguing in Publication Data
Data available

Library of Congress Cataloging in Publication Data
Data available

ISBN 978–0–19–959709–3 (Hbk.)
ISBN 978–0–19–877998–8 (Pbk.)

Award Statement
of the IZA Prize Committee

The IZA Prize in Labor Economics 2009 is awarded to Richard A. Easterlin (University of Southern California). In various seminal contributions, Easterlin has demonstrated the importance of material aspirations and relative economic status for human behavior. His work has laid the foundations for enlarging the scope of traditional economic analysis and has increased our understanding of behavior in several important domains, such as fertility choices, labor market behavior, or the determinants of individual well-being.

In two path breaking books – *Population, Labor Force, and Long Swings in Economic Growth (1968), Birth and Fortune (1980)* – and several influential papers, Richard Easterlin laid the ground for a novel view on the channels through which economic forces affect demographic magnitudes and are, in turn, affected by them. His central idea, the so-called "Easterlin Hypothesis" or cohort size hypothesis, posits that the economic and social fortunes of a cohort tend to vary inversely with its relative size.

According to Easterlin, this effect is caused by the material aspirations that a generation forms during adolescence, taking the economic outcomes of their parents as a benchmark of comparison. Members of a large birth cohort who grow up during a time of economic prosperity form high income aspirations for themselves. Compared to their expectations, such a cohort faces relatively bad prospects since crowding mechanisms in the family, the education system, and the labor market contribute to relatively lower economic success of the cohort: a larger birth cohort is likely to entail a higher number of siblings per family which in turn can lead to a dilution of parental time and family resources per child. Since the human and physical capital stock in the education system tends to be relatively inflexible, resources per student are also lower in larger birth cohorts. Both mechanisms contribute to a decrease in the quality of education for the cohort. Finally, the entry of a large cohort of young and inexperienced workers into the labor market tends to be accompanied with lower relative wages and higher unemployment rates. As a consequence, the cohort feels deprived compared to its aspiration level. In order to keep up with its aspirations, such a cohort is likely to exhibit lower birth rates than expected, breeding a smaller succeeding cohort with relatively low material aspirations. Richard Easterlin's findings have spurred the interest in the economic analysis of fertility and family decision-making. By integrating insights from demography, psychology, and sociology, the cohort size effect contributed to understanding phenomena such as long-term swings in fertility, but also swings in labor and goods market conditions.

Richard Easterlin also made pioneering contributions to the analysis of individual well-being. In his 1974 article *Does Economic Growth Improve the Human Lot?* he discovered what is now known as the "Easterlin Paradox": in cross-sectional analyses of subjective well-being within countries, people with higher income on average report higher levels of happiness. However, the relationship between income and subjective well-being does not hold in time series analyses, where it is usually found that countries which experience economic growth do not necessarily become "happier". Moreover, comparing well-being measures across countries, happiness does not vary much with national income once material wealth is sufficient to meet basic fundamental needs with respect to clothing, nutrition, or housing.

Again, Easterlin suggested that relative income concerns and aspiration processes are at the heart of this puzzling finding. Once basic needs are fulfilled, an increase in absolute income does not raise well-being anymore if it is not accompanied by an improvement of relative position within the society. At the same time, an increase in income tends to induce an adaptation of income and consumption aspirations. Easterlin's research on happiness has inspired many economists and other social scientists to systematically analyze the relationship between subjective well-being and socioeconomic characteristics such as marital status, health, employment status, or political institutions. The relevance of relative income concerns and material aspirations for economic behavior are now widely acknowledged. For instance they have contributed to a better understanding of female labor supply decisions and job search by the unemployed. Some of the most important theories that have recently been developed by "behavioral" economists, e.g., the theories on reference-dependent utility or inequity aversion, share the spirit of Easterlin's earlier work. Anticipating the potential of using psychological concepts for analyzing economic decision-making, Easterlin can thus be considered a pioneer of the ongoing integration of psychological motives into economic models of human behavior.

Easterlin's work has also shaped the political debate on how to measure societal development. Recently, several governments around the globe have launched initiatives to integrate insights from research on subjective well-being for assessing social prosperity instead of focusing only on a narrowly defined concept of national income. On a methodological dimension, Easterlin's careful use of survey techniques has increased economists' confidence in subjective measures as reliable tools for analyzing human preferences and decision-making. The recent developments in scholarly research – not least the more than 10,000 research papers listed in the "World Database of Happiness" – show that Easterlin's vision of regarding subjective and objective measures as complementary is increasingly coming true.

Apart from being one of the founding fathers of two important and growing fields of economic research, Richard Easterlin continues to be an extremely productive scholar himself. Over the last 50 years, he has published an impressive amount of articles in outlets such as American Economic Review, Quarterly Journal of Economics, Economic Journal, Proceedings of the National Academy of Sciences, Journal of Economic Behavior and Organization, and Journal of Economic History.

Richard Easterlin earned his Ph.D. in 1953 from the University of Pennsylvania and is currently professor of economics at the University of Southern California. He is Member of the National Academy of Sciences, a Distinguished Fellow of the American Economic Association, a Fellow of the American Academy of Arts and Sciences and the Econometric Society, and a former Guggenheim Fellow. Easterlin is past President of the Population Association of America and the Economic History Association. He served on the editorial board of journals such as American Economic Review, Journal of Economic Literature, Journal of Economic History, Journal of Population Economics, and Journal of Economic Behavior and Organization.

George A. Akerlof	University of California, Berkeley
Marco Caliendo	IZA
Richard Portes	London Business School; CEPR
Jan Svejnar	University of Michigan, Ann Arbor
Klaus F. Zimmermann	IZA; University of Bonn

Disclaimer

While every effort was made to contact the copyright holders of material in this book, for Table 1.1 we were unable to do so. If the copyright holders contact the author or publisher, we will be pleased to rectify any omission at the earliest opportunity.

*For my wife, my children,
and my grandchildren,
who make me very happy.*

Acknowledgments

I want to thank first Jacqueline Zweig who has patiently and professionally helped assemble and prepare the present manuscript. I also want to thank my co-authors who have kindly given their permission to publish our joint work in this volume: Laura Angelescu (Chapter 5), Enrico Marcelli (Chapter 8), Anke C. Plagnol (Chapter 9), and Onnicha Sawangfa (Chapters 3 and 10). The IZA Prize in Labor Economics made this volume possible, and for this I want to thank IZA Director Klaus F. Zimmermann and the other IZA Prize Committee members (George A. Akerlof, Marco Caliendo, Richard Portes, Jan Svejnar). I want to express my appreciation too to members of the IZA staff who have helped in many ways, and especially Holger Hinte.

Richard A. Easterlin

Contents

Contents

Contents

I

Shaping the Economics of Happiness: The Fundamental Contributions of Richard A. Easterlin

Holger Hinte and Klaus F. Zimmermann

Did it take a global economic and financial crisis to remind us that money and material wealth alone cannot make people happy? It almost seems that way. While countries around the world are dealing with the impact of the recent crisis, there have been increasing calls for alternative indicators of well-being, including happiness and life satisfaction as important criteria.

But this impression is misleading. A long-established subfield of economic science has provided in-depth analyses of the "economics of happiness and individual well-being," which increasingly take into account findings from behavioral economics. Widely regarded as the founding father of this discipline, Richard Easterlin has made a number of seminal contributions. His broad and innovative approach has had a profound impact on the entire research community and continues to be echoed in academic science and beyond.

The visibility of this research field and its pioneers has increased substantially in recent years. For instance, as shown by the Social Science Citation Index (SSCI), Easterlin's work is remarkably well cited, particularly in the recent past. Easterlin's fundamental 1995 article "Will Raising the Incomes of All Increase the Happiness of All?" in the Journal of Economic Behavior and Organization, to be found in revised form in this book, has been cited in scientific work on average 9 times per year between 1997 and 2004. Subsequently, the numbers went up dynamically to 26 citations in 2005 and peaked at 57 in 2008. Followed by 41 in 2009 the number of citations reached and additional 36 by October 2010; hence this influential paper has an impressive total of more than 270 citations so far. Other work by Richard Easterlin has experienced a similar rise in citations, particularly in journals with a high impact factor, which shows how influential Easterlin's work has been until this day.

The number of articles in this area has also grown fast and become increasingly diverse. Created a decade ago, the "World Database of Happiness" already contains more than 10,000 contributions to happiness research.[1] Innovative approaches to the relatively young field of behavioral economics are often strongly reminiscent of Easterlin's work, even if they arrive at different conclusions. The "economics of happiness" is also undergoing a dynamic development, which could hardly be imagined without the foundations laid by Richard Easterlin.

Overall, there is a strong and growing demand for deeper knowledge of the relationship between wealth and happiness. It is certainly no coincidence that this comes at a time when the limitations of the market model are becoming strikingly apparent in the light of climate change, fast structural change and an alarming North-South prosperity gap. For instance, the "Commission on the Measurement of Economic Performance and Social Progress" installed by the President of France in 2008 has been inspired to a large extent by Easterlin's work. As part of the Commission, a working group is dealing exclusively with issues of measuring quality of life beyond the established indicators of wealth.[2] In fact, several of the statements by the Commission could have been written by Easterlin himself:

> "Quality of life includes the full range of factors that make life worth living, including those that are not traded in markets and not captured by monetary measures. While some extensions of economic accounting allow including some additional elements that shape quality of life in conventional money-based measures of economic well-being, there are limits to the extent to which this can be achieved. Non-monetary indicators have an important role to play in measuring social progress, and recent advances in research have led to new and credible measures for at least some aspects of quality of life. These measures, while not replacing conventional economic indicators, provide an opportunity to enrich policy discussion and to inform people's view of the conditions of the communities where they live; today, they have the potential to move from research to standard statistical practice." (Stiglitz, Sen, Fitoussi et al. 2009, p. 216)

In its report, the Commission rightly emphasizes that sustainability and inequality should be more in the focus of and "that the time is ripe for our measurement to shift from measuring economic production to measuring people's well being."[3]

Against this background, the 2009 IZA Prize in Labor Economics is a long overdue honor for Richard Easterlin, whose original work has had a profound influence not only on today's research in economics but also on the recent policy debate on happiness. Running its own research programs on behavioral and personnel economics as well as on employment and development, the Institute for the Study of Labor feels a particularly close connection to Easterlin's work. An IZA Research Fellow for over ten years, Easterlin has published a number of influential IZA Discussion Papers. He also served since its beginning on the editorial board of the Journal of Population Economics, which is headquartered at IZA. Easterlin's impact on labor economics, which is the focus of IZA's activities, is indisputable. The relationship between well-being, social status, labor market status and income is a key determinant of such individual behavior as job search effort, female labor force participation, entrepreneurship or political activity. Moreover, Easterlin's relative income hypothesis of fertility is a core theory of population economics, a field that is closely associated with IZA's approach to labor economics.

In its Award Statement, the IZA Prize Committee emphasizes Easterlin's leading role in demonstrating the importance of material aspirations and relative economic status for human behavior.

> "His work has laid the foundations for enlarging the scope of traditional economic analysis and has increased our understanding of behavior in several important domains, such as fertility choices, labor market behavior, or the determinants of individual well-being. [...] His central idea – the so-called 'Easterlin Hypothesis' or cohort size hypothesis – posits that the economic and social fortunes of a cohort tend to vary inversely with its relative size. [...] Richard Easterlin's findings have spurred the interest in the economic analysis of fertility and family decision-making. By integrating insights from demography, psychology, and sociology, the cohort size effect contributed to understanding phenomena such as long-term swings in fertility, but also swings in labor and goods market conditions."

At least of equal importance is Easterlin's analysis of individual well-being. The "Easterlin Paradox" has become a household name for anyone involved in this field of research. While in cross-sectional analyses of subjective well-being within countries, people with higher income on average report higher levels of happiness, the relationship between income and subjective well-being does not hold in time series analyses: Countries which experience economic growth do not necessarily become "happier." At the same time, measuring across countries shows that happiness does not vary much with national income once material wealth is sufficient to meet basic fundamental needs.

These basic needs being fulfilled, an increase in absolute income does not further raise well-being if it is not accompanied by an improvement of relative position within the society. This paradox is of crucial relevance not only for the analysis of human behavior with respect to workplace motivation, incentives, and wages, but also for the study of social cohesion and welfare system reforms. If an increase in income tends to induce an adaptation of income and consumption aspirations, firm employment strategies as well as public policies cannot but calculate with such a rational paradox.

Based on Easterlin's findings, fundamental research has been done to explore the nexus between socioeconomic, health, and employment status, and individual well-being. There is a clear line from Richard Easterlin's inspiring work to the recent development of behavioral economics that aims at integrating psychology into economics. The international reputation of IZA in this area must to some extent be attributed to Easterlin as well.

Richard Easterlin considers himself a "reluctant economist." His work shows how effectively economics can be extended beyond its original realm, and that it is rightfully regarded as a social science. The 2009 IZA Prize laureate has managed throughout his career to transcend the borders of economics, thus broadening the horizon of the profession. The fact that economists, sociologists, psychologists and even neuroscientists are increasingly finding common ground and mutual benefits is a laudable trend that has been set by scientists like Richard Easterlin, according to his motto: "It is good to be an economist, it is better to be a social scientist."[4]

This volume provides an authentic account of a remarkable lifetime achievement. It contains a blend of Richard Easterlin's seminal papers. Newly arranged by the author and enriched with thoughtful introductions and an epilogue, the new volume is a must-read for anyone interested in a subfield of economics which is of great significance for shaping the future of the global society.

It will be interesting to witness how Easterlin's message continues to find its way into policymaking. The proposal of the above-mentioned "Commission on the Measurement of Economic Performance and Social Progress" to better integrate aspects of sustainability and subjective well-being into measures of wealth is no guarantee that this idea will actually be realized in practice. Achieving this would in fact be the ultimate triumph for the great pioneer in the economics of happiness – Richard A. Easterlin. He truly is the founding father of happiness research.

II

Growth and Happiness

Introduction

In 1970 I had the good fortune to be at the Center for Advanced Study in the Behavioral Sciences in Stanford, California, where economists have the opportunity to mix with scholars from other social sciences. It was a sociologist, I believe, who called my attention to public opinion surveys that occasionally include straightforward questions on personal happiness, such as "Taken all together, how would you say things are these days – would you say that you are very happy, pretty happy, or not too happy?"

As an economic historian trained under Simon Kuznets in the empirical study of economic growth, I was intrigued: Did modern economic growth bring about an increase in human happiness, as most economists firmly believed? My effort to answer this led to the paper comprising Chapter 1 of this book. The answer turned out to be paradoxical: At a point in time persons with higher income are, on average, happier than those with less; over time, however, as incomes increase generally in the course of modern economic growth, there is no improvement in the average level of happiness.

In the initial study the time series evidence for the paradox was for the United States only. The papers comprising the remainder of Part II reflect chiefly a progressive widening of the search to establish the empirical scope of the happiness-income paradox. Does it apply to other developed countries (Chapter 2)? To less-developed countries (Chapter 3)? To countries undergoing the transition from socialism to capitalism (Chapter 4)? This search reflects the gradual expansion of the happiness data base as new surveys, notably the Eurobarometer and World Values Surveys, came to provide time series of substantial length for analysis. It was also stimulated by the take off in the 1990s of economists' interest in empirical research on happiness, due in no small part to the work of Andrew Oswald and his collaborators. The answer to the empirical scope of the paradox, based on the evidence to date, is that it appears to hold in countries throughout the world, rich, poor, and transitional (Chapter 5).

Happiness does change, however, over the short term. Indeed, it is the failure to recognize the distinction between the shorter term association between happiness and income, which is positive, and the longer term relation, which is nil, that has led some analysts to question the happiness-income paradox. The initial finding of stability for the United States was, in fact, the outcome of a hill-shaped swing over a 25-year period in which happiness first rose, and then fell, returning at the end of the period to its initial level. Other researchers have found that happiness is positively associated with business cycle fluctuations in developed countries (Di Tella, MacCulloch and Oswald 2001). It is likely too that in developing countries there are fluctuations in happiness associated with short and long term movements in economic conditions. To date, however, the most dramatic evidence of sizable time series movements in happiness is found in the experience of the transition countries of central and eastern Europe, where a sharp collapse and recovery of economic output during the 1990s is accompanied by a similar swing in happiness (Chapter 4). Some analysts have pointed to the positive correlation of happiness and GDP per capita during the recovery period in these countries as contradicting the happiness-income paradox. This inference, however, fails to take adequate account of happiness prior to the recovery. When this is done, the contradiction no longer exists, and there is no significant long term trend in happiness accompanying the transition (Chapters 4 and 5).

How can we explain the happiness-income paradox? The key to the puzzle, I believe, lies in the interplay between a subjective variable, material aspirations, and an objective one, household income. At a point in time the dispersion among individuals in material aspirations is less than that in household income, and those with higher income are consequently better able to realize their aspirations, and are happier. Over time, however, material aspirations rise, on average, in about the same proportion as average income and undercut the increase in happiness that higher income would otherwise bring (see Chapters 2 and 5, and also Chapter 6 in Part III). Empirical research relating directly to aspirations is surprisingly hard to come by, not only in economics but other social sciences as well. (Important exceptions in happiness economics are the works of van Praag [see van Praag and Frijters 1999 for a good survey] and Stutzer [2004]). Some direct evidence on aspirations is given here in Chapters 1 and 2 and also in Part III (Chapters 6 and 9). One hopes that in the future, serious empirical research will be directed toward the explicit empirical study of aspirations, rather than the common practice currently of inferring aspirations from a theoretical model.

How can one reconcile the positive short term association between happiness and income with the absence of a long term relationship? The answer suggested in Chapter 5 is that there is an asymmetric response of happiness to income, reflecting the psychological phenomenon of "loss aversion." People adapt hedonically to an increase in income, their material aspirations tending to rise commensurately with income. But material aspirations are much less flexible downward, because once people have attained a given level of income, they cling to this reference point.

Why, despite the marked improvement in the flow of goods and services, has happiness failed to improve in the transition from socialism to capitalism? Evidence presented in Chapter 4 points to the widespread deterioration during the transition of personal security in regard to concerns other than material goods, such as jobs, health, and child care. Clearly this is an issue of substantial policy interest, but it is unlikely that we shall learn from these countries' experience under socialism so long as that experience, in contrast to the transition itself, remains a closed book to contemporary economic research.

In the present volume, concepts such as happiness, life satisfaction, net affect, and the like, are used interchangeably. There is ample research, especially in psychology, demonstrating that these concepts, though related, do not mean exactly the same thing. The problem of variant measures is not peculiar to happiness research; it applies equally to many concepts, such as poverty or unemployment in economics. My interest here is not in what is the correct measure of happiness. The pertinent question is whether different concepts yield substantially different pictures of change over time. A study about two decades ago by the U.S. Bureau of the Census (1992, p. xvii), for example, identified 15 measures of poverty, ranging in value in 1991 from a low of around 10 percent to more than twice that amount. But the picture of change given by these measures, year-to-year or over longer intervals, was remarkably consistent, e.g., over the longest period, 1979 to 1991, the percentage point increase in the poverty rate was between 2.2 and 2.7 points. The choice on the issue of the "best" definition of poverty made virtually no difference for the answer to whether poverty increased or decreased, and by how much. Little has been done to study different concepts of subjective well-being with regard to their consistency in indicating change over time. In comparisons of fairly reliable data attempted here, different measures of subjective well-being were found to move in strikingly similar ways (Chapter 3).

An important lesson of the happiness-income paradox is that point-of-time (cross-sectional) data are a questionable basis for inferring change over time. The positive cross-sectional relation of happiness and income that prevails both within and among countries is not reproduced in time series (Chapters 3, 5; Easterlin 2005a). Yet most generalizations about happiness, whether in economics, psychology, or other social sciences, are based on point-of-time data.

The preference for cross-sectional analysis is no doubt due in part to the readier availability of data for a single year than a succession of years. Moreover, time series data of the type used here have their own special problems, and little research is available to guide the analyst on how to deal with these problems systematically. Among the difficulties that have surfaced in the present research is that the happiness question or response categories may change from one time to another, and alter the answers given. When we know this to be the case here, we pool the data and use dummy variables for the segments with differing questions. The value of these dummy variables measures the average shift in response level attributable to a changed survey question or response option. Even if the happiness question itself remains the same, however, the predecessor question may change, and the change sometimes alters the subsequent response to the happiness question. One solution to this problem is to focus on happiness observations for the years in which the predecessor question is constant, a procedure used here in Chapter 5 in the analysis of the Eurobarometer surveys. Another problem, often encountered in World Values Surveys of developing countries, is that the geographic coverage of the surveys changes over time. When possible, we try to minimize the effect of such shifts by constructing series that cover the same population at different dates. Occasionally, a survey will include questions on different measures of subjective well-being, such as happiness, life satisfaction and/or financial satisfaction that make it possible for us to test the consistency of the time series movement of these measures. Or, different survey organizations may conduct separate surveys relating to the same measure, enabling us to examine the consistency of the time series results from different sources.

There has been a welcome development of interest in panel surveys that follow the same individuals over time. Panel surveys involve significant additional problems due to sample attrition and the incorporation of "refreshment" populations (Easterlin and Plagnol 2008, Appendix B), but they are not studied here simply for lack of data.

This Introduction has so far focused on the chapters that follow – findings, interpretation, concepts, methodology – and implicitly assumed an acceptance of measures of subjective well-being. But these measures are fairly new and concerns invariably arise about their meaningfulness. These concerns may be fairly general in nature or quite specific.

Some economists, for example, simply dismiss all subjective testimony of the kind collected in public opinion surveys, insisting that "what people *do* is more relevant than what people say" (Fuchs 1983, p. 14, emphasis in original). This belief has led to a distinction between "hard data", such as output or employment statistics, and "soft data" of the type collected in public opinion surveys. In a 2007 book review, for example, a Nobel Laureate states flatly "Being an economist, in this review I focus on the authors' sizable collection of hard statistics, not opinion polls" (Prescott 2007, p. F648).

The fact is that with regard to the supposedly "hard" data on the nation's output, issues of scope, netness, and valuation, so repeatedly stressed by the founding father of modern national income measurement, Simon Kuznets, have never been resolved, other than by convention (Kuznets, Epstein, and Jenks 1941, Kuznets 1948). And if measures such as the inflation and unemployment rates are "hard data", why, over the years, has there been a succession of governmental committees formed to examine, assess, and revise these measures? As noted above, a government publication on the "poverty rate," gives 15 variants of the measure. Hard data? Economists have so much come to live with the imperfect data central to most of their work, that they disregard the possible biases in these data or even forget about them.

But when less familiar data such as public opinion surveys are employed, economists are quick to note their shortcomings and dismiss the data as "soft", a euphemism for "meaningless," and a convenient way of avoiding findings undermining long held beliefs.

The truth, of course, is that no data conform to the conceptual ideal, and it is the task of disciplinary specialists to study and evaluate each piece of data potentially relevant to the problem at hand. The parent disciplines responsible for public opinion surveys, especially sociology and psychology, have developed a substantial methodological literature on data problems and their solutions. This literature, like that in economics on data problems, can be read either with a view to finding excuses to dismiss these data (Bertrand and Mullainathan 2001), or for helpful guidance on how the data may be intelligently used. One hopes that in time the artificial distinction between "hard" and "soft" data will disappear, and the recognition prevail that the operative research question is whether the biases in the data being used are likely to distort seriously the conclusions.

In contrast to the views of some economists, many psychologists are especially interested in what people say. This has led them to scrutinize intensely such data, and particularly self-reported data on subjective well-being such as those used in this volume.

There is the question for example, whether the self-reports of an individual are highly variable from day to day depending on one's momentary mood. The answer appears to be no; surveys following the same individuals over several months reveal a substantial consistency in self-reports, suggesting that the subjective well-being question is tapping a fairly stable feeling.

But are people truthfully reporting their feelings of well-being – is one really getting at concepts such as happiness? The answer appears to be yes. When other persons – a spouse, family members, relatives, friends, professional therapists – are asked to evaluate the psychological well-being of a survey respondent, there is substantial consistency between the evaluations of outside observers and self-reports. Also, measures of stress, studies of brain waves, and of facial expressions prove to be consistent with self-reports.

Are self-reports of different persons comparable – even if each person is truthfully reporting a basic feeling of well-being that is highly stable day to day, doesn't the meaning of happiness differ from person to person? It is true that when the question on happiness is posed, no guidelines are presented on the meaning of happiness, and each respondent is free to answer in terms of her or his particular concept. However, when respondents are asked what things make them happy, there is a high degree of consistency in their answers as to the sources of happiness. The circumstances cited most often are material living levels, family relationships, health, and work. Indeed, in countries throughout the world, these conditions are named by most people as most important for their happiness (Chapter 1; Easterlin 2000, p. 9, Table 1). That this consistency exists in the sources of well-being is, on reflection, not wholly surprising. The circumstances that are most important for happiness are those that take up most of the time in people's lives everywhere, and over which they usually feel they have some control. This suggests that the standards by which most people evaluate their well-being are fairly similar, and consequently the responses for groups of people, if not individuals, are reasonably comparable. Empirical support for this conclusion is provided by the highly consistent results across numerous countries found in microeconomic happiness equations (Oswald 1997; Blanchflower 2009).

In Parts II and III that follow, I have revised the original papers to eliminate repetition and to smooth transitions, leaving the substance of the paper unchanged. The exception is the original paper on happiness (Chapter 1) which, two small changes aside, remains the same as when it was first published.

1

Does Economic Growth Improve the Human Lot? Some Empirical Evidence

In 1959, Moses Abramovitz published an essay, "The Welfare Interpretation of National Income and Product," in which he concluded that "we must be highly skeptical of the view that long term changes in the rate of growth of welfare can be gauged even roughly from changes in the rate of growth of output,"[1] and called for "further thought about the meaning of secular changes in the rate of growth of national income and empirical studies that can fortify and lend substance to analysis."[2]

This paper is offered in the spirit of this little-heeded call. It brings together the results of surveys of human happiness that have been conducted in nineteen countries, developed and less-developed, during the period since World War II, to see what evidence there is of an association between income and happiness. Are the wealthy members of society usually happier than the poor? What of rich versus poor countries – are the more developed nations typically happier? As a country's income grows during the course of economic development, does human

This chapter is a revised version of: Easterlin, R. (1974). Does Economic Growth Improve the Human Lot?, in: David, P. A., Reder, M. W. (Eds.), Nations and Households in Economic Growth. Essays in Honor of Moses Abramovitz, New York, 89-125, reprinted with permission from Elsevier. The original paper was made possible by the opportunities and facilities offered by the Center for Advanced Study in the Behavioral Sciences, Stanford, California, where I was a Fellow in 1970–1971. It is not possible to acknowledge all those from whom I benefitted while at the Center, but special appreciation must be expressed to Elliot Aronson, Leonard Berkowitz, David Krantz, William H. Kruskal, Amos Tversky, and Stanton Wheeler. I am also grateful to Jack Meyer for statistical assistance. This research was partially supported by NSF grant GS-1563. A first draft of the paper was circulated during the academic year 1971–1972, and elicited many valuable and instructive reactions. It has been possible to take account of only a few comments in this revision, and for these I am especially grateful to Paul A. David, Stefano Fenoaltea, Henry A. Gemery, J. Robert Hanson, Alex Inkeles, John C. Lambelet, and Melvin W. Reder.

happiness advance – does economic growth improve the human lot?

Happiness is not confined, of course, to economic well-being. Abramovitz noted that "since Pigou … economists have generally distinguished between social welfare, or welfare at large, and the narrower concept of economic welfare," with "national product … taken to be the objective, measurable counterpart of economic welfare" [p. 3]. Happiness corresponds to the broader of these two concepts, that of social welfare, or welfare at large. However, as Abramovitz points out, economists have normally disregarded possible divergences between the two welfare concepts, and operated on Pigou's dictum "that there is a clear presumption that changes in economic welfare indicate changes in social welfare in the same direction, if not in the same degree" (p. 3). It is this dictum, as applied to the study of economic growth, that is the central concern of this paper. Is there evidence that economic growth is positively associated with social welfare, i.e., human happiness?

The term "happiness" is used intermittently, albeit loosely, in the literature of economics.[3] To my knowledge, however, this is the first attempt to look at the actual evidence. The initial section of this paper is devoted to a somewhat lengthy discussion of the concept and measurement of happiness, as the term is used in this study. The second section presents the results of the empirical analysis, and the third, an interpretation of the findings. The conclusions, in brief, are that the evidence supports Abramovitz's skepticism of a positive correlation between output and welfare, and for a good reason. The increase in output itself makes for an escalation in human aspirations, and thus negates the expected positive impact on welfare.

1.1. The Concept and Measurement of Happiness

1.1.1. Concept

The basic data used here are statements by individuals on their subjective happiness. These self-reports are sometimes designated "avowed" or "reported" happiness to underscore the possibility that they may not accurately reflect the true state of the respondents' feelings. This possibility will be examined shortly.

The data are of two types. The first consists of the responses to a Gallup-poll-type survey in which a direct question of the following sort was asked: "In general, how happy would you say that you are

– very happy, fairly happy, or not very happy?" Sometimes this was preceded by a question asking the respondent to state "in your own words, what the word 'happiness' means to you."

The other set of data comes from a more sophisticated procedure, devised by Cantril (1965) in a pioneering study of the hopes, fears, and happiness of persons in 14 countries of the world. Since Cantril's study figures prominently in the following analysis, it is worth quoting him at some length. He starts with a general description of the technique he calls the "Self-Anchoring Striving Scale":

> "A person is asked to define on the basis of his own assumptions, perceptions, goals, and values the two examples or anchoring points of the spectrum on which some scale measurement is desired – for example, he may be asked to define the 'top' and 'bottom', the 'good' and 'bad', the 'best' and the 'worst'. This self-defined continuum is then used as our measuring device.
>
> While the Self-Anchoring Striving Scale technique can be used on a wide variety of problems, it was utilized in this study as a means of discovering the spectrum of values a person is preoccupied or concerned with and by means of which he evaluates his own life. He describes as the top anchoring point his wishes and hopes as he personally conceives them and the realization of which would constitute for him the best possible life. At the other extreme, he describes the worries and fears, the preoccupations and frustrations, embodied in his conception of the worst possible life he could imagine. Then, utilizing a nonverbal ladder device [showing a scale from 0 to 10), symbolic of 'the ladder of life', he is asked where he thinks he stands on the ladder today, with the top being the best life as he has defined it, the bottom the worst life as he has defined it. ...
>
> The actual questions, together with the parenthetical instructions to interviewers, are given below:
>
> (A) All of us want certain things out of life. When you think about what really matters in your own life, what are your wishes and hopes for the future? In other words, if you imagine your future in the best possible light, what would your life look like then, if you are to be happy? Take your time in answering; such things aren't easy to put into words.
> PERMISSIBLE PROBES: What are your hopes for the future? What would your life have to be like for you to be completely happy? What is missing for you to be happy? [Use also, if necessary, the words 'dreams' and 'desires'.).
> OBLIGATORY PROBE: Anything else?
>
> (B) Now, taking the other side of the picture, what are your fears and worries about the future? In other words, if you imagine your future in the worst possible light, what would your life look like then? Again, take your time in answering.

> PERMISSIBLE PROBE: What would make you unhappy? [Stress the words 'fears' and 'worries'.)
> OBLIGATORY PROBE: Anything else?
> Here is a picture of a ladder. Suppose we say that the top of the ladder (POINTING) represents the best possible life for you and the bottom (POINTING) represents the worst possible life for you.
>
> (C) Where on the ladder (MOVING FINGER RAPIDLY UP AND DOWN LADDER) do you feel you personally stand at the present time? Step number." (pp. 22–23; italics in original)

This technique thus yields a rating by each individual of his personal standing on a scale from 0 (the worst possible life) to 10 (the best possible life), where "worst" and "best" are defined by each person for himself. The survey also asked for current evaluations of past and prospective personal standings, plus a similar set of evaluations by each individual of the situation of the nation as a whole. In the present analysis, use will be made only of the rating by each individual of his personal happiness at the time of the survey, since this is relevant to subjective well-being, and reports on one's feelings at the moment are likely to be more accurate than those on how one might feel or did feel in other situations.

Although the procedures differ in the Gallup poll and Cantril approaches, the concept of happiness underlying them is essentially the same. Reliance is placed on the subjective evaluation of the respondent – in effect, each individual is considered to be the best judge of his own feelings. He is seen as having a frame of reference that defines for him the range from unhappy to happy states of mind. His summary response – whether in terms of broad categories of happiness, as in the Gallup poll, or in terms of a numerical rating from 0 to 10, as in Cantril's approach – is a statement of his present position within that frame of reference.

The approach has a certain amount of appeal. If one is interested in how happy people are – in their subjective satisfaction – why not let each person set his own standard and decide how closely he approaches it? The alternatives of obtaining evaluations by outside observers or seeking to use objective indicators of happiness inevitably run into the problem of what observers or what indicators one should rely on. Moreover, despite the use of ratings based on a scale that varies from one individual to the next, it is possible to make meaningful comparisons. For example, consider two population groups. These might be two segments of a national population at a given time, say rich and poor, or the populations of an entire country at two different times, or the populations of two different countries at a given time. Whatever the case, it is of interest to ask whether on the average individuals in the first population differ significantly from those in the second in how high they rate themselves in terms of personal happiness, even though the scale being applied differs within each population and between the two. After all, in opinion surveys on the relative merit, say, of presidential aspirants, the criteria used by respondents in forming their evaluations doubtless differ. Indeed, it is of interest to ask whether there are systematic differences in the criteria used for the evaluations (a point we shall look into later). It may be argued, of course, that political opinion polls are of value because of their implications for prospective behavior of the respondents. But perhaps the same may be said of opinions on personal happiness – might not individuals with a low personal happiness rating be expected to behave differently from those with a high personal rating?

At the same time, a number of reservations on the meaningfulness of the data come to mind. There is first the question of the relevance of the happiness concept to populations differing widely in cultural characteristics. It is true that the present approach allows each individual to define his own standard of happiness. But is the idea itself present in all cultures? One indication that it is is the observation by Inkeles (1960) that happiness, in contrast to certain other concepts relating to emotional states, "may be translated fairly well from one language to another ..." (p. 15). Cantril (1965) devoted considerable effort to this translation issue:

> "One of the problems that had to be overcome was translating the original questions from English into the various languages used. In some cases this was by no means an easy task, and considerable time was spent with experts to be sure the translation contained the precise nuances wanted. One of the methods often utilized in this translation process was to have someone who knew the native language, as a native, for example, an Arab, and who also was completely fluent in English translate our questions into Arabic. Then someone whose native language was English but who had a perfect command of Arabic would translate the Arabic back into English so a comparison could be made with the original question and, through discussion and further comparisons, difficulties could be ironed out.
>
> Translations from English had to be made into the following twenty-six other languages which we list here alphabetically: Arabic, Bengali, Cebuano, German, Gujarati, Hausa, Hebrew, Hindi, Ibo, Ilocano, Ilongo, Malayalam, Marathi, Oriya, Polish, Portuguese, Serbo-Croatian, Slovenian, Spanish, Tagalog, Tamil, Telugu, Urdu, Waray, Yiddish, and Yoruba." (p. 26)

Apparently the effort paid off, for the non-response rate was generally low. To judge from this experience, happiness is an idea that transcends individual cultures.

Moreover, the considerations affecting personal happiness in different cultures turn out to be quite similar. In his survey, Cantril found that typically certain hopes and fears were more frequently expressed than others. Here, for example, is a tabulation he prepared of the things mentioned most frequently by Americans in discussing their hopes, and the proportion of the sample mentioning each item (Cantril 1965, p. 35):

Own health	40%
Decent standard of living	33
Children	29
Housing	24
Happy family	18
Family health	16
Leisure time	11
Keep status quo	11
Old age	10
Peace	9
Resolution of religious problems	8
Working conditions	7
Family responsibility	7
To be accepted	6
An improved standard of living	5
Employment	5
Attain emotional maturity	5
Modern conveniences	5

To facilitate handling such data, Cantril (1965, p. 36) further classified the items listed above into nine "general" categories of personal hopes:

Economic	65%
Health	48
Family	47
Personal values	20
Status quo	11
Job or work situation	10
International situation, world	10
Social values	5
Political	2

Table 1.1

Personal Hopes by Country, ca. 1960 [a,b]

Country	Economic	Family	Health	Values and character	Job/work	Social	International	Political	Status quo	Total
Brazil	68	28	34	14	8	1	1	-	1	115
Cuba	73	52	47	30	14	4	3	15	1	239
Dominican Republic	95	39	17	15	25	2	-	9	-	202
Egypt	70	53	24	39	42	9	2	4	-	243
India	70	39	4	14	22	8	-	-	2	159
Israel	80	76	47	29	35	10	12	2	4	295
Nigeria	90	76	45	42	19	14	-	-	-	286
Panama	90	53	43	26	26	3	-	1	1	243
Philippines	60	52	6	9	11	5	-	-	-	143
United States	65	47	48	20	10	5	10	2	11	218
West Germany	85	27	46	11	10	3	15	1	4	202
Yugoslavia	83	60	41	18	20	4	8	-	2	236

[a] From Patterns of Human Concerns by Hadley Cantril, Rutgers University Press, New Brunswick, New Jersey (1965).
[b] Percentage of population mentioning hopes that fall in indicated category. Sum of percentages exceeds 100 percent because some respondents mention hopes falling in more than one category.

Hopes relating to economic matters appear to be foremost in the minds of Americans, but clearly do not exhaust the content of happiness.

Similar classification of the replies for other countries enabled Cantril to compare the personal hopes of people in widely differing national and cultural circumstances (Table 1.1). What stands out is that hopes regarding economic, family, and health matters repeatedly dominate the perceptions of happiness by individuals in the various countries, with economic concerns typically the most frequently mentioned.

Needless to say, the specific nature of these concerns often differs (some evidence on this regarding economic aspirations is presented toward the end of this essay), and there are undoubtedly variations among people within countries as well. If one looks at a like tabulation for personal fears rather than hopes, a similarity among countries again appears, though the relative importance of the categories changes somewhat (e.g., typically health increases in relative importance). On reflection, the similarity in the results for different countries is plausible. In all cultures the way in which the bulk of the people spend most of their time is similar – in working and trying to provide for and raise a family. Hence the concerns that they express when asked about happiness are similar.

1.1.2. Measurement Problems

Let us turn to some technical issues regarding the data. For one thing, there is the question of the stability of the replies. Are emotional states so highly variable that the replies to questions about personal happiness tend to fluctuate widely over short periods of time, with the ups and downs of daily life? This problem has been studied by comparing the results of surveys of the same population run at short intervals. The conclusion, reported by Robinson and Shaver (1969, p. 17), is that "[o]ne of the most impressive features of the questions ... is the stable test–retest reliabilities they exhibit." This result is confirmed by the data used here. Two surveys by the American Institute of Public Opinion (AIPO) containing a happiness question were taken within two weeks of each other in September 1956. The results were virtually identical. A third poll taken six months later still showed very little change (see Table 1.8 below).

Another important issue is the validity of self-reports on happiness. Are people capable of assessing their own emotional states? One test, though hardly a definitive one, is to examine the consistency of self-reports with evaluations by outside judges – peers, professional psychologists, and so on. The results of such tests are summarized as follows by Wilson (1967):

> "Data from these several studies suggest that judges agree poorly among themselves, that judges vary in the extent to which they agree with self-ratings, and that few judges agree closely with self-ratings. At the same time, the data show that most judges agree with self-ratings to some extent and that the pooling of judges' estimates increases the agreement with self-ratings. These facts would seem, if anything, to support the validity of self-ratings." (p. 295)

Comparisons have also been made between self-reports on happiness and measures presumed to be indicative of happiness, e.g., indicators of physical health, and between self-reports on happiness and measures of other psychological states such as depression and self-esteem (Bradburn 1969, p. 39; Robinson and Shaver 1969, pp. 26–31). In both cases the self-reports show significant correlations with the other measures of the type expected. In all of these comparisons, there is inevitably the question of what is to be taken as the ultimate arbiter of "happiness." Perhaps the most that can be said is that the general consistency of self-reports with the other bases of evaluation bolsters one's confidence in the ability of people to assess with some validity their own feelings.

The result bears also on another issue – whether a person is likely to report his true feelings to an anonymous interviewer. The fact that the self-reports check out fairly well with other bases of evaluation suggests that the replies are reasonably honest. Indeed, in view of the considerable success in obtaining reports on such matters of intimate concern as personal income and sex, it might be felt that there would be no serious problem in getting people to state how happy they are. However, one possibly important source of bias exists. In formulating replies to survey questions, respondents are influenced by considerations of what they believe to be the proper or socially desirable response (Davis 1965).[4] Thus, if the social norm is that happiness is a good thing, there might be a tendency toward an upward bias in the replies due to considerations of social desirability.

Again, there have been attempts to test for this factor. Comparisons have been made between replies given to an interviewer and the responses on a self-administered questionnaire, the presumption being that one is likely to be more honest in the latter situation. Also, correlations have been run between people's statements of their happiness and their tendencies toward social conformity, as measured by standard psychological tests. Sometimes the tests suggest some influence of social desirability in the replies; sometimes they do not (Bradburn 1969, p. 38; Wilson 1967, p. 295).

Of course, if all responses were similarly biased, there would be no real problem for the present study. The concern here is with the relation of happiness to income, and the real question is whether there may be differential bias in the replies by income level. Is it likely, for example, that rich people would feel that they were expected to reply that they are "very happy," and conversely for poor people? On reflection it is not wholly certain what reply people might think was expected of them. While most respondents might feel that the social norm is that "money makes one happy," there is the possibility that others would be influenced by the notion of the "carefree, happy poor." The expected bias in the replies would clearly be different depending on which is perceived as the social norm. Beyond this there is the question of the universality of the norm. Has "the" norm been the same in the United States since 1946, or has it perhaps been altered by public attention in the 1960s to the "poverty problem"? Is the norm the same in 19 different countries ranging over the various continents of the world?

It is also pertinent to consider the context in which the happiness question is asked. If one were asked his income and then, immediately following, how happy he was, the respondent might link the two questions, and his awareness of a social norm might bias his reply. In the Gallup poll surveys used here, however, the happiness question is intermixed with 50 or more survey questions, most of which deal with current events, usually political. The question on economic status comes at the end of these surveys along with other inquiries as to personal characteristics. Under these circumstances, the respondent, in formulating his reply to the happiness question, is not likely to feel the interviewer is regarding him as a "rich person" or as "a poor person" and to answer the way he thinks such a person "ought" to answer. The Cantril survey is specifically focused on people's feelings – their hopes, fears, and how happy they are. Even in this case, however, the question on economic status comes at the end of the survey. It is far from clear that in considering questions a respondent would feel himself especially cast in the role, say, of a poor person, as distinct from that of one who is young or married or has any one of a number of other personal characteristics.

Finally, it is instructive to note the effect of variations in the wording of the happiness question. The National Opinion Research Center (NORC) has asked a question similar to that in the AIPO surveys, but the happiness categories differ as follows:

	(1)	(2)	(3)
AIPO	Very happy	Fairly happy	Not very happy
NORC	Very happy	Pretty happy	Not too happy

The first and third categories are virtually alike. It seems reasonable to suppose, however, that many individuals would consider the NORC's rating (2), "pretty happy," closer to (1) and farther from (3) than the AIPO's rating "fairly happy." Hence, one might expect that some respondents who chose category (1) in the AIPO poll would have chosen (2) in the NORC poll, and some who chose (2) in the AIPO poll would have chosen (3) in the NORC poll. The results of polls taken at similar dates confirm this expectation – the percentage in group (1) tends to run lower and the percentage in group (3) runs higher in the NORC polls (see Table 1.8, panels A and B). Moreover, a shift of this type is common to all income classes, with no systematic difference in magnitude.[5] The direction of the shift and the consistency by income level suggest that respondents throughout the population are placing similar interpretations on the question asked and are answering, at least to some extent, in terms of their real feelings.

However, when all is said and done, the possibility of differential bias in the replies by income level cannot be ruled out, though the magnitude remains uncertain, and this qualification must be borne in mind in interpreting the findings presented here. My own feeling is that while such bias may exist, it is not significant enough to invalidate the conclusions on the association between income and happiness. Perhaps the most important basis for this judgment is the impressive consistency of the results in a variety of times and places under widely differing cultural and socioeconomic circumstances.

1.2. The Evidence

1.2.1. Within-Country Comparisons

Does greater happiness go with higher income? Let us look first at the comparative status of income groups within a country at a given time.

Table 1.2 presents the data from the most recent survey of the American population, conducted in December 1970. Of those in the lowest income group, not much more than a fourth report that they are "very happy." In the highest income group the proportion very happy is almost twice as great. In successive income groups from low to high the proportion very happy rises steadily. There is a clear indication here that income and happiness are positively associated.

How typical is this result? Tables 1.3–1.5 summarize the results of 29 additional surveys. Sixteen of these surveys are of the Gallup-poll type; 13, of the Cantril type. Ten of the surveys relate to the United States between 1946 and 1966; 19 to other countries, including 11 in Asia, Africa, and Latin America. The classifications by socioeconomic status tend to differ among the surveys and are typically broad and nonnumerical, consisting of designations such as "poor," "wealthy," "lower class," and "upper class." But the results are clear and unequivocal. In every single survey, those in the highest status group were happier, on the average, than those in the lowest status group.

This finding is corroborated by the results of other studies of happiness and related emotional states. In an article published 10 years ago, Inkeles (1960) concluded:

> "Those who are economically well off, those with more education or whose jobs require more training and skill, more often report themselves happy, joyous, laughing, free of sorrow, satisfied with life's progress. Even though the pattern is weak or ambiguous in some cases, there has not been a single case of a *reversal* of the pattern, that is, a case where measures of happiness are inversely related to measures of status, in studies involving fifteen different countries – at least six of which were studied on two different occasions, through the use of somewhat different questions. There is, then, good reason to challenge the image of the 'carefree but happy poor'." (p. 17; italics in original)

Similar conclusions are reached by Bradburn (1969), Robinson and Shaver (1969), Wilson (1967), and Gurin, Veroff and Feld (1960). In a comprehensive study surveying the literature on mental health, Davis (1965, p. 68) reported that "study after study shows that mental health is positively related to socioeconomic status in a variety of measures of mental health and SES."

Table 1.2

Percentage Distribution of Population by Happiness, by Size of Income, United States, 1970[a,b]

Income (in $1000)	(1) Very happy	(2) Fairly happy	(3) Not very happy	(4) No answer
All classes	43	48	6	3
15+	56	37	4	3
10-15	49	46	3	2
7-10	47	46	5	2
5-7	38	52	7	3
3-5	33	54	7	6
Under 3	29	55	13	3

[a] Data from AIPO Poll of December 1970.
[b] $N = 1517$

Table 1.3

Percentage Not Very Happy in Lowest and Highest Status Groups, United States, 1946–1970[a]

Date	Number of groups	Lowest status group Designation	N.V.H. (%)	Highest status group Designation	N.V.H. (%)	N
Apr. 1946	4	Poor	11	Wealthy	3	3151
June 1947	4	Poor	9	Wealthy	0	3088
Dec. 1947	4	Poor	12	Wealthy	3	1434
May 1948	4	Poor	10	Wealthy	0	1800
Aug. 1948	4	Poor	15	Wealthy	4	1596
Nov. 1952	3	Poor	12	Average +	8	3003
Jan. 1960	3	Low income	6	Upper income	2	2582
July 1963	6	Income < $3000	10	Income = $15,000 +	0	3668
Oct. 1966	6	Income < $3001	6	Income = $15,000 +	0.3	3531
Dec. 1970	6	Income < $3002	13	Income = $15,000 +	4	1517

[a] Data from Table 1.2 and AIPO polls 369, 399, 410, 418, 425, 508, 623, 675, and 735. In No. 623 (Jan. 60), the responses were on a scale ranging from -5 to +5. For the present purpose, all negative values were classified as "not very happy (N.V.H.)." Comparisons among surveys are of uncertain reliability because of variations in the specific question asked and in the group designations.

Table 1.4

Percentage Not Very Happy in Lowest and Highest Status Groups, Seven Countries, 1965[a]

Country	Number of groups	Lowest status group Designation	N.V.H.[b] (%)	Highest status group Designation	N.V.H.[b] (%)	N
Great Britain	3	Very poor	19	Upper, upper middle, middle	4	1179
West Germany	3	Lower middle, lower	19	Upper, upper middle	7	1255
Thailand	2	Lower/middle	15	Middle/upper	6	500
Philippines	2	Lower middle, lower	15	Upper, upper middle	5	500
Malaysia	2	Lower/middle	20	Middle/upper	10	502
France	3	Lower	27	Upper	6	1228
Italy	3	Lower middle, lower	42	Upper, upper middle	10	1166

[a] Data from World Survey III 1965.
[b] Not very happy

25

Table 1.5

Personal Happiness Rating in Lowest and Highest Status Groups, Thirteen Countries, ca. 1960 [a,b]

	(1)	(2)	(3) Lowest status group	(4)	(5) Highest status group	(6)	(7) Difference, high minus low [(6)-(4)]	(8)
Country	Date	Number of groups	Designation	Rating	Designation	Rating		N
United States	Aug. 1959	5	Lower economic	6.0	Upper economic	7.1	1.1	1549
Cuba	Apr.-May 1960	3	Lower socioeconomic	6.2	High, upper middle socioeconomic	6.7	0.5	992
Israel	Nov. 1961-June 1962	3	Lower income	4.0	Upper income	6.5	2.5	1170
West Germany	Sept.1957	3	Lower economic	4.9	Upper economic	6.2	1.3	480
Japan	Fall 1962	3	Lower, middle lower socioeconomic	4.3	Upper, upper middle socioeconomic	5.8	1.5	972
Yugoslavia	Spring 1962	4	Lower, farmer	4.3	Upper, nonfarmer	6.0	1.7	1523
Philippines	Spring 1959	4	Lower economic	4.1	Upper economic	6.2	2.1	500
Panama	Jan.-Mar.1962	2	Lower socioeconomic	4.3	Upper socioeconomic	6.0	1.7	642
Nigeria	Sept. 1962-spring 1963	2	Lower socioeconomic	4.7	Upper socioeconomic	5.8	1.1	1200
Brazil	Late 1960-early 1961	5	Lower socioeconomic	3.9	Upper socioeconomic	7.3	3.4	2168
Poland	Spring 1962	5	Unskilled	3.7	White-collar	4.9	1.2	1468
India	Summer 1962	4	Income<R75	3.0	Income>R301	4.9	1.9	2366
Dominican Republic	Apr. 1962	2	Lower socioeconomic	1.4	Upper socioeconomic	4.3	2.9	814
Average				4.2		6.0	1.8	

[a] Data from Cantril 1965, pp.365-377.
[b] Minimum: 0, maximum: 10.

In addition to classification by income level, data on happiness are sometimes available by characteristics such as sex, age, race, education, and marital status. While the association of happiness with income is the most pervasive, some other patterns are apparent, though not without exception. Perhaps the firmest is a positive association between happiness and years of schooling. There is also some suggestion that the young are happier than the old, married persons than unmarried, and whites than blacks. Where the data permitted multivariate analysis, the independent association of income and happiness has been confirmed (Bradburn 1969, p. 294; Gurin, Veroff and Feld 1960, p. 221; Robinson and Shaver 1969, pp. 19–23). Also, the available evidence indicates low happiness levels among the unemployed and those on relief.

Inevitably, a question arises as to the direction of causality. Does higher income make people happier? Or are happier people more likely to be successful, i.e., receive higher income? It would be naïve to suppose that the issue is an either/or one. But emotional states are noticeably absent among the many factors usually cited by economists in explaining income differences. Factors such as education, training, experience, innate ability, health, and inheritance are among those principally mentioned. It might be felt that emotional well-being is implicit in the ability factor, or perhaps in that of health, though health is usually taken to refer to physical well-being. But it is doubtful that one would expect the influence of emotional well-being on earnings to stand out as clearly as in the simple bivariate comparisons shown here. Moreover, for some countries, some of the status designations, such as "upper class," are essentially hereditary. To argue that happiness causes such class differences is akin to arguing that, where happiness is correlated with age, happiness causes the age differences. Finally, as we have seen, when people are asked about the things that make them happy or unhappy, personal economic concerns are typically foremost (Table 1.1; cf. also Gurin, Veroff and Feld 1960, pp. 22–28). The worries of less-happy respondents differ most from those who are more happy in their emphasis on financial security (Gurin, Veroff and Feld 1960, p. 29; Wessman 1956, pp. 213, 216; cf. also Table 1.11 below). On the whole, therefore, I am inclined to interpret the data as primarily showing a causal connection running from income to happiness.[6]

1.2.2. International Comparisons

What happens when one looks at cross-sectional differences among countries? Are richer countries happier countries? Let us examine the Cantril data first, since that study made the greatest effort to assure comparability of approach among the various countries.

Table 1.6 presents the average personal happiness ratings for each of fourteen countries, along with figures on real GNP per capita. Cantril's own reading of these data is that they show a positive association between income and happiness and he presents correlation results to this effect (Cantril 1965, p. l94).[7] He generalizes this into a five-stage scheme, reminiscent of Rostow's stages of growth, to describe the phases of emotional well-being through which a country passes in the course of economic development (Rostow 1960; Cantril 1965, Chapter XV). However, as with Rostow's classification, countries do not fall neatly into one or another stage. One's confidence in the generality of the scheme is further undermined by the following passage, which concludes the presentation of the stage scheme:

> "It should be noted in passing, however, that people in some cultures or subcultures may seem to qualify for placement in this fifth [highest] stage of 'satisfaction and gratification' who have not gone through earlier stages of development but appear to outside observers to be stuck at relatively primitive levels. The Masai of Kenya and Tanganyika might be regarded as such a pocket of contentment within their microcosm. There is, of course, every likelihood that once the boundaries of such a microcosm are penetrated by 'advanced' cultures with the aspirations they intrude into people's minds, then the people within such a microcosm will alter the standards by means of which they judge satisfaction *and revert to an earlier stage of development.*" (Cantril 1965, p. 310; italics added)

To judge from this paragraph, some cultures or subcultures may "have it made" before they are touched by, or as long as they can remain free from, economic development.

Actually the association between wealth and happiness indicated by Cantril's international data is not so clear-cut. This is shown by a scatter diagram of the data (Figure 1.1). The inference about a positive association relies heavily on the observations for India and the United States. According to Cantril (1965, pp. 130–131), the values for Cuba and the Dominican Republic reflect unusual political circumstances – the immediate aftermath of a successful revolution in Cuba and prolonged political turmoil in the Dominican Republic.[8] What is perhaps most striking is that the personal happiness ratings for 10 of the 14 countries lie virtually within half a point of the midpoint rating of 5, as is brought out by the broken horizontal lines in the diagram. While a difference of rating of only 0.2 is significant at the 0.05 level, nevertheless there is not much evidence, for these 10 countries, of a systematic association between income and happiness. The closeness of the happiness ratings implies also that a similar lack of association would be found between happiness and other economic magnitudes such as income inequality or the rate of change of income.

Table 1.6

Personal Happiness Rating and Real GNP per Head, Fourteen Countries, ca. 1960[a,b]

County	Period of survey	(1) Rating of personal happiness (min: 0; max: 10)	(2) Real GNP per head 1961 ($U.S.)
United States	Aug. 1959	6.6	2790
Cuba	Apr.-May 1960	6.4	516
Egypt	Fall 1960	5.5	225
Israel	Nov. 1961-June 1962	5.3	1027
West Germany	Sept. 1957	5.3	1860
Japan	Fall 1962	5.2	613
Yugoslavia	Spring 1962	5.0	489
Philippines	Spring 1959	4.9	282
Panama	Jan.-Mar. 1962	4.8	371
Nigeria	Sept. 1962-spring 1963	4.8	134
Brazil	Late 1960-early 1961	4.6	375
Poland	Spring 1962	4.4	702
India	Summer 1962	3.7	140
Dominican Republic	Apr. 1962	1.6	313
Average		5.0	

[a] Data in column (1) from Cantril 1966, p. 184; data in column (2), except for West Germany, from Rosenstein-Rodan 1961, pp. 118, 126, 127; data in column (2) for West Germany from Table 1.7.
[b] For sample sizes see Table 1.5.

Of course, picking and choosing among points is a dubious practice. What one can perhaps safely say is this: In the within-country data shown in Table 1.5, the difference in happiness rating between low- and high-status groups averages almost 2 points, and for only 1 of the 13 countries is the difference less than 1 point. In contrast, in the comparison of national averages shown in Table 1.6, the ratings for 10 of 14 countries lie within a range of 1.1 points. The tenfold range in per-capita income covered by these countries almost surely exceeds the typical income range between low- and high-status groups covered in the within-country data. The happiness differences between rich and poor countries that one might expect on the basis of the within-country differences by economic status are not borne out by the international data.

Figure 1.1

Personal Happiness Rating and GNP per Head, 14 Countries, ca. 1960

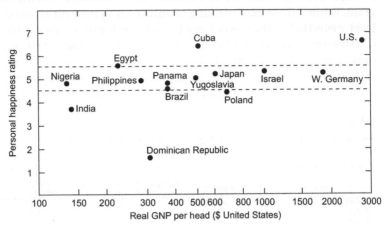

Source: Table 1.6.

Table 1.7

Percent Distribution of Population by Happiness, Nine Countries, 1965[a]

Country	Very happy	Fairly happy	Not very happy	Other	N	Real GNP per head 1961 ($)
Great Britain	53	42	4	1	1179	1777
United States[b]	49	46	4	2	3531	2790
West Germany	20	66	11	3	1255	1860
Thailand	13	74	12	1	500	202
Japan[c]	–	81	–	13	5	920	613
Philippines	13.5	73	13.5	0	500	282
Malaysia	17	64	15	4	502	552
France	12	64	18	5	1228	1663
Italy	11	52	33	4	1166	1077

[a] Happiness data are from World Survey III 1965, except those for the United States and Japan, which are from Table 1.8 and the 1958 survey of Japanese national character, respectively. GNP data are from Rosenstein-Rodan 1961, except those for Great Britain, France, West Germany, and Italy. For these countries GNP was estimated to bear the same proportion to the United States figure as that shown by the geometric mean estimates by Gilbert et al. 1958, p. 36, extrapolated from 1955 to 1961 by the per-capita volume indexes in OECD 1970, p.11.

[b] 1966.

[c] 1958. (Question read "not happy" rather than "not very happy".)

The other principal sources of international data are of the Gallup-poll type. In this case, the effort to secure comparability in asking the happiness question, which was only one of many questions, was less than in Cantril's study. In 1965, however, a survey obtained responses to a uniform inquiry in seven different countries. The results of this, plus that of a 1958 survey in Japan and a 1966 survey in the United States, are reported in Table 1.7.

There are four countries represented in both Tables 1.6 and 1.7 – the United States, West Germany, Japan, and the Philippines. One's confidence in the data is bolstered by the striking similarity in the results. In both cases the United States appears much happier than West Germany, and West Germany slightly happier than the Philippines. The Japanese data in Table 1.7 are least comparable with those of the other countries, but even the relative position of Japan vis-à-vis the other three is not much different in Table 1.7 from that in Table 1.6.

What association between happiness and income is indicated by the Table 1.7 data for all nine countries? The results are ambiguous. The four lowest-income countries are neither at the top nor at the bottom of the Table, but are clustered in the middle. This result cannot be attributed to the younger age of the populations in these countries, for it shows up in comparisons for individual age classes. (This is true also of the data in Table 1.6.) If there is a positive association between income and happiness, it is certainly not a strong one. In contrast, in the within-country comparisons by economic status, shown in Tables 1.3 and 1.4, the happiness differences are clear and consistent. The conclusion indicated by the Gallup-poll data is thus consistent with that shown by the Cantril data.

International happiness comparisons for 1946 and 1949 are given by Cantril (1951, p. 281), Wessman (1956, P. 166), and Inkeles (1960, p. 13). These are confined to a few Western European countries and their overseas descendants. The comparability of the questions is uncertain, but for what it is worth, the results are similar to those shown above – if there is a positive association among countries between income and happiness it is not very clear.

The international data are intriguing in various respects. For example, notice the high position of Great Britain compared with the United States in Table 1.7. This result is a persistent one, to judge from the polls mentioned in the preceding paragraph. Also, in those polls Canada and Australia show levels of happiness comparable in magnitude to Great Britain and the United States. There is also a noteworthy closeness in the results for the four Asian countries shown in Table 1.7. Perhaps there are cultural influences in the international happiness data, though one should hesitate before lumping together Thailand, Malaysia, the Philippines, and Japan as having a common culture. Of course, even if there are cultural influences, they would not necessarily systematically bias the relation of happiness to income indicated by the international data. Suppose, for example, one were to argue that cultural biases are obscuring a strong positive relation between income and happiness among countries. This implies that, ceteris paribus, in poorer countries cultural influences operate systematically to elevate happiness as compared to richer countries, an implication which seems doubtful in view of the cultural heterogeneity among countries within both the rich and poor categories.

1.2.3. National Time Series

What one would like most, of course, is historical series on happiness as countries develop. The crucial question is: "Will raising the incomes of all increase the happiness of all ...?" (Inkeles 1960, p.18). Unfortunately, as is too often the case, time series data are in short supply. In addition, comparability over time is impaired by variations in the wording of the happiness question. It was possible, however, to put together a series for one country, the United States, covering intermittent dates from 1946 through 1970. (Three of these dates, in 1956–1957, are only six months apart, and demonstrate the point made earlier regarding the short-run stability of the survey results.) In the first seven surveys the happiness classification was the same – "very happy," "fairly happy," or "not very happy." In the last three, "not happy" was used instead of "not very happy." This more negative designation of the lowest happiness category resulted, for the lowest happiness class, in a downward bias compared with the earlier data, and for the middle "fairly happy" category, in a corresponding upward bias. However, the "very happy" class seems comparable over all 10 surveys and reliance is therefore placed on the trend shown by this category. Fortunately, it is possible to utilize as a check happiness data obtained by NORC and Cantril, which overlap the AIPO data in the period when the change in AIPO question wording occurred.

The upper panel of Table 1.8 presents the results of the 10 AIPO surveys covering 1946–1970. From 1946 through 1956–1957, the proportion "very happy" drifts slowly but steadily upward. There is then a noticeable decline between 1957 and 1963, and a second one from 1966 to 1970. By 1970 the proportion "very happy" is just about the same as in 1947. If one views the period as a whole, there is a noticeable swing, but little indication of any net trend up or down.[9]

Table 1.8

Percent Distribution of Population by Happiness, United States, 1946–1970[a]

		A. AIPO Polls				
Date		Very happy	Fairly happy	Not very happy	Other	N
Apr.	1946	39	50	10	1	3151
Dec.	1947	42	47	10	1	1434
Aug.	1948	43	43	11	2	1596
Nov.	1952	47	43	9	1	3003
Sept.	1956	53	41	5	1	1979
Sept.	1956	52	42	5	1	2207
Mar.	1957	53	43	3	1	1627
July	1963	47	48	5[b]	1	3668
Oct.	1966	49	46	4[b]	2	3531
Dec.	1970	43	48	6[b]	3	1517

		B. NORC Polls			
Date		Very happy	Pretty happy	Not too happy	N
Spring	1957	35	54	11	2460
Dec.	1963	32	51	16	1501
June	1965	30	53	17	1469

[a] Data from Table 1.2 and AIPO Polls 369, 410, 425, 508, 570, 571, 580, 675, and 735. NORC data from Bradburn 1969, p.40.
[b] Question read "not happy" rather than "not very happy."

The finding of a downturn between 1957 and 1963 runs into the difficulty that the question wording changed between these two dates, though as indicated this should not have affected the "very happy" replies. However, three NORC polls were taken independently around this time. As noted earlier, the happiness categories in the NORC polls differ from those in the AIPO polls. Our interest, however, is in the change over time shown by the NORC polls (Table 1.8, panel B). The results confirm those shown by the AIPO polls – a decline in happiness between the late 1950s and mid-1960s. (The exact timing is obviously open to question because of the intermittent nature of both sets of survey data.) Further support is provided by two United States surveys reported by Cantril (1965, p. 43) which show a decline in the national average personal happiness rating between 1959 and 1963 from 6.6 to 6.2.

Table 1.9

Percent Very Happy by Size of Income, United States, 1946–1952[a]

Date		All classes	Average+ and wealthy	Average	Poor
Apr.	1946	39	47	43	34
Dec.	1947	42	52	46	37
Aug.	1948	43	54	50	37
Aug.	1948	43	51	51	37
Nov.	1952	47	51	51	42

[a] Data from AIPO Polls 369, 410, 425, 508.

To a limited extent, it is possible to follow the trends for individual income groups. Table 1.9 presents the data for the first four surveys, which appear to have had roughly consistent income classifications. (Unfortunately, no subdivision by income is available for the three 1956–1957 surveys.) To judge from the data in Table 1.9, there was a common advance in happiness in all major income groups through 1952.

The surveys relating to the period of declining happiness show a rather interesting difference from this pattern (Table 1.10). Whereas the national average shows a slight rise between 1963 and 1966, the data by income class show a decline for the poorest groups. Thus the slight rise shown by the national average reflects an upward movement for the higher income groups which more than offsets the decline among the lower. (Could this be partly due to the national prominence given to the poverty problem at this time?) Between 1966 and 1970, however, all income classes show a noticeable decline, and in 1970 there is no class which is higher than it was in 1963.

Table 1.10

Percentage Very Happy by Size of Income, United States, 1963–1970[a]

Date		All classes	$15,00+	$10,00-14,999	$5000-9999	$3000-4999	Under $3000
July	1963	47	59	50	50	46	40
Sept.	1966	49	67	62	50	42	34
Dec.	1970	38	56	49	43	33	29

[a] Data from Table 1.2 and AIPO Polls 675 and 735.

Certainly, one must be cautious about drawing any strong conclusions from the limited United States time series studied here. As in the case of the international cross-sections, however, it seems safe to say that if income and happiness go together, it is not as obvious as in the within-country cross-sectional comparisons.

1.3. Interpretation

1.3.1. Theory

Why do national comparisons among countries and over time show an association between income and happiness which is so much weaker than, if not inconsistent with, that shown by within-country comparisons? To economists, long accustomed to dealing with anomalies such as these, the possible relevance of Duesenberry's "relative income" explanation of the celebrated United States income–savings paradox will immediately spring to mind (Duesenberry 1952; cf. also Brady and Friedman 1947). The basic idea was stated quite simply by Karl Marx over a century ago: "A house may be large or small; as long as the surrounding houses are equally small it satisfies all social demands for a dwelling. But if a palace rises beside the little house, the little house shrinks into a hut."[10]

Suppose one assumes, following Duesenberry, that the utility a person obtains from his consumption expenditure is a function, not of the absolute level of his expenditure, but of the ratio of his current expenditure to that of other people, that is,

$$U_i = f\left[\frac{C_i}{\sum a_{ij}C_j}\right],$$

where U_i and C_i are the utility index and consumption expenditures, respectively, of the ith individual, C_j is consumption of the jth individual and a_{ij} is the weight applied by the ith consumer to the expenditure of the jth (Duesenberry 1952, p. 32). In the simplest case, in which the expenditures of every other person are given equal weight, the utility obtained by a given individual depends on the ratio of his expenditure to the national per-capita average. The farther he is above the average, the happier he is; the farther below, the sadder. Moreover, if the frame of reference is always the current national situation, then an increase in the level of income in which all share proportionately would not alter the national level of happiness. A classical example of the fallacy of composition would apply: An increase in the income of any one individual would increase his happiness, but increasing the income of everyone would leave happiness unchanged. Similarly, among countries, a richer country would not necessarily be a happier country.

The data are presently too limited to warrant pushing this line of explanation very far, and the illustration above is certainly too simple. An intriguing research issue, for example, is the appropriate values of the a_{ij}'s [which can be viewed as a variant of the sociologist's problem of "reference groups" (Merton 1968, Chapters X and XI)]. Any given individual in the population does not give equal weight to all others in forming his reference standard; among other things, "peer group" influences play a part. Thus, the reference standard of a rich man probably gives disproportionate weight to the consumption of his well-to-do associates vis-à-vis persons living in poverty, and conversely for the reference standard of the poor man.

Nevertheless, the general form of the argument remains valid. Despite peer group influences, there is a "consumption norm" which exists in a given society at a given time, and which enters into the reference standard of virtually everyone. This provides a common point of reference in self-appraisals of well-being, leading those below the norm to feel less happy and those above the norm, more happy. Over time, this norm tends to rise with the general level of consumption, though the two are not necessarily on a one-to-one basis.

Other possible interpretations of these data come to mind. For example, emphasis might be placed on external diseconomies of production. At a given time, it might be argued, the rich are better able to avoid these sources of "ill-fare" and hence are happier. But over time and across societies increases in income are largely or wholly offset by a corresponding growth in pollution, congestion, and so forth.

A radical interpretation of the data might emphasize power as the key factor in happiness. At any given time those who have more power (the rich) are happier. But over time and across societies, increases in income have not been accompanied by a wider diffusion of power among the various socioeconomic strata (the Establishment persists), and hence happiness has not grown.

1.3.2. Evidence for a "Relative Income" Interpretation

There are a number of reasons why an interpretation based chiefly on "relativity" notions seems more plausible. First, a certain amount of empirical support has been developed for the relative income concept in other economic applications, such as savings behavior and, more recently, fertility behavior and labor force participation (Duesenberry 1952; Easterlin 1973, 1969; Freedman 1963; Wachter 1971a,b). Second, similar notions, such as "relative deprivation," have gained growing theoretical acceptance and empirical support in sociology, political science, and social psychology over the past several decades (Berkowitz 1971; Davies 1962; Gurr 1970; Homans 1961; Merton 1968; Pettigrew 1967; Smelser 1962; Stouffer et al. 1949). Indeed, to scholars vitally concerned with professional reputation in a competitive field of learning, it should hardly come as a surprise that relative status is an important ingredient of happiness. Third, historical changes in the definition of poverty attest to the importance of relative position in society's thinking on this matter. For example, Smolensky (1965, p. 40) has pointed out that estimates of "minimum comfort" budgets for New York City workers throughout the course of this century "have generally been about one-half of real gross national product per capita." (cf. also Fuchs 1967; Rainwater 1974; Tabbarah 1972.)

Table 1.11

Relation of Economic Status and Major Worries, United States, 1946[a,b]

Major worry	Economic status (percent)		
	Upper	Middle	Lower
My family and children	20	20	24
Health (personal and family)	19	21	18
Financial worries, money	6	12	22
Security, job, future	13	17	12
World and national conditions	7	6	4
Work conditions	7	5	3
Personal traits	3	2	2
Housing	2	1	1
Miscellaneous	9	7	5
Nothing	13	10	10
No answer	5	7	5
	-	-	-
	104	108	106
Sample size	195	637	1506

[a] From Wessman(1956).
[b] The question asked was "What one thing do you worry about most?" Percentages add to more than 100 because some respondents gave more than one answer.

By no means least important are the statements in the surveys of the respondents themselves on what they take to comprise happiness. These statements overwhelmingly emphasize immediate personal concerns, such as adequacy of income, family matters, or health, rather than broader national or social issues such as pollution, political power, or even threat of war. Furthermore, economic

37

worries appear to be especially important among lower-income persons. Table 1.11, for example, reports on the "one thing" worried about most by Americans of upper, middle, and lower economic status in a 1946 survey. For all three groups worries about economic, family, and health matters predominate. However, the item on which the three groups most markedly differ is that labeled "financial worries, money." Such concerns increase significantly as economic status declines.

Finally, there is evidence that consumption norms vary directly with the level of economic development. Here, from Cantril's survey (1965), are some statements by Indians on their material aspirations, and, for comparison, those of Americans:

> "INDIA: I want a son and a piece of land since I am now working on land owned by other people. I would like to construct a house of my own and have a cow for milk and ghee. I would also like to buy some better clothing for my wife. If I could do this then I would be happy. (thirty-five-year-old man, illiterate, agricultural laborer, income about $10 a month)
>
> INDIA: I wish for an increase in my wages because with my meager salary I cannot afford to buy decent food for my family. If the food and clothing problems were solved, then I would feel at home and be satisfied. Also if my wife were able to work the two of us could then feed the family and I am sure would have a happy life and our worries would be over. (thirty-year-old sweeper, monthly income around $13)
>
> INDIA: I should like to have a water tap and a water supply in my house. It would also be nice to have electricity. My husband's wages must be increased if our children are to get an education and our daughter is to be married. (forty-five-year-old housewife, family income about $80 a month)
>
> INDIA: I hope in the future I will not get any disease. Now I am coughing. I also hope I can purchase a bicycle. I hope my children will study well and that I can provide them with an education. I also would sometime like to own a fan and maybe a radio. (forty-year-old skilled worker earning $30 a month)
>
> UNITED STATES: If I could earn more money I would then be able to buy our own home and have more luxury around us, like better furniture, a new car, and more vacations. (twenty-seven-year-old skilled worker)
>
> UNITED STATES: I would like a reasonable enough income to maintain a house, have a new car, have a boat, and send my four children to private schools. (thirty-four-year-old laboratory technician)
>
> UNITED STATES: I would like a new car. I wish all my bills were paid and I had more money for myself. I would like to play more golf and to hunt more than I do. I would like to have more time to do the things I want to and to entertain my friends. (Negro bus driver, twenty-four-years old)

UNITED STATES: Materially speaking, I would like to provide my family with an income to allow them to live well – to have the proper recreation, to go camping, to have music and dancing lessons for the children, and to have family trips. I wish we could belong to a country club and do more entertaining. We just bought a new home and expect to be perfectly satisfied with it for a number of years. (twenty-eight-year-old lawyer)." (pp. 205, 206, 222)

It is a well-accepted dictum among social scientists other than economists that attitudes or "tastes" are a product of the socialization experience of the individual. What more eloquent testimony could be provided than the foregoing statements?

In a comprehensive survey of long-term trends in American consumption, Brady has pointed out that "today, the great majority of American families live on a scale that compares well with the way *wealthy* families lived 200 years ago" (cf. Davis, Easterlin and Parker 1972, p. 84, italics added). But, as the above statements show, the typical American today does not consider himself wealthy. His consumption standards are not those of his colonial predecessors; rather they are formed by his personal experience with the human condition as evidenced in contemporary America. The same is true of the typical Indian living in modern India. Material aspirations or tastes vary positively with the level of economic development. Moreover, these changes in tastes are caused by the process of income growth itself (though the cause–effect relation may run both ways). As a result of secular income growth, the socialization experience of each generation embodies a higher level of living and correspondingly generates a higher level of consumption standards. Even within the life cycle of a given generation, the progressive accretion of household goods due to economic growth causes a continuous upward pressure on consumption norms. This upward shift in standards (tastes) tends to offset the positive effect of income growth on well-being that one would expect on the basis of economic theory. Supporting evidence is provided by the findings from a survey in Taiwan that included questions on goods aspirations:

"There is a positive relationship between income levels and aspirations. ... Although economic conditions improved markedly in Taiwan during the five years prior to the survey, most respondents failed to perceive any improvement in their financial situation – only 20 per cent felt that they were better off."(Freedman 1975, pp. 107-108)

It would be premature to assert that "everything is relative," but it is hard to resist the inference that relative considerations play an important part in explaining the evidence presented here.

1.3.3. An Analogy[11]

The present interpretation may be clarified by an analogy with comparisons of height. Americans today are taller than their forebears and than their contemporaries in present-day India. Suppose, however, that representative samples of Americans and Indians in 1970 were asked the following question: "In general, how tall would you say that you are – very tall, fairly tall, or not very tall?" It seems reasonable to suppose that this question would elicit a similar distribution of responses in the two countries, even though on an objective scale most Americans are, in fact, taller than most Indians. The reason for the similar distributions would be that, in answering, individuals in each country would apply a subjective norm of "tallness" derived from their personal experience. The reference standard in terms of which Americans would evaluate "tallness" would be larger than that applied by Indians, because Americans have grown up in and live in a society in which persons are generally taller. An American male (5 ft. 9 in.) in height living in the United States, though tall on an international scale, is not likely to feel tall. By the same token, Americans today are not likely to feel taller than their forebears, because today's standard of reference is higher.

What, then, are the "facts" of tallness? By an objective scale, current-day Americans are, indeed, taller. If, however, one is interested in feelings about height, the truth is quite possibly different. Today's Americans may not, on the average, feel any taller than do contemporary Indians or than their ancestors did. The reconciliation between the "objective facts" and "subjective states of mind" lies in the mediating role of the social norm for height, which enters together with one's actual height in determining feelings of tallness. This norm varies among societies both in time and space, and is a direct function of the heights typical of these societies.

The situation with regard to happiness is like that for height, but with one critical difference. It is similar in that each individual, in evaluating his happiness, compares his actual experience with a norm derived from his personal social experience. It is different in that there is no objective scale of measurement for happiness, independent of the individual. On the contrary, the concern is precisely with subjective states of mind. One may attempt to use "objective" indexes such as consumption, nutrition, or life expectancy to infer happiness. Or one may seek to gauge well-being from various behavioral indicators, for example, measures of the prevalence of social disorganization (delinquency, suicide, and so forth). Ultimately, however, the relevance of such measures rests on an assumed connection between external manifestations and internal states of mind – in effect, on a model of human psychology. And if it is feelings that count, there is a real possibility that subjective reports may contradict the "objective" evidence. To social scientists, and especially economists, this can be frustrating. As Mishan (1969) observes,

> "[t]here is a temptation ... to lose patience with human cussedness and to insist that if both the Smith family and the Jones family receive a 10 percent increase in their 'real' income they are better off, even if they both sulk at the other's good luck. But while this may be salutary morals, if welfare is what people experience there is no escape for us in honest indignation." (p. 821)

On the contrary, there are good psychological reasons why people may not feel better off, even though they "should." This is because the standard with reference to which evaluations of well-being are formed is itself a function of social conditions. As these conditions "improve," the norm tends to advance along with people's actual experience. Economic analysis has been able, for a long time, to resist the uncomfortable implications of this mechanism, by assuming that tastes are given and/or are unmeasurable. For many of the short-term problems with which economists have traditionally been concerned, this may not be seriously damaging. But with the growth in concern about long-term economic growth, on the one hand, and in evidence on people's feelings and aspirations, and the factors governing them, on the other, one can only wonder whether this view will be much longer defensible.

1.4. Summary and Concluding Observations

The concern of this paper has been with the association of income and happiness. The basic data consist of statements by individuals on their subjective happiness, as reported in thirty surveys from 1946 through 1970, covering nineteen countries, including eleven

41

in Asia, Africa, and Latin America. Within countries there is a noticeable positive association between income and happiness – in every single survey, those in the highest status group were happier, on the average, than those in the lowest status group. However, whether any such positive association exists among countries at a given time is uncertain. Certainly, the happiness differences between rich and poor countries that one might expect on the basis of the within-country differences by economic status are not borne out by the international data. Similarly, in the one national time series studied, that for the United States since 1946, higher income was not systematically accompanied by greater happiness.

As for why national comparisons among countries and over time show an association between income and happiness which is so much weaker than, if not inconsistent with, that shown by within-country comparisons, a Duesenberry-type model, involving relative status considerations as an important determinant of happiness, was suggested. Every survey that has looked into the meaning of happiness shows that economic considerations are very important to people, though by no means the only matters of concern. In judging their happiness, people tend to compare their actual situation with a reference standard or norm, derived from their prior and ongoing social experience. While norms vary among individuals within a given society, they also contain similar features because of the common experiences people share as members of the same society and culture. Thus, while the goods aspirations of higher status people probably exceed those of lower status people, the dispersion in reference norms is less than in the actual incomes of rich and poor. Because of this, those at the bottom of the income distribution tend to feel less well off than those at the top. Over time, however, as economic conditions advance, so too does the social norm, since this is formed by the changing economic socialization experience of people. For the same reason, among different societies at a given time, there tends to be a rough correspondence between living levels and the social norm. As a result, the positive correlation between income and happiness that shows up in within-country comparisons appears only weakly, if at all, in comparisons among societies in time or space. Various pieces of evidence were noted in support of this interpretation.

In a sense, these results are a testimony to the adaptability of mankind. Income and aspirations in time and space tend to go together, and people seemingly can make something out of what appears, in some absolute sense, to be a sorry lot. At the same time, the conclusions raise serious questions about the goals and prospective efficacy of much social policy. As sociologist George C. Homans remarks (1961, p. 276) regarding similar findings on another subject, "[t]hings like this have persuaded some people who would prefer to believe otherwise that any effort to satisfy mankind is bound to be self-defeating. Any satisfied desire creates an unsatisfied one."

The present results do not necessarily imply that a redirection of attention is needed from economic growth to income redistribution as a vehicle for improving welfare. The data themselves give no indication that international differences in happiness are systematically related to inequality. And the theoretical relationship is uncertain – if relative positions were unchanged and income differences halved, would happiness be greater? It is at least plausible that sensitivity to income differences might be heightened, so that lower income people might suffer as much in the new situation from an income spread of 50% as they previously had from a spread of 100%. If this were so, then subjective welfare would be unchanged.

The only sure conclusion is that we need much more research on the nature and causes of human welfare. Bradburn (1969, p. 233) makes the point simply and effectively: "Insofar as we have greater understanding of how people arrive at their judgments of their own happiness and how social forces are related to those judgments, we shall be in a better position to formulate and execute effective social policies."

The present analysis also points to a clear need for research on the formation of preferences or tastes. Economists have generally insisted that the determination of tastes is not their business. But on this matter there are hopeful signs of change in economists' tastes themselves. Katona (1951, 1971), Morgan (1968), Strumpel (1973), and their associates at the Survey Research Center in Michigan have been doing pioneering studies on this subject (cf. also Pfaff 1973). In the 1950s, Siegel (1964) did some little-noticed work modeling the formation of aspirations. A central tenet of Galbraith's (1958, 1967) assault on economic theory has been the "dependence effect," that tastes are subject to substantial manipulation by the business system.[12]

In the area of growth economics, the present findings raise doubt about the importance of the "international demonstration effect." If those in rich and poor countries shared a common scale of material aspirations, then countries higher on the scale of actual income should show a higher level of happiness. At the same time, the within-country cross-sectional findings, indicating a similarity in the aspirations of members of the same society, lend support to the concept of an internal demonstration effect.[13]

Economists' models of economic growth tend uniformly to exclude tastes as a variable.[14] But it is possible that not only are tastes affected by economic growth, but that taste changes serve as a spur to growth, in the manner suggested by Mack some years ago (1956). Thus one might conceive of a mutually reinforcing interaction between changes in tastes and changes in per capita income, which, *ceteris paribus,* drive the economy ever onward and per capita income ever upward.

Another interesting analytical possibility opened up by recognition of taste changes is in the relation of economic changes to political behavior. Recent work on the causes of political agitation and revolution has stressed the importance of disparities between the aspirations of the population and their fulfillment (Davies 1962; Gurr 1970). Since economic goods form such an important part of human concerns, a growth model which included material aspirations as a variable might incorporate also the political consequences of unfulfilled expectations, and possible feedback effects of any resultant political activity on the growth process itself.

Finally, with regard to growth economics, there is the view that the most developed economies, notably the United States, have entered an era of satiation. Economic growth, it is said, tends to eventuate in the "mass consumption society" (Rostow 1960), the "affluent society" (Galbraith 1958), the "opulent society" (Johnson 1967), or the "post-industrial society" (Bell 1970). The present analysis raises serious doubts whether the United States is in such an era, or, indeed, whether such a terminal stage exists. Long-term fluctuations aside, the present generation is not noticeably more advanced over its predecessor than has been the case for over a century – the long-run growth rate of per-capita income has been remarkably steady since at least the first half of the nineteenth century (Davis, Easterlin and Parker 1972, Chapter 2). The view that the United States is now in a new era is based in part on ignorance of the rapidity of growth in the past. Consider the following statement: "The advancement of the arts, from year to year, taxes our credulity, and seems to presage the arrival of that period when human improvement must end" (as quoted by Davis, Easterlin and Parker

1972, p. 177). This was made by Henry L. Ellsworth, Commissioner of Patents, in 1843! Similarly, a writer in the Democratic Review of 1853 predicted that electricity and machinery would so transform life that fifty years thereafter: "Men and women will then have no harassing cares, or laborious duties to fulfill. Machinery will perform all work – automata will direct them. The only task of the human race will be to make love, study and be happy."[15] Brady's recent work catalogs in great detail the myriad advances in food, clothing, housing, transportation, and style of life in general that followed one upon the other throughout the nineteenth century (Davis, Easterlin and Parker 1972, Chapter 2). Is there any reason to suppose that the present generation has reached a unique culminating stage in this evolution, and the next will not have its own catalog of wonders, which, if only attained, would make it happy? An antimaterialistic cultural revolution may be in the making, but it seems dubious that a major cause is an unprecedented affluence which American society has recently attained. If the view suggested here has merit, economic growth does not raise a society to some ultimate state of plenty. Rather, the growth process itself engenders ever-growing wants that lead it ever onward.

2

Will Raising the Incomes of All Increase the Happiness of All?

Will raising the incomes of all increase the happiness of all? The answer to this question can now be given with somewhat greater assurance than twenty years ago. It is "no". The following gives a brief summary of the model and evidence.

2.1. Model

A simple thought experiment may convey the basic reasoning. Imagine that your income increases substantially while everyone else's stays the same. Would you feel better off? The answer most people would give is 'yes'. Now suppose that your income stays the same while everyone else's increases substantially. How would you feel? Most people would say that they feel less well off. This is because judgments of personal well-being are made by comparing one's objective status with a subjective living level norm, which is significantly influenced by the average level of living of the society as a whole. If living levels increase generally, subjective living level norms rise. The individual whose income is unchanged will feel poorer, even though his or her objective circumstances are the same as before.

Put generally, happiness, or subjective well-being, varies directly with one's own income and inversely with the incomes of others.

This chapter is a revised version of: Easterlin, R. (1995). Will Raising the Incomes of All Increase the Happiness of All?, in: Journal of Economic Behavior and Organization, 27(1), 35–47, reprinted with permission from Elsevier. The author is grateful to Donna Hokoda Ebata and Christine M. Schaeffer for excellent assistance, to Richard H. Day and Morton O. Schapiro for comments, to Ed Diener and Alan Heston for helpful data, and to the University of Southern California for financial support. The title of this article comes from Inkeles (1960, p. 18).

Raising the incomes of all does not increase the happiness of all, because the positive effect of higher income on subjective well-being is offset by the negative effect of higher living level norms brought about by the growth in incomes generally.

As discussed in Chapter 1, formally this model corresponds to a model of interdependent preferences in which each individual's utility or subjective well-being varies directly with his or her own income and inversely with the average income of others.[1] At any point in time average income is given; and happiness varies directly with individual income. Over time, however, a general increase in individual incomes raises the societal average. The increase in happiness that one might have expected based on the growth in individual incomes is offset by a decrease in happiness due to the rise in the average, yielding, on balance, no net growth in well-being.

Although this model generates paradoxical cross-sectional and time series relationships between happiness and income of the type actually observed, a more realistic model would, in addition, take account of habit formation, in which the utility one attaches to one's current income level depends also on one's past income (Modigliani 1949; Pollak 1970; Day 1986).[2] Many of those with higher incomes come from higher income backgrounds, and conversely for those with lower incomes. The difference in living level experience implied by the difference in income history might be expected to give rise to similar differences in living level norms–higher norms for the affluent and lower norms for the poor. Indeed, if habit formation alone shaped norms, one might arrive at a dispersion in norms in direct proportion to the dispersion in income, and no significant income-happiness relationship even in the cross-section. With the more realistic assumption of habit formation plus interdependent preferences, however, the dispersion in norms is less than that in income, because norms at all income levels are pulled toward the income average. The result is a positive happiness–income relationship in the cross-section, but one weaker than that which would prevail in the absence of habit formation.

2.2. Evidence

The evidence that income growth in a society does not increase happiness comes from time series studies of the United States, nine

European countries, and Japan. For the United States, on which the most work has been done, the most comprehensive studies of historical experience are those of Smith (1979) and Campbell (1981, Chapter 3). In a detailed analysis of data from 45 happiness surveys taken between 1946 and 1977, Smith arrives at the same conclusion as in Chapter 1 here, that there is a swing in American happiness with a peak in the late 1950s, but little indication of a trend. The absence of a trend in happiness is noted also by Campbell, and extended by him to include questions on general life satisfaction. Campbell also points out that movements in happiness sometimes occur in direct opposition to what one would have expected based on economic trends (1981, pp. 29-30). Drawing on a small area survey, O.D. Duncan (1975) reports that "there was no change in the distribution of satisfaction with the standard of living among Detroit area wives between 1955 and 1971, although ... constant dollar [median family] income increased by forty percent."

Figure 2.1

Percent Very Happy, United States, 1972–1991

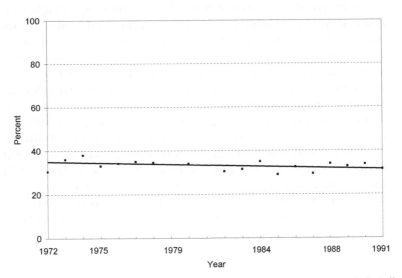

Source and Notes: National Opinion Research Center 1991. The question is, "Taken all together, how would you say things are these days – would you say that you are very happy, pretty happy, or not too happy?" An ordinary least squares regression line is fitted to the data; the time trend is not statistically significant.

These studies cover the post-World War II period through the 1970s. What of experience since then? The answer is, again, no trend in happiness. The evidence for this is annual data from the General Social Survey from the year when the survey was initiated, 1972, through 1991 (Figure 2.1). In this period, real per capita disposable income rose by a third. Together with the results for the earlier part of the post-World War II period, the conclusion is that there has been no improvement in happiness in the United States over almost a half century in which real GDP per capita more than doubled (Maddison 1991).

Trends in life satisfaction in nine European countries from 1973 to 1989 are much like that just reported for happiness in the United States (Figure 2.2; for a similar figure for happiness in these countries covering a somewhat shorter period, see Inglehart and Rabier 1986, pp. 49). Satisfaction drifts upward in some countries, downward in others. The overall pattern, however, is clearly one of little or no trend in a period when real GDP per capita rises in all of these countries from 25 to 50 percent (OECD 1992).

Figure 2.2

Percent Very Satisfied With Their Lives in General,
Nine European Countries, 1973–1989

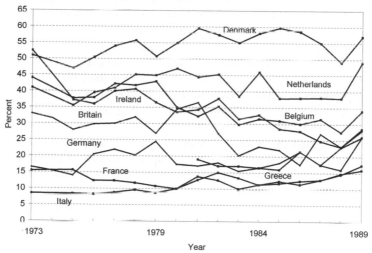

Source and Notes: Inglehart and Reif 1992. The question asked is, "Generally speaking, how satisfied are you with your life as a whole? Would you say that you are very satisfied, fairly satisfied, not very satisfied, or not at all satisfied?" Ordinary least squares regressions (not shown) yielded time trends that were not significant for five countries, significant and positive for two, and significant and negative for two.

The experience of Japan after recovery from World War II is of special interest, because it encompasses much lower levels of income than those of the United States and Europe. The best historical estimates of real GDP per capita put Japan's living level in 1958 at only about one-eighth that of the United States in 1991 (Summers and Heston 1991). In 1991 in Third World areas other than Africa a number of countries already equaled or exceeded Japan's 1958 income level:

Table 2.1

	Number of countries with estimates for 1991	Number of countries equal to or higher than Japan in 1958
Asia (excluding Japan)	24	16
Latin America and Caribbean	24	15
Africa	43	11

Hence, in considering the experience of Japan, one is looking at a country advancing from an income level lower than or equal to those prevailing in a considerable number of today's developing countries.

Between 1958 and 1987 real per capita income in Japan multiplied a staggering five-fold, propelling Japan to a living level equal to about two-thirds that of the United States (Summers and Heston 1991). Consumer durables such as electric washing machines, electric refrigerators, and television sets, found in few homes at the start of the period, became well-nigh universal, and car ownership soared from 1 to about 60 percent of households (Yasuba 1991). Despite this unprecedented three decade advance in level of living, there was no improvement in mean subjective well-being (Figure 2.3; cf. also Inglehart and Rabier 1986, p. 44).

When Japan's population near the start of this period is classified into three income groups, average happiness in the highest group is substantially greater than in the lowest (Chapter 1, Table 1.5). Given the remarkable growth of incomes that occurred, the proportion of the population at the end of the period with incomes equaling or exceeding that of the highest group at the beginning must have risen substantially. Yet the average level of satisfaction was unchanged.

Some scholars of subjective well-being argue that the relation of subjective well-being to income is curvilinear, that it may be nil in richer countries, but that it is positive in poorer countries, although no time series evidence to this effect has been presented (Inkeles 1993; Veenhoven 1991). Presumably a positive relation will be observed in poorer countries as the population is freed from subsistence level needs for food, clothing, and shelter. In 1958, Japan was beyond this stage, as are a number of Third World countries today. Yet the magnitude of Japan's subsequent advance in living levels does encompass a transformation from a 'subsistence level' of consumer durables to plenitude, with no impact on subjective well-being. One would suspect that the spread of consumer durables among the Japanese must have involved widespread satisfaction of perceived needs. The total absence of any subjective welfare effect would seem to raise doubts about the hypothesized curvilinear relationship.

Figure 2.3

Mean Subjective Well-Being, Japan 1958–1987

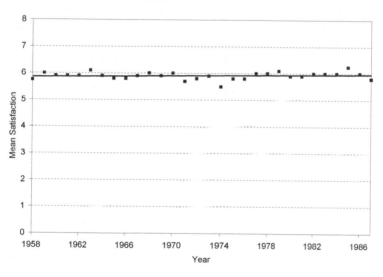

Source and Notes: Veenhoven 1993. An ordinary least squares regression is fitted to the data; the coefficient of mean satisfaction on year is not statistically significant.

There is also evidence relating to norms that supports the notion that higher incomes do not lead to greater happiness because material aspirations increase with a society's income. As discussed in Chapter 1, in an international inquiry into people's hopes and fears, social psychologist Hadley Cantril asked an open-ended question on what was needed to make the respondent 'completely happy.' After comparing responses of those in rich countries with those in poor, he concluded that

> "[p]eople in highly developed nations have obviously acquired a wide range of aspirations, sophisticated and expensive from the point of view of people in less-developed areas, who have not yet learned all that is potentially available to people in more advanced societies and whose aspirations concerning the social and material aspects of life are modest indeed by comparison." (Cantril 1965, p. 202)

Time series comparisons of aspirations yield similar results. When Americans are asked to think about the 'good life - the life you'd like to have,' the proportion identifying goods such as 'really nice clothes' and 'a vacation home' as essentials of the good life is considerably higher in 1988 than in 1975 (Easterlin and Crimmins 1991, p.526). Perhaps most important are findings indicating that material norms and income increase, not only in the same direction, but at the same rate. Thus, 'minimum comfort' budgets of New York city workers in this century 'have generally been about one-half of real gross national product per capita' (Smolensky 1965, p. 40). Similarly, Rainwater (1990) concludes that the income perceived as necessary to get along rose between 1950 and 1986 in the same proportion as actual per capita income.

Theoretical expectations of a positive within-country relationship between happiness and income are also supported by the data (cf. Chapter 1). A survey article summarizes as follows:

> "There is an overwhelming amount of evidence that shows a positive relationship between income and SWB [subjective well-being] within countries. This relationship exists even when other variables such as education are controlled ... Although the effect of income is often small when other factors are controlled, these other factors may be ones through which income could produce its effects ..." (Diener 1984, p. 553; see also Andrews 1986, p. xi; for a seemingly contrary reading of the literature, see Lane 1993)

As mentioned, the expectation of a positive happiness-income relation within a society assumes that the dispersion in material norms is less than that in actual incomes, although the two are positively related. Rainwater's analysis of perceptions of 'get along' income supports this view of the dispersion in norms. He concludes that there is

> "a rather high degree of consensus about perceived living levels in society. Even high income people do not exaggerate very much the needed

income of [a family of four]. The same conclusion can be drawn from the two studies which ask about a wider range of living levels from poor to rich [those by Rainwater 1974 and Dubnoff 1985]." (Rainwater 1990, p. 11)

What of point of time comparisons among countries at different levels of income? On this, the theoretical expectation is uncertain. At one extreme, one might imagine a replication of the within-country situation – a substantial convergence in norms between rich and poor resulting in a positive happiness–income relation. At the other extreme, one might suppose that norms would vary in direct proportion to actual income, resulting in no significant association between happiness and income. Put differently, the expected happiness–income relation in international cross-sections would depend on the extent to which trans-national material norms have come to prevail throughout the world.

Figure 2.4

Mean Satisfaction with Life in General and Real Gross National Product per Capita, 24 Countries

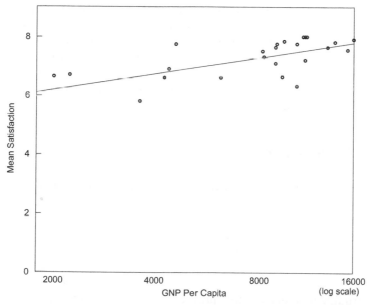

Source and Notes: From Inglehart 1988, based on Euro-Barometer surveys. Eighteen European countries are included plus the United States, Canada, Australia, Japan, Argentina, and the Union of South Africa. An ordinary least squares regression is fitted to the data; the coefficient of satisfaction on GNP per capita is statistically significant.

There is considerable agreement among scholars involved in international comparisons that material aspirations vary positively with the level of economic development.[3] However, the dispersion in norms appears to be, on average, less than that in incomes, because a positive happiness–income relationship typically turns up in international comparisons (Figure 2.4, see also Gallup 1976-77; Inkeles 1993; Inkeles and Diamond 1980).[4] It would be of interest to assess the size of the cross-sectional income–happiness relation among countries relative to that found within countries. This undertaking is complicated, however, by the now well-established finding that bivariate international comparisons of happiness and income are significantly influenced by cultural factors.

For example, the substantial stability in the relative positions of the nine European countries throughout the period shown in Figure 2.2 is taken in the study in which a similar figure originally appeared to indicate a 'durable cultural component' that varies by country in reports on subjective well-being (Inglehart 1988, p. 1207; see also Inglehart and Rabier 1986). Inkeles (1993, p. 12) states it as follows: "... [N]ational groups display a response propensity – evidently an aspect of their cultural orientation – to see most things either in a positive or negative light."[5] These observations on cultural influences on international happiness comparisons underscore the importance of national time series evidence, such as that emphasized here, for inferring the relationship between subjective well-being and economic development.

2.3. Conclusion

Today, as in the past, within a country at a given time those with higher incomes are, on average, happier. However, raising the incomes of all does not increase the happiness of all. This is because the material norms on which judgments of well-being are based increase in the same proportion as the actual income of the society.

Although the evidence in support of these conclusions continues to grow, there is need for more work. Despite the fact that time series studies are crucial to the question of how subjective well-being and economic development are related, surprisingly little analysis of this type has been done, especially in poorer countries. Moreover, happiness does sometimes rise or fall over time, and these movements deserve study. There is also need for more empirical work on how material norms change with the level of economic development, and of the mechanisms shaping such norms. Finally, there is need to develop international cross-sections of the happiness–income relationship that are free of cultural biases.

In a survey done by Diener (1984) of well over 200 studies on the measurement and determinants of subjective well-being only two references appear to articles in economics journals. With a few exceptions (Abramovitz 1979; Frank 1985a; Layard 1980; Morawetz et al. 1977; Ng 1978; Scitovsky 1976; Scitovsky 1986; van Praag and Kapteyn 1973), economists tend to ignore or dismiss the present findings, holding to 'the more comfortable conclusion that when incomes generally increase people, on the average, feel better off' (Silver 1980, p. 160). This resistance is no doubt due in part to reluctance to abandon the Benthamite conception of the social good that has prevailed in traditional welfare economics and served as a justification for public policy. Recent work in normative economics, however, has increasingly focused on alternative approaches to the social good and their policy implications (see Anand and Ravallion 1993; Hahnel and Albert 1990; Hausman and McPherson 1993, and the review of Sen's research by Sugden 1993). The empirical results here would seem to underscore the importance of such work. As Hausman and McPherson (1993, p. 723) observe: "An economics that is engaged actively and self-critically with the moral aspects of its subject matter cannot help but be more interesting, more illuminating, and ultimately more useful than one that tries not to be."

3

Happiness and Economic Growth: Does the Cross-Section Predict Time Trends? Evidence from Developing Countries

Little is known about happiness trends in the developing world. As a result, point-of-time comparisons between richer and poorer countries have typically been used to infer the likely course of happiness as GDP per capita rises. In this chapter we bring together some of the limited evidence available on happiness in the developing world to examine whether trends over time are consistent with expectations based on cross-sectional data. The developing countries are of special interest, because, according to the cross-sectional comparisons, this is where economic growth would be expected to have its biggest impact on happiness. As it turns out, for the limited number of countries studied here, we find that the actual trends do not conform to those predicted by the cross-sectional relationship.

We examine three specific questions: (1) What is the nature of happiness trends in the developing countries? (2) Does the commonly observed international cross-sectional pattern of diminishing mar-

This chapter is a revised version of: Easterlin, R., Sawangfa, O. (2010). Happiness and Economic Growth: Does the Cross Section Predict Time Trends? Evidence from Developing Countries, in: Diener, E., Kahneman, D., Helliwell, J. (Eds.), International Differences in Well-Being. New York, reprinted with permission of Oxford University Press. All those who have used the World Values Survey must be grateful for this impressive undertaking by Ronald Inglehart and his collaborators that has placed in the public domain information on subjective attitudes and well-being for so many countries throughout the world over the past two to three decades. Without these data Chapters 3, 4, and 5 of Part II would not have been possible. We have benefited from suggestions made by Timothy Biblarz, Ed Diener, John Ham, John Helliwell, Betsey Stevenson, and Justin Wolfers, and the generous assistance of Jacqueline Zweig and Laura Angelescu. For their help in providing data and comments thereon, special thanks go to Valerie Møller (South Africa) and Takayoshi Kusago (Japan). Financial support was provided by the University of Southern California.

ginal utility of income predict the time trend in happiness? (3) Are higher rates of economic growth typically accompanied by more positive trends in happiness? We start with no preconceptions as to what the answers should be. Our interest is factual: to find out what the evidence is on these questions.

Studies of time trends in happiness in developing countries are virtually non-existent due to the limited and fragmentary nature of the available data. In the economics literature the most notable exception is a recent paper by Stevenson and Wolfers (2008), discussed in Chapter 5. Outside of economics, there is a time series study by two quality-of-life specialists, Michael Hagerty and Ruut Veenhoven (2003) which, like the Stevenson and Wolfers paper, claims to find that happiness is positively associated with economic growth. The data and methods used in this study have been critiqued by Easterlin (2005b). (See also the reply by Hagerty and Veenhoven 2006). Also, political scientist Ronald Inglehart and his collaborators in an analysis of World Values Survey data for recent decades report that "happiness rose in 45 of 52 countries for which substantial time series data were available" (Inglehart, Foa, Peterson and Welzel 2008, p. 264). As explained in Chapter 4, this inference appears to result from an upward bias between waves 2 and 3 of the WVS in the happiness measure on which the authors' conclusion relies.[1]

Our criterion for including a country to study happiness trends is that there be at least three comparable observations on subjective well-being spanning at least ten years; the average period spanned is actually about 16 years. This is a short time series for studying happiness. The original time series study of happiness and economic growth found that, when comparing identical happiness questions, there was an increase in happiness in the United States from 1946 to 1956–57, followed by a decline to 1970, with a negligible net change over the entire period (Chapter 1). The rise and fall observed in the United States over more than two decades suggests that even a ten- or fifteen-year period may fail to give a valid indication of the long-term trend. But even when we set minima as low as a ten-year period and comparable observations at three, we are left with fairly few developing countries – a total of only thirteen. This small number is somewhat compensated for by the fact that most are quite populous, and several have very high rates of economic growth. Indeed, four (Brazil, China, Japan, and South Korea) have the distinction of being among the thirteen "success stories" of economic growth recently featured in a World Bank Report (Commission on Growth and Development 2008).

Happiness depends on many factors (Bruni and Porta 2005; Frey and Stutzer 2002a; Layard 2005). Generalizations about growth and happiness in developing countries, however, have typically been based on bivariate cross-sectional comparisons of national measures of subjective well-being and per capita income. A succinct example of inferring time trends of subjective well-being for developing countries from a bivariate multi-country cross-section appears in the valuable survey volume by two of the leading economists in the study of the economics of happiness:

> "Comparing across countries, it is true that income and happiness are positively related and that the marginal utility falls with higher income. Higher income clearly raises happiness in developing countries, while the effect is only small, if it exists at all, in rich countries." (Frey and Stutzer 2002a, p. 90)

Hence, in testing here such generalizations against time series evidence we too employ a bivariate methodology. Some analysts look at happiness in relation to the absolute amount of change in income; others, the percentage change. In the analysis below, we look at both.

In keeping with much of the literature the term "happiness" has been used to this point as a proxy for measures of subjective well-being (SWB) in general. The following analysis is based specifically on two measures of SWB, overall life satisfaction and satisfaction with finances. Although satisfaction with finances is less comprehensive than overall life satisfaction, one might expect it to be even more closely related to economic growth and thus an even better measure to test the happiness–growth relationship. Most importantly, by using two measures we are able to gauge whether they provide consistent answers to our three questions. In what follows, the term "subjective well-being" is used when referring to the two measures either separately or together.

3.1. Data and Measures

The principal data set is the World Values Survey (WVS), conducted in an increasing number of countries throughout the world in five waves: 1981–84, 1989–93, 1994–99, 1999–2004, and 2005–2007 (World and European Values Surveys Four-Wave Integrated Data File 2006; World Values Survey 2005 Official Data File V.20081015, 2008). Most of the developing countries included here were first surveyed in wave 2, but four (Argentina, Japan, South Korea, and Mexico) were covered in wave 1. A second major source is the Latinobarometer, conducted almost annually since 1995. For the six Latin American countries studied here – Argentina, Brazil, Chile, Mexico, Peru, and Venezuela – we rely on the Latinobarometer once it is available rather than the WVS, because of its fuller time series coverage. Two African countries, Nigeria and South Africa, are included. For South Africa, besides the WVS, there is a separate survey, the South African Quality of Life Trends Study commissioned to MarkData (hereafter SA MarkData) that provides a check on the WVS data.[2] Five Asian countries are studied – China, India, Japan, South Korea, and Turkey. For China two other survey sources, Gallup and the Asiabarometer are used to check the WVS. For Japan the primary series comes from the "Life in Nation" surveys. These surveys start in 1958 when Japan's GDP per capita, at 11 percent of the U.S. level in 2000, put it well within the developing bloc (Chapter 2). The series extends through 2007, and is complemented by the WVS and a survey conducted by the Cabinet Office of Japan and kindly provided by Takayoshi Kusago covering the period 1978–2005 (Kusago 2007).[3] The three surveys for Japan all terminate at a point when Japan's GDP per capita is upwards of 80 percent of the U.S. 2000 level, and thus span the widest range of growth experience covered here.

In the Japanese "Life in Nation" surveys there are several changes in the survey question between 1958 and 2007 (Hirata 2001; Stevenson and Wolfers 2008). Stevenson and Wolfers 2008, Table 3.5 gives a valuable digest of these data. We therefore divided the series into three segments that we analyze separately, Japan 1 (1958–1969), Japan 2 (1970–1991), and Japan 3 (1992–2007). The 11-year Japan 1 series comprises two shorter segments that we pool in order to satisfy our 10 year minimum criterion, using a dummy variable to account for the difference in response level attributable to the change in survey question. The WVS data for Japan (1981–2005), used in the analysis of satisfaction with finances, are labeled Japan 4.

The GDP data are those of the World Bank 1975 onwards (World Development Indicators Online 2008). Those for Japan prior to 1975 are based on a backward extrapolation of the World Bank series using the Penn World Table (Heston, Summers, and Aten 2006).

We date the observations on subjective well-being here, not at the actual survey dates, but to match the annual GDP observations that they most likely reflect. The GDP data are for calendar years while the SWB surveys typically relate to a single month or span only a few months. If a survey is conducted early in a year it would clearly be meaningless to link it to a GDP estimate covering the entire twelve months of the same year. Our procedure, therefore, is as follows. An SWB survey conducted within the first four months of a year, say, January–April 1991, is linked to 1990 GDP; a mid-year survey, conducted in the period May through August 1991 is compared to the GDP average of 1990 and 1991 and dated 1990.5; and a survey conducted in the latter part of the year, September–December 1991, is compared with 1991 GDP and dated 1991.

In the WVS life satisfaction and satisfaction with finances are measured on a response scale ranging in integer values from 1(= dissatisfied) to 10 (= satisfied). The specific question for each subjective well-being measure used here is given in Appendix A. We do not use the 4-category happiness measure from the WVS, except for India from wave 3 onward. The 10-response categories of the other two measures have the obvious advantage of greater sensitivity, but as mentioned earlier and discussed in Chapter 4 the happiness measure is biased upwards between waves 2 and 3.

For overall life satisfaction there is also a bias problem, one that would tend to reduce life satisfaction in waves 3 and 4 compared to the earlier and later waves. In this case it is a "focusing bias", due to placing the question on financial satisfaction before that on overall life satisfaction in waves 3 and 4 (cf. Stevenson and Wolfers 2008). However, the question on financial, as opposed to life satisfaction appears to be comparable across waves in terms of both content and context. Both life and financial satisfaction typically exhibit similar directions of change between waves 2 and 3, suggesting that the bias in the question on life satisfaction, to the extent it exists, is not as serious as that in the happiness measure.

The Latinobarometer, used here together with the WVS for all six Latin American countries, also has comparability problems. The response categories for life satisfaction in the first two surveys (1997 and 2000) differ from those in subsequent surveys; hence the observations for the first two years are not used here. Also, the 2006 Latinobarometer data on financial satisfaction are omitted. In this case, a focusing bias occurred in 2006, because of the placement before the financial satisfaction question of a new question involving comparison with one's parents' situation that tended to bias upward the subsequent response on financial satisfaction. [4]

3.2. Methods

We compute the long-term growth rate of SWB by regressing it on time, taking as our period of analysis for each country the longest time span available. The long-term growth rate of GDP per capita is computed from the GDP per capita values at the start and end of the period covered by the SWB observations. When more than one data set is available for SWB, as in the case of the Latin American countries, we compute a pooled regression with a dummy variable to identify the different data set. Growth rates for both SWB and GDP per capita are per year; the change in SWB is measured in absolute terms, that in GDP per capita, in percentage terms.

In taking long periods for analysis the purpose is specifically to distinguish the longer-from the shorter-term relationship between SWB and GDP per capita. There is ample evidence that short term fluctuations in SWB are positive correlated with macroeconomic conditions. This is nowhere more apparent than in the massive economic collapse and subsequent recovery of the transition countries, but it is also evident in developed countries (Chapter 4; Di Tella, MacCulloch and Oswald 2001). This shorter-term positive association between fluctuations in SWB and GDP per capita should not be mistaken for the longer term relation. Imagine, for example, two series, one of SWB and one of GDP per capita, exhibiting synchronous sawtooth movements but those in SWB are around a horizontal trend line, while those in GDP per capita are about a positive trend. The shorter-term relationship between the growth rate of SWB and that of GDP per capita is positive, but the longer-term one is not. As shown in Chapter 5, if data with shorter and longer time spans for different countries are pooled, the shorter-term positive relationship will tend to dominate a regression of SWB on GDP per capita. This is because shorter-term growth rates of GDP per capita, both positive and negative, are larger (disregarding sign) than long-term growth rates; hence the short-term rates are more likely to be the outlying observations and disproportionately affect the regression results.

As mentioned, the WVS response scale for the two SWB questions used here ranges in integer values from 1 (= dissatisfied) to 10 (= satisfied). In other surveys included in this chapter, the response options are typically categorical, not numerical. In keeping with the usual practice in the literature, we have assigned integer

values to each category from 1 (= the worst response option) up
to the number corresponding to the best response option (e.g., 4
if there are four response categories). We then compute the mean
SWB from the integer responses for all respondents for each year
that data are available.

Because the WVS satisfaction questions are on a 1–10 scale,
while the non-WVS questions are on a 1–4 or 1–5 scale, we rescale
the WVS responses to conform to the non-WVS scale. In rescaling
the WVS to a 1–4 response scale, for example, we assume a WVS
response of 10 corresponds to a non-WVS response of 4, a WVS response of 1 to a non-WVS response of 1, and make a linear transformation using the formula:

$$y = 0.3333x + 0.6667,$$

where $y = $ SWB on the non-WVS scale, and $x = $ SWB on the WVS
scale. In the regression results in the analysis below the slope coefficients are those based on the rescaled WVS responses.

The WVS surveys are imperfect. In the preceding section we
noted that the wording or context of the SWB questions sometimes changes from one survey to another. Another problem is
that for some countries the geographic coverage of the surveys
changes over time. Sometimes sample weights are provided to adjust for variations in sample coverage, but weights are generally
not given regularly enough to yield time series comparable for our
purpose.

A valuable summary based on WVS documentation of shifts in
survey coverage is given by Stevenson and Wolfers (2008, Appendix B). Their criterion for including a WVS survey in their analysis
appears to be that the survey must be nationally representative.
As a result they discard a number of surveys for seven of the countries studied here. Although a nationally representative survey is
clearly preferable, it seems premature to dismiss other surveys as
unusable. Invariably, when the WVS surveys are not nationally
representative, they cover the more literate and urbanized segments of the population. These are precisely the groups that are
most likely to be experiencing the income benefits of economic
growth. Hence if economic growth is raising subjective well-being,
it is these population groups that one would expect to show the
improvement in SWB most clearly.

The real problem for comparability over time arises when the survey coverage changes, typically to a nationally representative survey. We try to minimize the effects of such shifts in several ways, depending on the nature of the available data. For two countries, Argentina and Chile, we use only the earlier WVS surveys that appear to be comparable over time in geographic coverage; these surveys cover about 70 percent of the population. For two other countries, Mexico and Nigeria, where the survey coverage is shifting, especially in regard to coverage of the rural population, we base our analysis on the SWB means for the population living in places of 100,000 population or more, those likely to be covered fairly consistently. Finally, for two other countries, China and South Africa, we have independent surveys by other organizations that provide support for the time series change in SWB reported in the WVS. Of the seven countries included here whose surveys are largely or wholly discarded by Stevenson and Wolfers we are left with only India, a country that appears here solely in the analysis of life satisfaction, and whose exclusion would not alter the results. The basic data for all thirteen countries studied here and the rationale for the data chosen are given in Appendix B. We do not show there the results of an additional test that we ran – an estimate of the SWB mean at each date after controlling to the extent possible for shifts in population composition by gender, age, education, and size of place of residence. This analysis yielded patterns of change much like those in the data selected.

For countries for which we use two surveys to establish the trend in SWB, we compute the ordinary least squares (OLS) time trend for each series separately, and then a pooled regression that includes a dummy variable for one of the series. Because the wording of the SWB question and/or response categories change from one series to another, the dummy variable tells one whether the change has a significant effect on the level of the series. The detailed regression results for each country are given in Appendix B.

3.3. Results

Trends in subjective well-being. Within a country, life satisfaction and financial satisfaction almost always trend in the same direction, providing mutually consistent evidence of the longer-term movement in subjective well-being. In nine of the twelve countries for which the two measures are available, they both move upward, and in two, downward (compare the upper right and lower left quadrants of Figure 3.1). Peru is a borderline exception.

Life satisfaction is often seen as the net outcome of satisfaction with various domains of life – finances, family, health, work, friends, and so on (see Part III). The significant relation between financial and life satisfaction found here provides new evidence consistent with the view that satisfaction with economic conditions is an important determinant of the time series movement in life satisfaction (cf. Easterlin and Plagnol 2008). This relationship holds in Figure 3.1 despite the fact that the number of years spanned by the financial satisfaction series is sometimes different from that for life satisfaction. In four countries the difference is about one year, but in one (South Africa) it is around 9 years (see column 2 of Tables 3.1 and 3.2).

Figure 3.1

Annual Rate of Change in Life Satisfaction and Financial Satisfaction

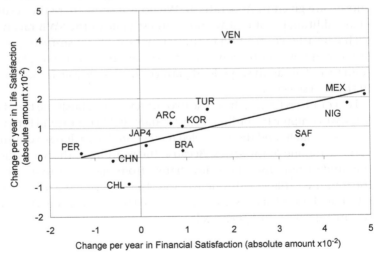

Source: Column 4 of Tables 3.1 and 3.2. The fitted OLS regression is $y = 0.47081 + 0.35442x$; $n = 12$; adjusted $R^2 = 0.24$; t-statistics in parentheses.   (1.19)   (2.12)

Table 3.1

Annual Growth Rates of Life Satisfaction and GDP per Capita in Specified Country during Specified Period
(countries arrayed from high to low by growth rate of GDP per capita)

	(1)	(2)	(3)	(4)	(5)
				Life satisfaction	GDP per capita
Country	Period	Years	Number of observations	Change per year $*10^{-2}$ (1-4) scale	% change per year (PPP 2000 international dollars)
Japan 1	1958-1969	11	12	1.37*	9.4
China	1995-2007	12	3	-0.16	8.61
South Korea	1980-2005	25	4	1.04	5.4
India	1995-2006	11	3	0.28	4.95
Chile	1989.5-2006	16.5	7	-0.94	4.04
Japan 2	1970-1991	21	25	0.56**	3.29
Turkey	1990-2007	17	4	1.6	2.33
Peru	1995.5-2006	10.5	7	0.15	2.18
Mexico	1989.5-2006	16.5	8	2.10*	1.63
Brazil	1991-2006	15	7	0.22	1.28
Argentina	1984-2006	22	8	1.13	1.15
Japan 3	1992-2007	15	14	-1.22**	1.12
Venezuela	1995-2006	11	7	3.90*	0.53
Nigeria	1989.5-2000	10.5	3	1.8	0.19
South Africa	1981-2007	26	5	0.37	0.17
Addendum					
Japan	1958-2007	49	51	0.13	4.03
Japan 4	1981-2005	24	5	0.42	1.97

Notes: + significant at 10%; * significant at 5%; ** significant at 1%
Source: Life satisfaction, Appendixes B and C. GDP, World Bank 2007. The World Bank series for Japan was extrapolated from 1975 back to 1958 using the annual rate of change in the Penn World Table 6.2.

Table 3.2

Annual Growth Rates of Financial Satisfaction and GDP per Capita in Specified Country during Specified Period
(countries arrayed from high to low by growth rate of GDP per capita)

	(1)	(2)	(3)	(4)	(5)
	Period			Financial satisfaction	GDP per capita
Country	Period	Years	Number of observations	Change per year $*10^{-2}$ (1-5) scale	% change per year (PPP 2000 international dollars)
China	1995-2007	12	3	-0.58	8.61
South Korea	1980-2005	25	5	0.92	5.4
Chile	1989.5-2005	15.5	12	-0.27	4.11
Turkey	1990-2007	17	4	1.47	2.33
Japan 4	1981-2005	24	5	0.13	1.97
Peru	1994.5-2005	10.5	10	-1.34	1.01
Mexico	1989.5-2005	15.5	12	4.91*	1.5
Brazil	1991-2005	14	12	0.93	1.19
South Africa	1990-2007	17	4	3.55	0.98
Argentina	1984-2005	21	13	0.65	0.86
Nigeria	1989.5-2000	10.5	3	4.53	0.19
Venezuela	1994.5-2005	10.5	10	1.98	-0.14

Notes: + significant at 10%; * significant at 5%; ** significant at 1%
Source: See Table 3.1.

In most countries the rates of change in subjective well-being are not very great, and, in all but Mexico and Venezuela, not significantly different from zero (Tables 3.1 and 3.2, column 4; the Japan 4 series, available for both life and financial satisfaction, is used in the Figure 3.1 analysis). It is noteworthy, however, that in nine of twelve countries, the regression coefficients for both life and financial satisfaction are positive, signifying some improvement over time, if not enough to achieve statistical significance. Possibly the lack of significance for six of the twelve countries is because the number of observations is only 3 to 5. If, however, we regress log GDP instead of SWB on time, using only the dates for which there are SWB values, the trend coefficient is significant at the 5-percent level or better for three of the same six countries despite the few observations. Moreover, the issue of significance, or lack thereof, does not affect the findings on the two main questions below with which this chapter is primarily concerned.

Figure 3.2

Regression of Life Satisfaction on GDP per Capita, WVS Cross-Section (GDP per capita on absolute scale; 195 observations for 89 countries)

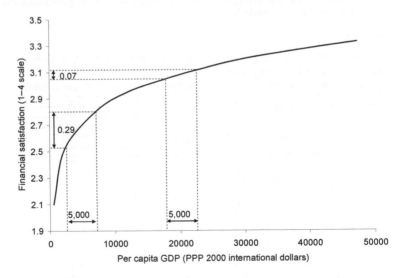

Source: WVS, Waves 1–4. The fitted regression is $y = 0.405 + 0.270\ln(x)$ $(n = 195,$ adjusted $R^2 = 0.452)$; *t*-statistics in parentheses. $\qquad$ (2.05) $\quad$ (12.68)

Figure 3.3

Regression of Financial Satisfaction on GDP per Capita, WVS Cross-Section (GDP per capita on absolute scale; 136 observations for 54 countries)

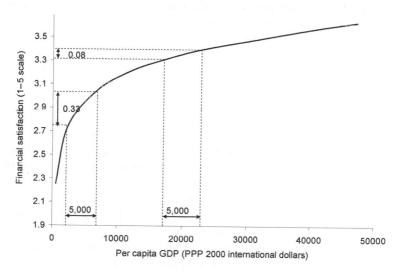

Source: WVS, Waves 1–4. The fitted regression is $y = 0.338+0.305\ln(x)$ $(n = 136,$ adjusted $R^2 = 0.31)$; t-statistics in parentheses.   (0.96) (7.85)

The principal issue is whether countries with better economic performance exhibit more positive trends in SWB. To answer this, we turn to two specific questions:

(1) Do the actual trends in SWB conform to what might be expected based on the cross-sectional relation of SWB and GDP per capita?
(2) Are the trends in SWB positively associated with the rate of economic growth?

Predicted and actual trends in SWB. The predicted trends in SWB are estimated here by the practice common in the literature of using a point-of-time comparison between richer and poorer countries to infer the likely course of happiness as GDP per capita rises (Frey and Stutzer 2002a; Layard 2005; Stevenson and Wolfers 2008). We then compare the actual trends in SWB in our thirteen countries with the predicted trends to see to what extent the international cross-sectional relation of SWB to GDP per capita predicts the observed trends. Our finding is that the actual trends are not significantly related to the predicted trends. Put more strongly: knowing the actual change over time in a country's GDP per capita and the multi-country cross-sectional relation of SWB to GDP per capita adds nothing, on average, to one's ability to predict the actual time series change in SWB in a country.

Our procedure in general is as follows. We first estimate the cross-sectional relation between SWB and log GDP per capita by pooling all of the observations from all countries included in waves 1–4 of the WVS (the regression equations are reported in the source notes to Figures 3.2 and 3.3). We then estimate from the regression equation the predicted change in SWB by entering the change in log GDP per capita between the initial and terminal dates of observation for each country. Finally, we compare the predicted change in SWB with the actual change between these dates as estimated from a regression on time of the observed values of SWB.

The cross-sectional relation of both life and financial satisfaction to absolute GDP per capita exhibits the typical pattern of diminishing marginal utility of income (Figures 3.2 and 3.3). A $5,000 increment of GDP per capita from an initial level of $2,500, for example, raises life satisfaction by almost 0.3 points on a 1–4 scale; in contrast, from an initial level of $17,500, the increment in life satisfaction for the same absolute change in GDP per capita is less than one-fourth as much, 0.07 points (Figure 3.2). The increments in financial satisfaction for corresponding changes in GDP per capita are respectively 0.33 and 0.08 on a 1–5 scale (Figure 3.3). Thus, the cross-sectional regressions in Figures 3.2 and 3.3 demonstrate the assertion commonly made that a given absolute increase in GDP per capita has a greater impact on SWB in a poor than a rich country.

The calculation of the time series changes in life satisfaction predicted by the WVS cross-section of Figure 3.2 can be illustrated by comparing the prediction for China, which comes close to the poorer country's situation in Figure 3.2, with that for Japan 1992–2007 (the Japan 3 segment), which illustrates the richer country's situation. In the period under study China's absolute growth in GDP per capita is $4,631; Japan's, not much different, $4,409 (Table 3.3, column 4). But China's mean GDP per capita is about one fifth of Japan's – $5,047 compared with $26,372 (column 2). Consequently, the slope of the regression curve, which indicates the increment in life satisfaction associated with a given increment in the dollar amount of GDP per capita, is considerably greater at China's GDP level than Japan's (column 3). To calculate

Table 3.3

Full-Period Change in Life Satisfaction, Actual and that Predicted from Figure 3.2 Cross-Section (Countries Arrayed From Low to High by Mean GDP per Capita in Specified Period)

	(1)	(2)	(3)	(4)	(5)	(6)	(7)
				Δ GDP per capita			
Country	Period	Mean GDP per capita (PPP 2000 international dollars)	Predicted Δ LS per $1000 GDP per capita	PPP 2000 international dollars	Natural log	Predicted Δ LS, full period	Actual Δ LS, full period
Nigeria	1989.5-2000	838.10	0.322	16.40	0.020	0.005	0.189
India	1995-2006	2,626.00	0.105	1,363.80	0.532	0.144	-0.030
China	1995-2007	5,047.00	0.058	4,631.10	0.992	0.268	-0.019
Peru	1995.5-2006	5,145.10	0.053	1,160.00	0.226	0.061	0.016
Venezuela	1995-2006	6,301.70	0.043	367.20	0.058	0.016	0.429
Turkey	1990-2007	6,778.30	0.040	2,623.70	0.392	0.106	0.271
Brazil	1991-2006	7,148.50	0.038	1,354.50	0.190	0.051	0.033
Japan 1	1958-1969	7,591.50	0.038	6,946.90	0.988	0.267	0.151
Chile	1989.5-2006	8,314.90	0.034	5,247.30	0.653	0.177	-0.154
Mexico	1989.5-2006	8,800.60	0.031	2,333.30	0.267	0.072	0.346
South Africa	1981-2007	10,562.40	0.026	453.90	0.043	0.012	0.096
Argentina	1984-2006	12,135.10	0.022	3,034.60	0.251	0.068	0.248
South Korea	1980-2005	12,461.50	0.025	14,364.10	1.314	0.355	0.261
Japan 2	1970-1991	18,079.20	0.016	11,830.50	0.679	0.184	0.117
Japan 3	1992-2007	26,372.00	0.010	4,408.90	0.168	0.045	-0.183
Addendum							
Japan	1958-2007	16,347.20	0.021	24,458.40	1.937	0.524	0.062
Japan 4	1981-2005	22,222.80	0.012	10,243.50	0.469	0.127	0.100

the change in life satisfaction that one would predict for China based on the observed change in GDP per capita, we express China's GDP per capita at the beginning and end of the period in log terms, compute the difference (0.992; column 5) and multiply it by the slope coefficient (0.270) of the cross-sectional regression equation underlying Figure 3.2 (given in the source note for Figure 3.2). The result is a predicted change in China's life satisfaction of 0.268 for its GDP change of $4,631. The same procedure for Japan yields a predicted change of 0.045 – about one-sixth of that for China – for its GDP change of $4,409.

Figure 3.4

Actual Change in Life Satisfaction and that Predicted from Change in GDP per Capita Using WVS Cross-Sectional Regression in Figure 3.2

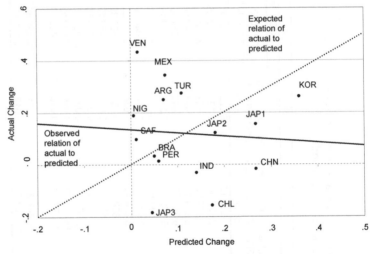

Source: Table 3.3, columns 6 and 7; regression statistics, Table 3.5. For each country the change in life satisfaction is measured over the full period spanned by the life satisfaction data.

The actual change in life satisfaction for each country is estimated from a regression on time of the life satisfaction values actually observed. For China, the slope coefficient of the regression, the change per year in life satisfaction is -0.0016 on a 1–4 scale (Table 3.1, column 4). Multiplying this by the number of years in the period under study, 12, yields the actual change in life satisfaction, -0.019, as estimated from the time trend. For Japan, the slope coefficient of observed life satisfaction on time is -0.0122; the period, 15 years; and the estimated actual change in life satisfaction, -0.183. Thus we obtain for China a predicted change in life satisfaction from the WVS cross-section of 0.268, and an actual change, based on the observed life satisfaction time trend, of -0.019. For Japan, the corresponding values are: predicted, 0.045; actual, -0.183 (these are the values for China and Japan that appear in columns 6 and 7 of Table 3.3).

Figure 3.5

Actual Change in Financial Satisfaction and that Predicted from Change in GDP per Capita Using WVS Cross-Sectional Regression in Figure 3.3

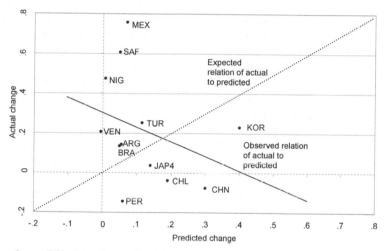

Source: Table 3.4, columns 6 and 7; regression statistics, Table 3.5. For each country the change in financial satisfaction is measured over the full period spanned by the financial satisfaction data.

For life satisfaction there are 13 other cases – yielding a total of 15 altogether – for which we can estimate the actual change in life satisfaction and compare it with that predicted from the WVS cross-section. These fifteen paired observations (listed in columns 6 and 7 of Table 3.3) are plotted in Figure 3.4. If the actual changes corresponded to those predicted from the cross-sectional relationship, the 15 observations would fall along the positively sloped dotted line in Figure 3.4, a line with a slope of 1.0. For 9 of the 15 life satisfaction observations the actual change is less than the predicted change (the points falling below the dotted line), and in four of these cases (China, Chile, India, Japan 3) the actual change is negative while the predicted change is positive. Six countries (Venezuela, Mexico, Turkey, Argentina, Nigeria, and South Africa) have changes in life satisfaction considerably in excess of what one would expect based on the cross-sectional relation. For financial satisfaction the distribution of countries above and below the dotted line is quite similar to that for life satisfaction, except that Brazil shifts from slightly below to slightly above the dotted line (Figure 3.5).

A regression line fitted to the 15 observations in Figure 3.4 – the solid line plotted in the figure – actually has a somewhat negative slope, -0.152, though it is not statistically significant (the regression statistics are reported in Table 3.5). Moreover, the dotted line slope coefficient of 1.0 lies outside a two-standard-error range of the solid line slope coefficient of -0.152. The same conclusions hold for the coefficients in the analysis of financial satisfaction in Figure 3.5. We conclude, therefore, that for the thirteen countries studied here the actual changes in SWB typically have no relation to the cross-sectional pattern. The practice common in the literature, to infer time trends in SWB from the cross-sectional relationship of SWB to GDP per capita, finds no support in this analysis.

Japan is of special interest, because it traverses such a broad range of GDP per capita. Compared to the United States GDP per capita level in 2000, Japan moved from 11 percent in 1958 to about 80 percent in 2006. Based on the international cross-sectional pattern in Figure 3.2 this impressive growth in GDP per capita should have raised life satisfaction by 0.52 points, about one-sixth of the way along a 1–4 scale.

Table 3.5

Regression Relationships between Full-Period Actual Change in Subjective Well-Being and Change Predicted from WVS Cross-Section

	Actual Change	
	Life satisfaction	Financial satisfaction
Predicted change	-0.15191	-0.72643
	-0.744	-0.305
Constant	0.13662	0.30221
	(0.084)[+]	(0.024)*
Observations	15	12
R^2	0.008	0.104

Notes: + significant at 10%; * significant at 5%; ** significant at 1%; *p* values in brackets
Source: Life satisfaction, Table 3.3, columns 6 and 7; financial satisfaction, Table 3.4, columns 6 and 7. For each country the change in SWB is measured over the full period spanned by the SWB data.

Table 3.4

Full-Period Change in Financial Satisfaction, Actual and that Predicted from Figure 3 Cross-Section (Countries Arrayed From Low to High by Mean GDP per Capita in Specified Period)

Country	(1) Period	(2) Mean GDP per capita (PPP 2000 international dollars)	(3) Predicted Δ LS per $1000 GDP per capita	(4) Δ GDP per capita PPP 2000 international dollars	(5) Δ GDP per capita Natural log	(6) Predicted Δ LS, full period	(7) Actual Δ LS, full period
Nigeria	1989.5-2000	838.1	0.364	16.4	0.02	0.006	0.475
Peru	1994.5-2005	4,890.30	0.063	970	0.199	0.061	-0.141
China	1995-2007	5,047.00	0.065	4,631.10	0.992	0.303	-0.07
Venezuela	1994.5-2005	6,020.40	0.051	-88.5	-0.015	-0.004	0.208
Turkey	1990-2007	6,778.30	0.046	2,623.70	0.392	0.12	0.25
Brazil	1991-2005	7,055.10	0.043	1,167.80	0.166	0.051	0.13
Chile	1989.5-2005	8,156.90	0.039	4,931.20	0.624	0.19	-0.042
Mexico	1989.5-2005	8,625.90	0.036	1,983.90	0.231	0.071	0.762
South Africa	1990-2007	9,968.30	0.031	1,642.20	0.165	0.05	0.604
Argentina	1984-2005	11,663.50	0.026	2,091.50	0.18	0.055	0.137
South Korea	1980-2005	12,461.50	0.028	14,364.10	1.314	0.401	0.231
Japan 4	1981-2005	22,222.80	0.014	10,243.50	0.469	0.143	0.032

The actual change in life satisfaction over this 48-year period, as estimated from a pooled regression of life satisfaction on time, is slightly (but not significantly) positive, 0.06 points. (The regression is given in Appendix B.)

Subjective well-being and economic growth. When plotted against the natural log, rather than the absolute value of GDP per capita, the cross-sectional regressions underlying Figures 3.2 and 3.3 above imply that higher rates of economic growth are accompanied by greater improvements in SWB. In the Figure 3.6 cross-section, for example, where GDP is now on a logarithmic scale, an increase in GDP per capita from $1,000 to $2,000 (an increase in log GDP per capita from 6.91 to 7.60) raises life satisfaction by 0.18 points. Doubling the rate of economic growth, i.e. raising GDP per capita from $1,000 to $4,000 (log GDP per capita, from 6.91 to 8.29) doubles the increase in life satisfaction to 0.36 points. Figure 3.7 indicates for financial satisfaction a similar relationship, a doubling of the rate of economic growth accompanied by a doubling of the increase of subjective well-being.

The relationship that one would predict from the cross-sectional regression between the rate of change per year in GDP per capita (in percentage terms) and that in SWB (in absolute amounts) is shown by the dotted lines marked "Predicted Relation" in Figures 3.8 and 3.9. The points in these lines are obtained by using the regression equations given at the bottom of Figures 3.2 and 3.3 to estimate the improvement in SWB that would result from annual growth rates of GDP per capita of 1, 3, 5 percent, and so on. The dotted lines demonstrate that higher growth rates of SWB are expected to be associated with higher rates of economic growth.

Table 3.6

Regression Relationships between Annual Growth Rates of Subjective Well-Being and GDP per Capita

	(1) Δ Life satisfaction	(2) Δ Financial satisfaction
Δ GDP per capita	-0.10084	-0.4007
	-0.419	(0.096)[*]
Constant	1.08787	2.37295
	(0.050)[*]	(0.010)[**]
Observations	15	12
R^2	0.051	0.252

Notes: + significant at 10%; * significant at 5%; ** significant at 1%; *p* values in brackets
Source: Column 1 from Table 3.1, columns 4 and 5; column 2 from Table 3.2, columns. 4 and 5. Growth rates of SWB are in absolute amount per year; of GDP per capita, percent per year.

Figure 3.6

Life Satisfaction and GDP per Capita, WVS Cross-Section
(GDP per capita on logarithmic scale)

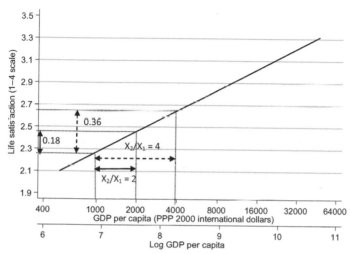

Source: The regression equation is the same as that for Figure 3.2.

Figure 3.7

Financial Satisfaction and GDP per Capita, WVS Cross-Section
(GDP per capita on logarithmic scale)

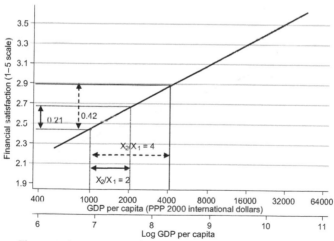

Source: The regression equation is the same as that for Figure 3.3.

Figure 3.8

Annual Rate of Change in Life Satisfaction and in GDP per Capita, Actual and that Predicted from WVS Cross-Section

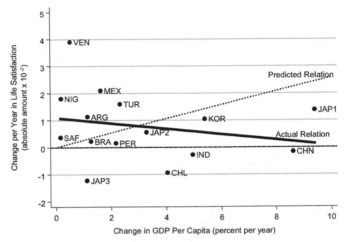

Source: Table 3.1, columns 4 and 5; regression statistics, Table 3.6.

Figure 3.9

Annual Rate of Change in Financial Satisfaction and in GDP per Capita, Actual and that Predicted from WVS Cross-Section

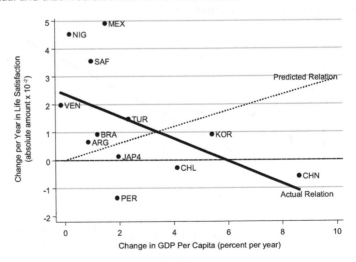

Source: Table 3.2, columns 4 and 5; regression statistics, Table 3.6.

Is a higher growth rate of GDP per capita in fact accompanied by a higher growth rate of SWB? To assess this, we plot in Figures 3.8 and 3.9 the values for each country of the actual rates of change per year in SWB and GDP per capita (given in columns 4 and 5 of Tables 3.1 and 3.2). Without exception, countries with quite high rates of growth in GDP per capita, 4 percent per year or more, fall below the dotted line, indicating that the improvement in SWB is less than what one would expect based on the cross-section. In contrast, countries with growth rates of GDP per capita lower than 4 percent fall on either side of the dotted line – some have a greater improvement in SWB than would be predicted from the cross section; others less. Regression lines fitted to the country data on growth rates of SWB and GDP per capita – the solid lines in Figures 3.8 and 3.9 marked "Actual Relation" – are, in fact, negatively, not positively inclined. For one of them, financial satisfaction, the slope coefficient is statistically significant at the 10-percent level (Table 3.6). In both figures the dotted line ("Predicted Relation") slope coefficient is significantly different from the solid line ("Actual Relation") slope coefficient. For life satisfaction the slope coefficient of the predicted relation is 0.270 [0.228, 0.312]; the slope coefficient of the actual relation is -0.101 [-0.362, 0.160]. For financial satisfaction the slope coefficient of the predicted relation is 0.305 [0.227, 0.382]; of the actual relation, -0.401 [-0.887, 0.086]. (Numbers in brackets are 95% confidence intervals.) A conservative conclusion would seem to be that for the thirteen developing countries studied here there is no evidence that more rapid economic growth is accompanied by a greater improvement in happiness.

3.4. Conclusion

The experience of thirteen developing countries, scattered across three continents, fails to show any consistent relation between long-term economic growth and the growth rate of subjective well-being. This is true for two measures of subjective well-being that were separately analyzed, life satisfaction and financial satisfaction. The absence of any relationship between financial satisfaction and GDP per capita is especially noteworthy, because this is the SWB measure that one would expect to be most strongly affected by economic growth. However, the two measures of subjective well-being themselves typically trend similarly within a country, providing mutually supporting evidence of the movement in subjective well-being.

Point-of-time cross-sectional regressions of SWB on GDP per capita are often used as a basis for asserting that economic growth raises subjective well-being, especially in poorer countries. For the developing countries studied here there is no relation between expectations based on cross-sectional data and actual time series experience – one more bit of evidence that cross-sectional relationships are a questionable basis for inferring change over time (cf. Chapter 5 in this volume; also Easterly 1999). Of course, we are examining here only the simple bivariate relation between the growth rates of SWB and GDP per capita, but it is the bivariate relation between SWB and GDP per capita that has provided the cross-sectional evidence underlying generalizations that economic growth would raise subjective well-being.

Our conclusions are subject to a number of qualifications. We consider only thirteen of the world's developing countries, though a number of them are the most populous in the world and several have quite high rates of economic growth. Our time series for subjective well-being are short, averaging 16 years. We have tried to minimize shorter-term disturbances by computing growth rates over the full time span covered by the data for each country, but we cannot rule out the possibility that shorter-term influences still affect our estimates of the long-term trend. To maximize the time span covered, we use for some countries data from two different sources. We have tried to screen and test all of the data for comparability over time, but there is no assurance that our procedures are foolproof.

We do find that countries that have higher growth rates of satisfaction with finances typically have higher growth rates of overall life satisfaction. One might reasonably ask, therefore, if financial satisfaction is closely linked to life satisfaction, as this result indicates, why doesn't subjective well-being improve with economic growth? One possible answer to this question is that there are offsetting changes in other happiness domains such as family life. Another is that while economic growth raises objective living conditions, it also raises the standards by which people judge their living conditions (cf. Chapters 1 and 2; also Clark, Frijters and Shields 2008). There is nothing to suggest that those in developing countries are immune to this rise in material aspirations, and that this aspiration mechanism operates only beyond some unspecified "basic needs" point. This rise in standards would undercut the positive impact on well-being of objectively improved living conditions, as measured by GDP per capita. As a result, perceptions of one's financial situation, which is what the survey questions here capture, do not rise commensurately with the objective improvement in living conditions.

Clearly, the results here point to the need for deeper research into the happiness–growth relationship – to the need for consideration of the various effects of economic growth – not only via the accumulation of material goods, but also through aspirations, and work, health, and family concerns (see, for example, Knight and Gunatilaka 2009, 2010). They suggest too the urgency of time series study to test the current plethora of SWB generalizations based only on point-of-time cross-sections.

Appendix A: Survey Questions
World Values Survey

Life satisfaction: All things considered, how satisfied are you with your life as a whole these days? Please use this card to help with your answer.

1 'Dissatisfied' 2 3 4 5 6 7 8 9 10 'Satisfied'

Financial satisfaction: How satisfied are you with the financial situation of your household? If '1' means you are completely dissatisfied on this scale and '10' means you are completely satisfied, where would you put your satisfaction with your household's financial situation?

1 'Dissatisfied' 2 3 4 5 6 7 8 9 10 'Satisfied'

Happiness: Taking all things together, would you say you are:

1 = Very happy; 2 = Quite happy; 3 = Not very happy;
4 = Not at all happy

Latinobarometer

Life satisfaction: In general terms, would you say that you are satisfied with life?
1 = Very satisfied; 2 = Pretty satisfied; 3 = Not very satisfied;
4 = Not satisfied at all

Financial satisfaction: How would you define, in general, the current economic situation of yourself and your family? Would you say that it is...

1 = Very good; 2 = Good; 3 = Regular; 4 = Bad; 5 = Very bad

Gallup Survey (China)

Life satisfaction: Overall, how satisfied or dissatisfied are you with the way things are going in your life today? Would you say you are:
4 = Very satisfied; 3 = Somewhat satisfied; 2 = Somewhat dissatisfied; 1 = Very dissatisfied?

Life in Nation Survey (Japan)

1958–1963:   How do you feel about your circumstances at home? Please choose one of the following: satisfied, not satisfied/not dissatisfied, somewhat dissatisfied, or extremely dissatisfied.

1964–1969:   How do you feel about your life at home? Please choose one of the following: completely satisfied, satisfied, somewhat dissatisfied, or completely dissatisfied.

1970–1991:   How do you feel about your life now? Please choose one of the following: completely satisfied, satisfied, somewhat dissatisfied, or completely dissatisfied.

1992–2007:   Overall, to what degree are you satisfied with your life now? Please choose one of the following: satisfied, somewhat satisfied, somewhat dissatisfied, or dissatisfied.

Cabinet Office of Japan

Life satisfaction: Are you happy with your life overall?

1 = Very satisfied; 2 = Satisfied; 3 = Not satisfied or unsatisfied; 4 = Unsatisfied; 5 = Never satisfied

Eurobarometer

Life satisfaction: On the whole, how satisfied are you with the life you lead?

1 = Not at all satisfied   2 3 4 5 6 7 8 9   10 = Absolutely satisfied

South African Quality of Life Trends Study (Mark Data)

Life satisfaction: [1983, 1999 wording] (revised phrasing)
Taking all things together in your life, how satisfied are you with your life as a whole these days? [On the whole] (Generally speaking) would you say you are very satisfied, satisfied, dissatisfied, or very dissatisfied? (neither/nor, don't know)
(At other dates "neither" is the middle item.)

Happiness:
5 = Very happy; 4 = Fairly happy; 3 = Neither happy nor unhappy; 2 = Fairly unhappy; 1 = Very unhappy

Appendices B and C

Appendices B and C are available at http://www-rcf.usc.edu/~easterl/ and published in the original version of this chapter: Easterlin, R. A., Sawangfa, O. (2010). Happiness and Economic Growth: Does the Cross-Section Predict Time Trends? Evidence from Developing Countries, in: Diener, E., Helliwell, J. F., Kahneman, D. (Eds.), International Differences in Well-Being, New York, NY: Oxford University Press, 166–216.

4

Lost in Transition:
Life Satisfaction on the Road
to Capitalism

What has happened to subjective well-being as the former communist nations of Europe transitioned from centrally planned to market economies? Are people more or less satisfied with their lives? Have disparities in life satisfaction within the population widened or lessened? Are there differences between women and men, young and old, and the more and less educated? Although one might suppose these questions are of interest – some might even say, fundamental interest, considering that they involve comparing capitalism and socialism – they have received little attention in the voluminous literature on transition economies. This chapter seeks to help fill this gap. The geographic scope is central, southern, and eastern Europe; the time, the first decade of transition, 1989–1999, followed by an attempt to place this period in the perspective of recent and earlier experience.

The broad economic facts of the transition have been spelled out numerous times, especially for the period of the 1990s (see, for ex-

This chapter is a revised version of: Easterlin, R. (2009). Lost in Transition: Life Satisfaction on the Road to Capitalism, in: Journal of Economic Behavior and Organization, 71(2), 130–145, reprinted with permission from Elsevier. The present analysis has benefited from excellent research work and comments by Laura Angelescu and Onnicha Sawangfa. Anke C. Plagnol, co-author with me of a paper on Germany, has very generously responded to numerous requests relating to additional tabulations for East Germany, and provided useful comments. Helpful suggestions were also provided by Timothy Biblarz, Nauro F. Campos, John Ham, Timur Kuran, Jeffrey Nugent, Dimiter Philipov, Olga Shemyakina, John Strauss, Tomáš Sobotka, and participants in a University of Southern California seminar. I want also to acknowledge the extremely valuable studies and data compilations of transition analysts cited here, without which this study would not have been possible. Financial support was provided by the University of Southern California.

ample, Campos and Coricelli 2002; Havrylyshyn 2006; Mickiewicz 2005; Murrell 1996; Philipov and Dorbritz 2003; Simai 2006; Svejnar 2002; UNICEF 2001; World Bank 2002). Most notable was an abrupt and massive economic collapse, with measured GDP falling to levels of around 50 to 85 percent of the 1989 level, usually in a few years or less. Subsequently GDP recovered somewhat, though rarely by 1999 to the initial level. A visiting economist from Mars, confronted only with these GDP data, might well conclude that an economic disaster on the scale of the Great Depression had befallen some 400 million of the world's population.[1] On the plus side, consumer goods shortages – a chronic condition under socialism – largely disappeared. With regard to factor inputs, capital shrank and there was a significant increase in flows out of the labor force. Unemployment rates rose from near zero to double digit levels in many countries. "[P]overty and inequality ... both increased sharply in the beginning of the transition and have so far [1999] not shown signs of declining" (Campos and Corticelli 2002, 816; cf. also World Bank 2000b). The social safety nets that prevailed under socialism were severely ruptured (Fox 2003; Orenstein and Haas 2005; Pascall and Manning 2000; Simai 2006; UNICEF 1999, 2001; World Bank 2000a). Accompanying these striking socio-economic developments were equally dramatic changes in the political system. Former police states were replaced by new, often democratic, regimes, and the populations endowed with much wider civil and political rights.

Exactly how such massive changes should play out in terms of people's feelings of well-being is far from clear a priori. On the economic side, there is the debate on whether absolute or relative income determines well-being. If absolute income, then one might expect well-being more or less to follow the course of GDP. If relative income, then well-being might remain unchanged, people simply adapting hedonically to economic vicissitude.

There is also the question of how political change might weigh against economic in its impact on life satisfaction. On the one hand, there is the evidence that, when asked about their sources of well-being, people worldwide rarely mention political circumstances. Rather, they put foremost those concerns that principally occupy their time, most notably making a living, family life, and health (Chapter 1). On this basis, one might argue that economic circumstances would carry the day. On the other hand, there are findings for Switzerland that direct democracy, in the form of access to initiatives and referenda, has a significant positive effect on well-being, other things equal (Frey and Stutzer 2000). Also, a recent cross-country analysis of mostly European nations finds a significant positive relation between democracy and happiness, controlling for income, language, and religion (Dorn et al. 2007).[2] If political change were particularly stressed as determining life satisfaction, one might expect a rise in subjective well-being despite adverse economic events.

The few published empirical studies of trends in life satisfaction during transition usually relate to only one country, cover varying time periods, and give no consistent picture. Frijters and his collaborators find life satisfaction rising along with income in East Germany from 1991 to 2001 (Frijters, Haisken-DeNew and Shields 2004; Frijters, Shields and Haisken-DeNew 2004) and also varying directly with ups and downs in income in Russia between 1995 and 2001 (Frijters et al. 2006). These results are, in their view, vindication of the importance of absolute income in determining well-being. Saris (2001) and Veenhoven (2001) both report declines in life satisfaction in Russia between 1988 and the late 1990s, and Lelkes (2006), a decline in Hungary from the early to late 1990s. Hayo and Seifert (2003) consider economic, as opposed to overall, well-being from 1991 to 1995 and find in seven of ten transition countries declines in the proportion saying their economic situation is satisfactory or very satisfactory. All in all, neither theory nor the existing evidence point conclusively to the course of life satisfaction during the transition. (A recent article by Sanfey and Teksoz [2007] is discussed in the final section of this chapter.)

The analysis that follows first describes briefly the concept and methods employed. It then turns to evidence on the course of life satisfaction during the decade of the 1990s, and, following this, an analysis of who in the population gained and lost in life satisfaction. Finally, the movement of life satisfaction both before and after the 1990s is considered. The primary aim is to present the facts, but the facts immediately raise questions of "why", and so some tentative explanations are ventured, essentially hypotheses deserving further exploration. As will be seen, life satisfaction gives a rather different perspective on the transition than that common in economic studies that seek to evaluate different types of economic reform.

4.1. Concept, Data, Methods

The concept of central interest here is that of overall satisfaction with life, the response to the question: "All things considered how satisfied are you with your life as a whole these days?", asked in the World Values Survey (WVS, cf. Chapter 3). The response scale ranges in integer values from 1 (= dissatisfied) to 10 (= satisfied). The basic data are given in Appendix Table A-1. Transition countries first make their appearance in wave 2 of the WVS (except for Hungary which is included in wave 1), some very shortly after the start of the transition. Wave 5 of the WVS was done in 2005–2007 and some initial results published in Inglehart et al. (2008). The Ingelhart et al. paper and a newly published Eurobarometer survey make possible an update of the change in life satisfaction to 2005 presented in the last section of this chapter. Also included in the present analysis are annual data for East Germany (the former GDR) from June 1990 onward gathered in the German Socio-Economic Panel, and given in Appendix Table A-2.[3] This longitudinal survey contains a general satisfaction question very similar to that in the WVS. In all, the analysis covers thirteen transition countries spanning central Europe, the Baltic States, the Balkans, and the former Soviet Union. The transition countries of central Asia are not represented, because they were not surveyed until wave 3 of the WVS.

The 4-category happiness measure from the WVS is not used here. The 10-response life satisfaction measure has the obvious advantage of greater sensitivity, but there is a more fundamental reason for not using the happiness measure. In most of the transition countries, the happiness measure rises between waves 2 and 3 despite marked declines in life satisfaction. The reason for the increase appears to be a "primacy" bias resulting from a change in the instruction accompanying the happiness question. In wave 2, interviewers were instructed to alternate the order of response choices from one respondent to the next. Thus respondent 1 would be presented with choices ranging from "very happy" down to "not at all happy," while respondent 2 would be presented with "not at all happy" first. There are a number of survey studies demonstrating a tendency for respondents to favor earlier over later choices (Belson 1966; Chan 1991; Schuman and Presser 1981, pp. 56–77). In wave 2, therefore, half the respondents would have been more inclined toward less happy choices by virtue of being presented with the more negative options first. In wave 3, the "very happy" option appears first, and the instruction to alternate response options no longer appears. Hence happiness responses in wave 3 would tend to be biased upward relative to wave 2.

In any given wave the WVS surveys often differ from one country to another in both the year and month of the survey. As in Chapter 3, the life satisfaction observations have been dated here to match the annual GDP observation that they most likely reflect.[4] For six countries (Poland, Czech Republic, Slovakia, Hungary, Bulgaria, Romania) the surveys in waves 3 and 4 both fall in years close together toward the end of the 1990s decade, and these surveys have been merged for simplicity and increased reliability.

Table 4.1

GDP Index and Unemployment Rate at Date of Earliest Life Satisfaction Observation, 13 Transition Countries

	(1)	(2)	(3)
	Date of earliest LS observation	GDP index (1989=100)	Registered Unemployment Rate, (%)
GDP Index > 90			
Former GDR	1989.5	92	0
Poland	1989	100	1.3
Hungary	1990	96	1.7
Estonia	1989.5	96	1.6
Latvia	1989.5	101	2.3
Lithuania	1989.5	98	3.5
Belarus	1990	98	0.5
Russian Federation	1990	97	0.8
GDP Index < 90			
Slovenia	1991	84	10.1
Czech Republic	1991	87	4.1
Slovakia	1991	83	11.8
Bulgaria	1991	83	11.1
Romania	1993	82	10.4

Source: Column 2, Economic Commission for Europe 2003, Table B-1. Column 3, ibid, Table B-7, except Poland, from WVS, and former GDR, from GSOEP. For the Baltic states, Belarus, and the Russian Federation, the date for the unemployment rate is the earliest available, 1992.

Based on the data for which the earliest life satisfaction observation is available, the thirteen countries fall into two groups. For eight, the first observation occurs early in the transition, when GDP is typically 95 percent or more of its 1989 level and the unemployment rate around 2 percent or less (Table 4.1). For the other five, the first observation comes later in the transition when GDP is on the order of 85 percent of its 1989 level and the unemployment rate, usually 10 percent or more. The eight countries for which early-transition life satisfaction observations are available provide the fullest picture of the trend in life satisfaction in the first decade of transition and are principally relied on here.

4.2. The Trend in Well-Being

What can be said about the course of life satisfaction in transition countries during the 1990s? The data for the countries available, although less than comprehensive, give a fairly consistent picture. They suggest two generalizations.

First, life satisfaction plummets and then recovers, roughly following the course of the economy as indexed by real GDP. Second, the recovery of life satisfaction falls short of that in GDP.

The evidence for the first is as follows. Of the eight countries in the upper panel of Table 4.1 with early transition observations, there is one, the former GDR, for which annual life satisfaction data are available, and five with life satisfaction observations for the mid-nineties as well as the late nineties. When the observations for these six countries are plotted against time and compared with annual GDP data, life satisfaction in all six follows a V-shaped pattern fairly similar to that of GDP (Figure 4.1). In a seventh country, Slovenia, which also has three well-spaced observations in the 1990s, with the first falling close to the GDP trough, life satisfaction conforms to the recovery phase of GDP.

Such sizeable and rapid declines in life satisfaction as those in Figure 4.1 are very rare. The magnitudes of the decline from peak to trough in the six transition countries of Figure 4.1 fall outside the range of virtually all of the between-wave changes (both positive and negative) observed in fourteen non-transition European countries in the entire survey period since 1980–84. Moreover, these declines are doubtlessly foreshortened, because the data rarely, if ever, traverse the full peak-to-trough movement.

Figure 4.1

Life Satisfaction c. 1990, 1995, and 1999, and Index of Real GDP, Annually 1986–1999[a]

Former GDR

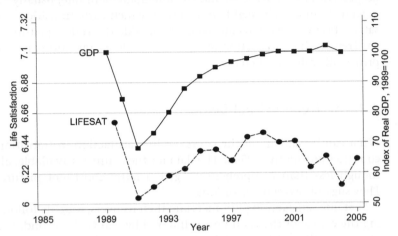

Estonia

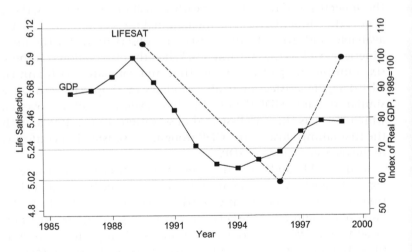

Figure 4.1 (continued)

Life Satisfaction c. 1990, 1995, and 1999, and Index of Real GDP,
Annually 1986–1999[a]

Belarus

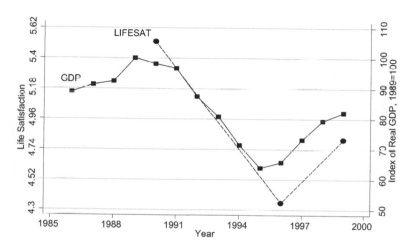

Latvia

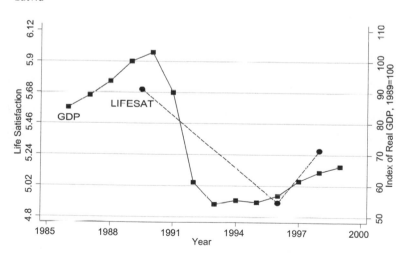

Figure 4.1 (continued)

Life Satisfaction c. 1990, 1995, and 1999, and Index of Real GDP, Annually 1986–1999[a]

Russian Federation

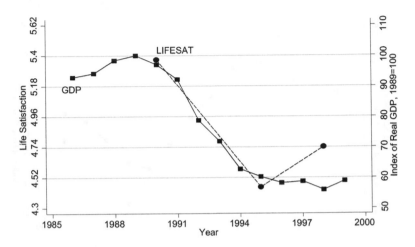

Lithuania

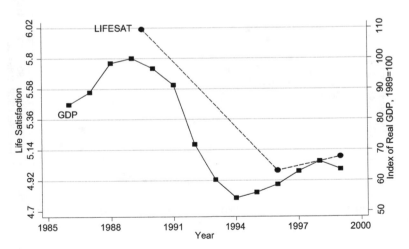

Figure 4.1 (continued)

Life Satisfaction c. 1990, 1995, and 1999, and Index of Real GDP, Annually 1986–1999[a]

Slovenia

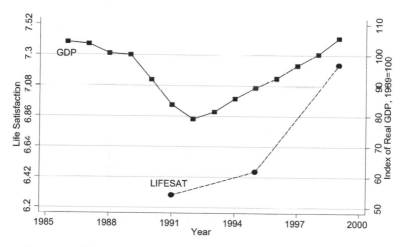

Source: Real GDP, Economic Commission for Europe 2003, Appendix Table B-1. For Former GDR, GDP 2003 on is extrapolated from 2002 via real household income from GSOEP. Life satisfaction, Appendix Tables A-1, A-2.
[a] Former GDR, 1989-2005

The evidence for the second generalization, that the 1990s recovery of life satisfaction falls short of that in GDP, is presented in Figure 4.2. For the eight countries in the upper panel of Table 4.1, those with both an early transition and late 1990s observation, the change in life satisfaction over the full period is plotted against the change in the GDP index, and an OLS regression line fitted to the data. If life satisfaction typically recovered to its 1989-90 level when GDP did, then the regression line would go through the origin. In fact, the y-axis intercept is a significant negative .25 when GDP fully recovers to its initial level (zero change in GDP). Given that the peak to trough decline in life satisfaction is typically around 1.00 or less, the .25 shortfall is sizeable.

Figure 4.2

Changes in Life Satisfaction and Index of Real GDP (1989=100), c. 1990 to 1999, Eight Countries with Early Transition Observations of Life Satisfaction

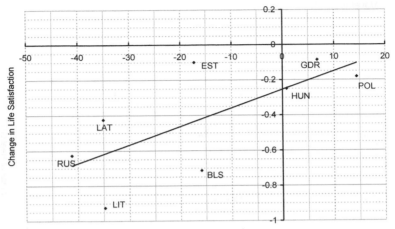

Change in index of Real GDP, 1989=100

Note: The equation for the OLS regression is: $y = 0.010x - 0.251$ (the *t*-stats are respectively 2.44 and -2.34; the adjusted R^2 = 0.414). The countries are those in the upper panel of Table 4.1.
Source: Same as Figure 4.1.

Why does life satisfaction fail to recover commensurately with GDP? The most obvious hypothesis is the sharp deterioration in employment conditions in the transition countries. In the WVS data in every one of the thirteen transition countries included here the employment rate, the percentage of the population employed, decreases substantially between the first and last dates for which life satisfaction is observed, with most countries experiencing double-digit declines. The declines reflect increases in both the unemployment rate and the proportion not in the labor force, with increased unemployment typically the larger of the two, especially for men (Table 4.2). As one might expect, the declines in the employment rate are less for the group of five countries whose initial observation occurs later in the transition, but the same pattern is observed in both groups of countries with regard to the increase in the unemployment rate and labor force exit (cf. panels A and B).

Table 4.2

Change in Employment Status of Persons Ages 20–59,
by Gender, c. 1990 to 1999

Country		(1) Per cent employed first date	(2) Employed	(3) Unemployed	(4) Not in labor force
			Percentage point change, first to last date		
A. Eight countries, initial GDP index > 90					
Females					
	Mean	80.2	-14.9	8.4	6.5
	(s.d.)	(9.0)	(6.3)	(4.4)	(6.5)
Males					
	Mean	90.6	-15.6	13.0	2.6
	(s.d.)	(4.9)	(6.1)	(6.6)	(3.4)
B. Five countries, initial GDP index < 90					
Females					
	Mean	74.1	-11.4	5.8	5.6
	(s.d.)	(6.4)	(9.6)	(6.4)	(10.1)
Males					
	Mean	86.6	-9.3	7.7	1.6
	(s.d.)	(7.2)	(7.3)	(6.8)	(4.2)

Source: WVS except former GDR, from GSOEP. The countries are grouped as in Table 4.1.

Trends in the absolute level of real wages also provide evidence of the deterioration of employment conditions. In 1999, average real wages ranged from around 40 to less than 90 percent of those in 1989, save for the Czech Republic, at 107 percent and Poland, 96 percent (UNICEF 2001, Appendix Table 10.9). But while deterioration in employment and wages in the 1990s is universal in the countries under study here, there is considerable variation in the specific form this takes. In the Russian Federation, for example, labor hoarding by state firms occurred along with growing wage arrears of sizeable magnitude. Such variations make difficult simple overall quantitative comparisons of countries' labor market conditions (Barr 2005 provides a good overview).

The significance of the deterioration in employment conditions goes beyond the direct economic effect, for it is also symptomatic of the deterioration of the social support system. Prior to transition there was what has been called the "socialist greenhouse", "an artificial environment typical for the state socialist societies of Eastern Europe..." (Sobotka 2002, p. 41 and Chapter 4). A key feature of this system was that many social benefits were tied to employment, "[w]ith a huge appetite for able labour, the state encouraged women to study, marry and have jobs and babies, and, where kinship support was weak, the state provided the means to help women manage competing demands" (UNICEF 1999, p. viii). With the collapse of employment and the socialist state there occurred a substantial reduction in these additional sources of support (World Bank 2000a).

Table 4.3

Satisfaction With Specified Domains of Life
A. Former GDR, 1990 and 1999

	(1)	(2)	(3)
	1990	1999	Change 1990 to 1999
Satisfaction with:			
Childcare	7.54	6.48	-1.06
Work	7.23	6.48	-0.75
Health	6.62	6.20	-0.42
Household income	5.54	5.55	+0.01
Standard of living	6.36	6.56	+0.20
Dwelling	6.93	7.32	+0.39
Goods availability	3.18	6.17	+2.99
Environment	3.13	6.50	+3.37

B. Hungary, 1992 and 1997

	1992	1997	Change 1992 to 1997
Satisfaction with:			
Work	7.4	6.7	-0.7
Home	7.1	6.5	-0.6
Neighborhood	7.3	6.5	-0.8
Health	6.4	5.8	-0.6
Household income	3.6	3.4	-0.2
Standard of living	4.6	4.5	-0.1

Source: Former GDR, GSOEP. Hungary, Spéder, Paksi and Elekes 1999. In both countries the scale is 0–10.

The implications for life satisfaction of the loss or reduction of such benefits is suggested by data for two countries, the former GDR and Hungary, for which evidence is available on satisfaction with specific domains of life. What stands out is that satisfaction declines in domains with formerly assured support. Thus, in the former GDR satisfaction with health, work, and childcare all decline (Table 4.3, panel A). In contrast, satisfaction with conditions relating to living level is typically greater in 1999 than 1990 – indeed, much greater in the case of goods availability and the environment, two notably deficient areas under socialism. In Hungary, where the first observation is unfortunately not until 1992, satisfaction with work, home, neighborhood, and health are all lower in 1997, while satisfaction with income and standard of living are virtually unchanged (Table 4.3, panel B).

The experience of another transition country, China, perhaps provides additional support for the importance for life satisfaction of employment and social support conditions. The reported growth of China's real GDP has been truly stunning – the 2004 level is estimated to be almost three times that in 1990 (Maddison 2003). Despite such unprecedented growth, life satisfaction has declined. Based on Gallup World Poll data for four dates between 1994 and 2004, Kahneman and Krueger (2006) report a steady decline in the percent of the population somewhat or very satisfied with life. The WVS data span a longer period and give a similar picture:[5]

1990	1995	2001	2007
7.29	6.83	6.53	6.76

Though China did not experience the severe economic collapse of the European countries, several features of the European transition are evident there, notably rising unemployment, increasing inequality, and dismantling of the social safety net. It is possible that these conditions have exerted both in China and Europe a similar drag on life satisfaction.[6]

4.3. Winners and Losers

Those with the biggest loss in life satisfaction during the 1990s are the less educated and the population aged 30 and over; women and men are about equally affected.[7] Disparities in life satisfaction, as measured by the Gini coefficient, typically widened.

The impact of the transition on different demographic groups is evidenced by comparing the coefficients of a multiple regression on end-of-decade data with those on beginning-of-decade data, where the regression is life satisfaction on gender, age, and education.[8] In the case of education the gradient in life satisfaction is typically negligible at the start of the transition, but turns noticeably and significantly positive over the course of the decade (Figure 4.3 first panel). Education is measured here by the age at which education is completed, the only education measure available in the WVS at both dates, with 7 years or less typically the minimum value and 23 years or more, the maximum. Both panels of the figure are plots based on coefficients from a multiple regression with country dummies on pooled data for the seven WVS countries in the upper panel of Table 4.1. Regressions on the individual country data yield quite similar results.

There is fairly little evidence of an age gradient in life satisfaction at the start of the transition, a result similar to that for education (Figure 4.3, second panel). By the late 1990s, however, a significant negative gradient emerges. The age categories here are less than 30 years, 30–44, 45–59, and 60 +, and the end-of-decade coefficients for the last three are all significantly less than that for the youngest group. The two oldest age groups suffer, on average, the largest declines in life satisfaction relative to those under 30 years old. Regressions on data for each country separately typically yield similar results, except that for those 60 years old and over there is more variation among countries, probably due to differences in pension policy.

It is plausible to suppose that the leveling of life satisfaction within the population at the start of the transition is linked to the socialist policies of wage equalization (political standing aside) and full employment, and that the appearance of the differentials just noted is to a considerable extent a reflection of the growth of income and unemployment differences as free market forces take hold. A simple comparison of the change in the Gini coefficient for life satisfaction with that for income provides some support for this hypothesis. In almost all of the eight countries in the upper panel of Table 4.1, inequality in life satisfaction rose in the 1990s and this rise tends to be associated positively with the rise in income inequality (Figure 4.4; the slope coefficient of the regression line is slightly short of significance at the 10 percent level).[9] The rise in income inequality is probably due to several things – the emergence of substantial wage differentials (Brainerd 1998; Milanovic 1999), the growth and differential incidence of unemployment in the population, and the associated demise of the social support system.

Figure 4.3

Life Satisfaction by Education and Age at Start and End of 1990s, Seven Countries with Early Transition Observations

By Education

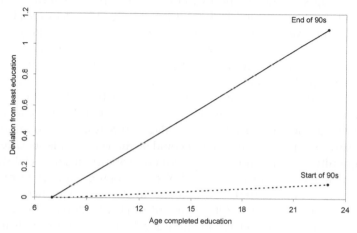

By Age

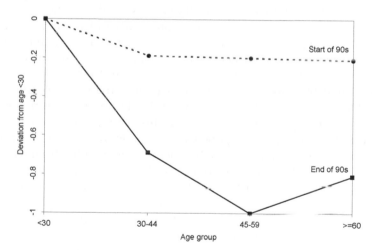

Note: In first panel, controlling for gender and age; in second panel, gender and education. Country dummies are also used. The countries are those in the upper panel of Table 4.1, except the former GDR. The GDR's education categories differ somewhat from the WVS; a separate analysis for the GDR, however, revealed the same patterns. *Source:* WVS, waves 3 and 4.

Why, controlling for education, is there a greater decline in life satisfaction among those in the population 30 and over than among young adults? For those ages 60 and over, the answer probably lies largely in the deterioration of old-age pension support. For those between ages 30 and 59, the answer is perhaps that, when free market conditions were established, most persons age 30 to 59 were already well-embarked on a life course set under the conditions of the socialist greenhouse – both spouses working, career paths set, and families established with housing and child-rearing arrangements in place. The collapse of the established system left many such families in turmoil, seeking to cope with family responsibilities while job opportunities and social support were disappearing.[10] Some families were literally uprooted, moving back to small villages in reasonable proximity to urban centers where an attempt could be made to couple subsistence agriculture with non-farm employment.[11] Symptoms of social stress grew markedly – increased alcoholism, smoking, and use of drugs; increased male mortality; and a rise in domestic violence against women (UNICEF 1999, 2001; Brainerd and Cutler 2005). Though not confined to those over age 30, these developments were usually more pronounced in the older age groups.

In contrast, those under age 30 were less wedded to the "socialist greenhouse". Raised, so to speak, more nearly in the wild, younger adults were in a better position to adapt to the new environment. Consistent with this greater degree of adaptation, Alesina and Fuchs-Schündeln (2007) find that younger cohorts in the former GDR are less favorably disposed toward welfare policies than their elders.

Many of those under 30 years old at the start of the transition had the option of postponing marriage and/or having children. This demographic strategy for coping with economic stress was a feature of the Great Depression, and, as the evidence shows, it has been widely exercised in the transition countries (Philipov 2002; Philipov and Dorbritz 2003; Sobotka 2002, 2003; Szivós and Giudici 2004). Some of these demographic changes were already underway in a few countries before the transition, but in the 1990s they appear in virtually every transition country, usually at an accelerated pace. They are not the result of young adults reducing their family size goals as free market forces replace the socialist greenhouse. Surveys conducted in seven of the transition countries included here typically find that the completed family size expected by women ages 20–24 in the mid-1990s is no different from that for women fifteen years older (Philipov and

Dorbritz 2003, p. 115, Table 2.5.2). Rather, they reflect decisions to postpone family formation as a way of coping with the less stable economic environment.

Figure 4.4

Change in Inequality of Life Satisfaction and of Income, c. 1990 to 1999, Countries With Early Transition Observations of Life Satisfaction

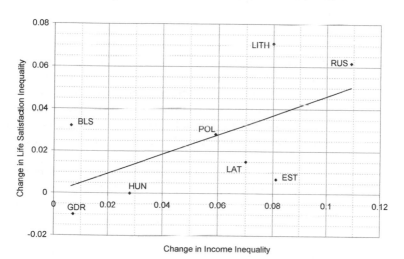

Change in Income Inequality

Note: The equation for the OLS regression is: 0.4603x+0.0003 (the t-stats are respectively 1.84 and 0.02; the adjusted R^2 = 0.254). The countries are those in the upper panel of Table 4.1.
Source: Income inequality: UNICEF 2001, Appendix Table 10.11, except GDR from GSOEP, with 1992 observation extrapolated to 1990 via Schwarze 1996, Table 4.2; life satisfaction inequality: WVS, except GDR from GSOEP.

Why do women and men have about equal declines in life satisfaction? The answer may lie in two parallel and related developments. On the one hand, unemployment rises and this affects men more than women; on the other, family dissolution increases and this impacts women more than men. Both cross-sectional and panel studies in the SWB literature repeatedly indicate sizeable negative effects on life satisfaction of both unemployment and marital dissolution (Blanchflower and Oswald 2004; Diener, Lucas and Scollon 2006; Frey and Stutzer 2002a,b; Helliwell and Putnam 2004; Winkelmann and Winkelmann 1998; Zimmermann and Easterlin 2006). End-of-decade regressions for the countries included here give the same result.

4.4. The 1990s in Current and Historical Perspective

In the half-decade after the late 1990s, GDP per capita grew rapidly in all but one of the transition countries included here. Leaving aside the former GDR, the total increase from the late nineties through 2004 averaged 36 percent, with a range from 18 to 56 percent. In addition, unemployment rates declined in most countries (TransMONEE 2008, Tables 10.1 and 10.6).

How has life satisfaction fared? To answer this, there are data available for every country except Belarus. The series already used here for the former GDR extends through 2005 (Table A-2). For ten other countries there is a Eurobarometer survey conducted in the first two months of 2005 that included a question on life satisfaction similar to that in the WVS (Directorate of General Research, European Commission 2005). Finally, the wave 5 life satisfaction value for Russia has been published in a paper by Inglehart et al. (2008, p. 283).[12]

Consistent with the recovery of GDP, life satisfaction has rebounded sharply almost everywhere (Table 4.4, column 2). Slight declines occurred only in the former GDR, where economic growth was slow, and Bulgaria. By early 2005, in every country except Bulgaria mean life satisfaction was above 6.0 and in two cases above 7.0, a marked contrast with the values for the mid- and late-1990s, which were often in the 4's and 5's (compare Table 4.4, column 1, and Table A-1, columns 5 and 8). Moreover, if life satisfaction around early 2005 is compared with that at or near the start of the 1990s, life satisfaction is higher in nine of the twelve countries for which a comparison is possible (Table 4.4, column 4). An ordinary least squares regression fitted to the observations for each country from the early 1990s to 2005 yields a positive coefficient of life satisfaction on time except for Slovakia and Bulgaria; the only significant coefficient, however, is that for Slovenia. Thus when the time span is lengthened from the decade of the 1990s to include early 2005, the typical picture is recovery of life satisfaction to its early 1990s level or better. However, as implied by Figure 4.3, this recovery in life satisfaction typically required a growth of GDP to well above its early transition level; the average increase in GDP from the base year life satisfaction observation in Table 4.1 to 2004 is 26 percent.

Although comparison is made difficult by differences in survey questions and response options, the results for life satisfaction in Table 4.4 are reasonably consistent with those reported in a 2006 survey conducted by the European Bank for Reconstruction and Development (2007). When presented with the statement "all things considered, I am satisfied with my life now," respondents in the central European and Baltic states who agreed with the statement typically outnumbered those who disagreed by 2 to 1. In Russia those who agreed just slightly outnumbered those who disagreed. Belarus, for which 2005 data are not available in Table 4.4, was among those with the highest levels of satisfaction, but in Romania and Bulgaria, those dissatisfied outnumbered the satisfied.

Table 4.4

Mean Life Satisfaction in 2005 and Change from Early and Late 1990s

	(1)	(2)	(3)	(4)
	Mean Life Satisfaction 2005	Change in L.S., late '90s to 2005	Date of early 1990s Observation	Change in L.S., early '90s to 2005
Countries with early transition observations:				
Former GDR	6.32	-0.19	1989.5	-0.27
Poland	6.98	0.58	1989	0.40
Hungary	6.30	0.52	1990	0.27
Estonia	6.32	0.42	1989.5	0.32
Latvia	6.31	1.04	1989.5	0.61
Lithuania	6.29	1.20	1989.5	0.28
Belarus	n.a.	n.a.	1990	n.a.
Russian Federation	6.09	1.35	1990	0.72
Countries starting with later transition observations:				
Slovenia	7.48	0.25	1991	1.19
Czech Republic	7.04	0.32	1991	0.35
Slovakia	6.47	0.42	1991	-0.15
Bulgaria	4.85	-0.15	1991	-0.18
Romania	6.30	1.26	1993	0.42

Sources:
Column 1: Directorate of General Research, European Commission 2005, except Russia (Inglehart et al. 2008, p. 283), and the former GDR, Table A-2. The European Commission survey is for January to February, 2005.
Column 2: Column 1 minus column 8 of Appendix Table A.1.
Column 3: Table 4.1.
Column 4: Column 1 minus column 2 of Table A.1.

The European Bank for Reconstruction and Development (EBRD) survey also elicited valuable comparisons of 2006 with 1989. Respondents were asked whether they agreed that "the economic situation in this country is better today than around 1989." On this question, respondents in central Europe and the Baltic countries were about evenly divided pro and con; elsewhere they leaned toward the negative side, either slightly (Russia) or strongly (Bulgaria and Romania). A similar comparison with regard to the political situation typically found more negative views than for the economic situation. A striking exception with regard to both economic and political conditions was Belarus, where positive responses outnumbered negative by a very large margin, about 4 to 1.

On all three questions (satisfaction, economic, and political conditions) the age pattern of responses in the EBRD survey is much like that in Figure 4.3 above. In every country, those ages 18 to 34 were much more favorably inclined than other age groups. Persons age 18 to 34 in 2006 comprise a cohort that in 1989 was under 18 years old; hence few were embarked on their careers at that time. In contrast, the most negative views were expressed by persons 50 years of age and older. In this cohort, it was not uncommon for respondents to view conditions in 1989 as better than currently. Although responses by level of education are not given, there are replies by income group – lower, middle, and upper. In keeping with the education pattern in Figure 4.3, those at the higher socio-economic level tend to be more satisfied, and view 2006 conditions more favorably than those at the lower level.

The dissolution of the police states and increase in political and civil rights in many of the transition countries might have been expected to increase life satisfaction. The sharp declines that initially occurred suggest that adverse economic and social conditions trumped the political in their impact on subjective well-being.

A different view is offered in the paper by Ronald Inglehart and his collaborators (2008, p. 277), who suggest that the WVS measures of life satisfaction and happiness reflect different determinants, the former, economic conditions, and the latter, political circumstances. In their interpretation "many ex-communist countries experienced democratization accompanied by economic collapse, resulting in rising happiness and falling life satisfaction." As explained earlier, the upward movement in happiness between waves 2 and 3 of the WVS appears to result from a "primacy bias" due to a change in the instructions to interviewers. Moreover, the argument that democratization raised happiness seems at variance with the findings of the EBRD survey, that in most countries respondents viewed the political situation in 2006 as worse than that in 1989, and the change in the political situation since 1989 more negatively than that in economic conditions.

A more direct test is possible of the hypothesis that the increase in happiness in the transition countries is due to democratization there. In nine of the twelve WVS countries included here happiness increases between waves 2 and 3; in the other three, it declines. During this period, the following question was asked in the Eurobarometer surveys: "On the whole, are you very satisfied, fairly satisfied, not very satisfied, or not at all satisfied with the way democracy works in (your country)?"[13] The Eurobarometer question specifies four response options, and the WVS happiness question also contains four response options. If the rise in happiness is due to democratization, a regression for all twelve countries of the change in happiness on the change in satisfaction with democracy should yield a positive slope coefficient. Actually, the regression yields a negative, though not statistically significant, coefficient. For two of the three countries that have the highest increase in mean happiness between waves 2 and 3, the mean value of satisfaction with democracy declines (Bulgaria and Slovenia). For two of the three countries in which mean happiness declines between waves 2 and 3, mean satisfaction with democracy increases (Belarus and Romania). These results do not support the hypothesis that democratization increased happiness in the transition countries.

There is evidence, however, that democratization may increase happiness at least temporarily, but if it does, it affects life satisfaction similarly. There are almost no surveys like the WVS which ask both happiness and life satisfaction questions, but the SA MarkData survey for South Africa, used in Chapter 3, does. In May 1994, one month after the country's first democratic election, a survey was conducted that included questions about both happiness and life satisfaction. Here, for both measures is the percentage of the black population in the top two (out of five) categories at that time and the corresponding percentages at the two adjacent dates when similar surveys were conducted:

	1988	1994	1995
Happiness	32	80	39
Life satisfaction	37	86	45

Note how by both measures the well-being of blacks soared at the time of the election. But as Valerie Møller (2007, p. 248) observes: "[P]ost-election euphoria was short-lived. Satisfaction levels have since returned to ones reminiscent of those under the former regime." This return is registered by both SWB measures. Moreover, the magnitude of rise and fall is virtually identical for the two measures. This evidence suggests that democratization may temporarily affect subjective well-being, but this effect appears not only in happiness but in life satisfaction as well.

Does the recovery of life satisfaction to 2005 in the transition countries mean that life satisfaction under capitalism is now typically greater than it was under socialism? If the early 1990s observation is assumed to be a reasonable approximation to the peak value of life satisfaction under socialism, the answer is yes. But there is reason to believe that this may not be a good assumption. Although the evidence is limited, it is consistent in suggesting that life satisfaction in the 1980s was higher than at the beginning of the 1990s transition, and higher also than in 2005.

There are 1980s life satisfaction data comparable to those used here for two countries, one in central Europe (Hungary) and one in Eastern Europe (Russia). Also, Veenhoven (2001, p. 115) gives a 1984 estimate for Belarus, though with some reservations. Here is the mean value of life satisfaction for Hungary in 1982, and, for comparison, the values for 1990 and 2005:

1982	1990	2005
6.93	6.03	6.30

These numbers indicate that there was a substantial decline in life satisfaction there during the 1980s and that even by 2005, life satisfaction was still considerably less than in 1982. Indirect support for a decline in life satisfaction in Hungary in the 1980s comes from surveys indicating a marked rise in anomie between 1978 and 1990 (Spéder, Paksi and Elekes 1999; cf. also Andorka et al. 1999). Surveys in the former GDR and Czechoslovakia also point to rising mental stress in those countries (Noelle-Neumann 1991; Glatzer and Bös 1998, p. 178; Boguszak, Gabal and Rak 1990, pp. 15–18).

In 1981 a WVS survey was conducted in the Russian *oblast* Tambov, about 250 miles southeast of Moscow. Although small (the population is somewhat over a million), it is reported to be "a region that [the Russians conducting the survey] considered representative of Russia as a whole" (Inglehart and Klingemann 2000, p. 175). As a check on the representativeness of Tambov *oblast*, a WVS survey was conducted there again in 1995 at the same time that the survey of the Russian Federation was being carried out. Given below is mean life satisfaction for Tambov in 1981 and 1995 and, for comparison, that in Russia as a whole in 1990 and 1995 and Belarus in 1984, 1990 and 1995:

	early 1980s	1990	1995
Tambov	7.26	n.a.	4.23
Russia	n.a.	5.37	4.45
Belarus	7.20	5.51	4.35

The 1995 observations for all three areas are quite similar in magnitude, as are the early 1980s values for Tambov and Belarus. The overall pattern is consistent with the inference that there was a marked decline in life satisfaction during the 1980s in both Russia and Belarus.

Other evidence suggesting that life satisfaction declined in Russia between the 1980s and 1990s comes from a longitudinal survey initiated in 1993 (Saris and Andreenkova 2001; the data given here are from http://www.vanderveld.nl/russet.html). At that time, respondents were asked about their current life satisfaction on a 1 to 10 scale and also their life satisfaction five years earlier, in 1988. Similar questions were asked about financial satisfaction. Here are the results for 1988 and 1993 with the WVS responses for 1990 placed between them:

	1988	1990	1993
Life satisfaction	6.46	5.37	5.05
Financial satisfaction	5.81	4.98	3.04

Even though the retrospective estimate is close to the end of the 1980s, both life and financial satisfaction give a picture consistent with that based on Tambov and Belarus, one of a marked decline from the 1980s to the 1990s. Moreover, the life satisfaction values for the 1980s given here – around 6.5 for Russia in 1988 and 7.2 for Tambov and Belarus earlier in the 1980s – are all similar in magnitude to the 1982 value of 6.9 for Hungary, and above the 2005 values for Russia (6.09) and Hungary (6.30). If these data are reasonably representative, life satisfaction in

2005 in the transition countries may have been less than in the 1980s.

Although the evidence for the 1980s presents a consistent picture, it is nowhere nearly as complete as one would like. But if it is reasonably correct, one might plausibly ask how it is possible that in the transition countries life satisfaction under socialism might at one time have been higher than it is currently under capitalism? A speculative answer to this question is suggested by the data on domain satisfaction for the former GDR and Hungary presented earlier (Table 4.3). Although the socialist system was notably deficient in its ability to supply material goods, it provided substantial security for individuals in other domains important for personal happiness such as job security, provision of child care, health insurance, and support in old age for oneself and one's parents. One might suppose that the authoritarian communist state and limited civil and political rights, coupled with often-empty store shelves, might have kept life satisfaction lower than currently. But the limited evidence above suggests that greater security with regard to other personal concerns may have outweighed the negatives.

While this study was in preparation, Sanfey and Teksoz (2007) published a valuable analysis of life satisfaction trends in the transition countries. There is substantial agreement between some of their conclusions and those of the present study, most notably with regard to the V-shaped pattern of life satisfaction in the transition countries and the differential impact of the transition by demographic group. This consistency is reassuring because the data set on which their study is based is also the WVS (waves 2–4). In other respects, however, there are important differences. Perhaps most fundamental is the answer to the question posed in the title of their paper, "Does transition make you happy?" Their response is that by the end of the 1990s "life satisfaction levels have returned close to pre-transition levels in most cases" (p. 707). This conclusion is not borne out by the analysis here, which finds a considerable shortfall still prevailing at the end of the 1990s, and, based on data not available for the Sanfey-Teksoz analysis, recovery to or above early transition levels not occurring until 2005. The difference between the two studies in the interpretation of the 1990s stems from their including all wave 2 transition countries covered in the WVS in their analysis of the degree of recovery in life satisfaction, while the present study focuses on seven WVS countries plus the former GDR, countries that all have an initial life satisfaction reading falling at or close to the date of the pre-transition levels of GDP and unemployment (Table 4.1). Clearly the larger set of WVS countries studied by Sanfey and Teksoz start, on average, later in the transition and consequently with life satisfaction values already depressed below the pre-transition level by the collapse of GDP and rise in unemployment. Given the lower initial reference point, it is not surprising that they find a greater degree of recovery in life satisfaction by the end of the 1990s. Moreover, the present analysis also suggests that if the baseline for analyzing the trend in life satisfaction were moved back to the 1980s, it is possible that even by 2005 recovery to earlier levels had not yet been achieved.

The present study differs from that of Sanfey and Teksoz in other respects. It adds an analysis of inequality of life satisfaction and it includes data on domain satisfaction that reveal the differing directions of change in satisfaction with material living levels versus work, family, and health. The domain satisfaction results suggest that while the transition from socialism to capitalism in Eastern Europe has, on average, been raising satisfaction with material living levels, this has occurred at the expense of satisfaction with employment, health, and family security, with the net balance in well-being at best not yet clearly better.

4.5. Conclusions and Implications

To sum up, the collapse of output and employment in the European transition countries precipitated a sharp drop in life satisfaction. Subsequently GDP improved, but throughout the 1990s stagnating labor market conditions and a deteriorating social safety net prevented a commensurate recovery of life satisfaction. Within the population differences in life satisfaction rose noticeably as wage and employment disparities increased, and family life was disrupted. Those hardest hit were the less educated and persons over age 30, with women and men suffering about equally. The observed movement of life satisfaction implies that economic circumstances trumped political in their impact on subjective well-being.

By 2005, life satisfaction had recovered to its early 1990s level or better, but this return required an increase in GDP per capita averaging about 25 percent above the early 1990s value. Moreover, the available evidence, though quite limited, suggests that even in 2005 life satisfaction may have been below the levels prevailing before the 1990s. The explanation of the 2005 shortfall relative to pre-1990s levels may be that the positive contribution to life satisfaction of improved material living levels was outweighed by losses in employment security, health and child care, and provision for old age.

The present analysis is based on intermittent observations of life satisfaction for a limited number of countries. Indeed, when one tries to identify countries with life satisfaction observations close to the start of the transition, the number is reduced to only eight. Moreover, the new republics of central Asia are wholly omitted because none were included in wave 2 of the WVS. The generalizations here refer to the "transition countries" as a whole, but even with the limited data available more might still be done to differentiate among the experiences of different countries. It is possible too that there are unpublished surveys conducted in some countries under communism that might throw light on subjective attitudes under socialism prior to the transition (cf. Kuran 1991).

The study by economists of life satisfaction and happiness is new, and we are only beginning to understand what these measures tell us about well-being. It seems reasonable to suggest, however, that they add a dimension to the evaluation of well-being that is a useful complement to the standard armory.[14] The human cost of the economic transition was enormous, with the lives of millions of people turned upside down. In a statement specifically about Russia, but representative of the transition countries generally, Brainerd and Cutler (2005, p. 125) point out that "[b]efore 1989, Russians lived in a country that provided economic security: unemployment was virtually unknown, persons were guaranteed and provided a standard of living perceived to be adequate, and microeconomic stability did not much affect the average citizen." All or most of this went by the board with the transition to free markets. So too did provision of health and child care. Family life was torn apart as divorce rates soared. Alcoholism, smoking, and drug use grew markedly. Suicide rates increased, and domestic violence against women rose. Families were uprooted, some moving back to villages where subsistence agriculture might provide some economic support.

The impact of these changes on people's personal lives and their well-being is almost totally missed by GDP per capita. Even a measure of income inequality – an increasingly popular supplement to GDP – barely hints at what happened. In contrast, the life satisfaction measure, which reflects not only material well-being, but the everyday concerns and worries of women and men about work, health, and family, is more indicative of the far-reaching changes that were taking place. Life satisfaction is not an exhaustive measure of well-being. But if, in formulating transition policy, some consideration had been give to this measure, perhaps there would have been fewer "lost in transition."

Appendix: Basic Data

Table A-1

Mean and Inequality of Life Satisfaction, Twelve Countries, c. 1990 to c. 1999

	(1) Initial date	(2) (3) Life satisfaction		(4) Mid-period date	(5) (6) Life satisfaction		(7) Terminal date	(8) (9) Life satisfaction	
		Mean	Gini coef.		Mean	Gini coef.		Mean	Gini coef.
Poland	1989	6.58	0.193	n.a.	n.a.	n.a.	1997.5	6.40	0.221
Hungary	1990	6.03	0.230	n.a.	n.a.	n.a.	1998.5	5.78	0.230
Estonia	1989.5	6.00	0.200	1996	5.00	0.256	1999	5.90	0.207
Latvia	1989.5	5.70	0.242	1996	4.90	0.256	1998	5.27	0.257
Lithuania	1989.5	6.01	0.221	1996	4.99	0.299	1999	5.09	0.292
Belarus	1990	5.52	0.228	1996	4.35	0.282	1999	4.81	0.260
Russian Federation	1990	5.37	0.252	1995	4.45	0.318	1999	4.74	0.314
Slovenia	1991	6.29	0.197	1995	6.46	0.184	1999	7.23	0.165
Czech Republic	1991	6.69	0.180	n.a.	n.a.	n.a.	1998	6.72	0.165
Slovakia	1991	6.62	0.205	n.a.	n.a.	n.a.	1998	6.05	0.208
Bulgaria	1991	5.03	0.258	n.a.	n.a.	n.a.	1998	5.00	0.288
Romania	1993	5.88	0.225	n.a.	n.a.	n.a.	1998	5.04	0.298

Source: WVS. Columns 1–3 from wave 2, and columns 4–6 from wave 3. Columns 7–9 are from wave 4, except the following countries for which waves 3 and 4, both in the late 1990s, are merged: Poland, Hungary, Czech Republic, Slovakia, Bulgaria, and Romania.

Table A-2

Mean and Inequality of Life Satisfaction, Former GDR, 1990 to 2005

Date	Mean	Gini coef.	Date	Mean	Gini coef.
1990	6.59	0.164	1998	6.48	0.152
1991	6.04	0.183	1999	6.51	0.154
1992	6.12	0.164	2000	6.44	0.149
1993	6.20	0.174	2001	6.45	0.151
1994	6.25	0.165	2002	6.26	0.160
1995	6.38	0.160	2003	6.34	0.156
1996	6.39	0.157	2004	6.13	0.173
1997	6.31	0.156	2005	6.32	0.173

Source: GSOEP (Haisken-DeNew and Frick 2005)

5

Happiness and Growth the World Over: Time Series Evidence on the Happiness–Income Paradox

> *"It's a small world after all."*
> *Disney theme song*

Simply stated, the happiness–income paradox is this: at a point in time happiness varies directly with income, but over time happiness does not increase when a country's income increases. This chapter pulls together the time series results of the two preceding chapters, and adds an updated analysis for 17 developed countries based chiefly on the Eurobarometer – a total of 37 countries in all. Our primary interest is factual: when the empirical scope of the time series is expanded to include not only a larger number of developed countries but transition and developing nations as well, are happiness and economic growth still unrelated? The answer suggested by the evidence continues to be yes.

The happiness–income paradox has recently received mixed reviews. Some analysts look rather favorably on it (Clark, Frijters and Shields 2008; Di Tella and MacCulloch 2008); others do not (Stevenson and Wolfers 2008). As will be seen, the dissenting view appears to be largely the result of failing to distinguish between the short- and long-term time series relationship between happiness and income. Over the short term, when

This chapter was co-authored by Laura Angelescu (University of Southern California). I would like to express my gratitude for her invaluable contributions. A first draft of the paper was published as: Easterlin, R., Angelescu, L. (2009). Happiness and Growth the World Over: Time Series Evidence on the Happiness-Income Paradox. IZA Discussion Paper No. 4060. We are grateful for helpful comments to Andrew Oswald, Mariano Rojas, Onnicha Sawangfa, and Jacqueline Zweig. Happiness data for Norway were kindly provided by Ottar Hellevik. For guidance on Northern Ireland GDP we are grateful to José L.I. D'Elia and Victor Hewitt. Financial support was provided by the University of Southern California.

fluctuations in macroeconomic conditions dominate the relationship, happiness and income are positively related. Over the long term, happiness and income are unrelated. After analyzing the long term relationship, we demonstrate the short term one, and the effect of mixing the two. In the final section of this paper we speculate on the reasons for the disconnect between the short- and long-term relationship.

5.1. Concepts and Methods

As in Chapter 4 our happiness measure is overall life satisfaction, the response to the question "All things considered, how satisfied are you with your life as a whole these days". We have adjusted for survey differences in the number of response categories by rescaling to a 1–10 scale, following a procedure like that described in Chapter 3. Economic growth is measured in terms of the percentage growth per year in real GDP per capita; the data are the same as those in Chapter 3.

We compute the long-term growth rate of life satisfaction from an OLS regression on time, taking as our period of analysis for each country the longest time span available. The long-term growth rate of GDP per capita is computed from the GDP per capita values at the start and end of the period covered by the life satisfaction observations. When more than one data set is available for a country's life satisfaction, as in the case of the Latin American countries, we compute a pooled regression with a dummy variable to identify the different data set. Growth rates for both life satisfaction and GDP are per year; the change in life satisfaction is measured in absolute terms on a 1–10 scale; that in GDP per capita, in percentage terms.

In our analysis of long-term rates of change the minimum time span for any country is 12 years. In taking long periods for analysis the purpose is specifically to distinguish the longer from the shorter term relationship between life satisfaction and GDP per capita, although even 12 years may be too short a period. For most countries the period actually spanned is usually longer, as can be seen from the following:

	Time span	
	Mean	Range
17 developed countries	29	21–34
11 transition countries	15	12–22
9 developing countries	19	15–33

The small number of transition and developing countries relative to developed is because of the limited happiness data available. As previously discussed, both the life satisfaction and GDP data are imperfect. We summarize here the principal problems with the life satisfaction data and what we have done to improve comparability over time.

First, the question on life satisfaction may change over time, as in the case of Japan.[1] For such cases, we pool the data and use dummy variables for the different segments to account for the difference in response level attributable to the change in survey questions.

Second, the context of the life satisfaction question may change. In the Eurobarometer, for example, there are a few surveys in which a question on satisfaction with finances is inserted before that on overall life satisfaction. People generally are less satisfied with their finances than with life in general, and the replacement of a neutral question with one on financial satisfaction tends to bias downward responses on life satisfaction. We have deleted the life satisfaction observations in the years that are so biased.[2]

Third, the geographic coverage of the surveys may change over time, especially for the developing countries. We try to minimize the effects of such shifts by constructing series that cover the same population at different dates. Typically the coverage is for at least 70 percent of the population and comprises the more literate and urbanized segments of the population, those most likely to be experiencing the income benefits of economic growth. Also, for two countries, China and South Africa, there are independent surveys by other organizations that provide support for the time series change indicated by the series we use.

We make no claim that the time series analyzed here are faultless. We have, however, done our best to make the series for the various countries reasonably comparable over time.

5.2. Results

5.2.1. The Cross-Sectional Relationship

We start with a point-of-time comparison of happiness and income in richer and poorer countries. The contradiction between this cross-sectional relationship and the time series one is the essence of the happiness–income paradox, but curiously – as will be seen below – the cross-sectional relationship is frequently cited as though it disproves the time series evidence.

Figure 5.1

Diminishing Marginal Utility of Income
(life satisfaction and GDP per capita (absolute scale) based on WVS cross-section ($n = 195$))

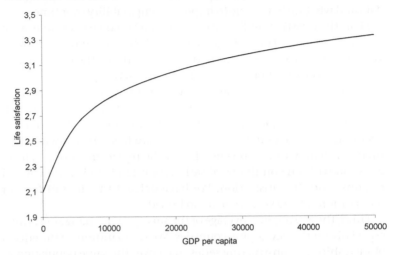

Source: The basic data are 195 pooled observations for 89 countries surveyed in waves 1–4 of the World Values Survey. Individual country observations are omitted from the figure. The fitted regression is $y = 0.405 + 0.270\ln(x)$ (adjusted $R^2 = 0.452$); t-statistics in parentheses. (2.05) (12.68)

Two main conclusions emerge from the cross-sectional analysis:

1. If richer and poorer countries are compared at a point in time, life satisfaction increases with the absolute amount of GDP per capita, but at a diminishing rate (Figure 5.1). As noted in Chapter 3, this cross-sectional relationship has led some analysts to assert that a given increase in GDP per capita has a much bigger impact on happiness in poorer than richer countries.

2. If richer and poorer countries are compared at a point in time, "[e]ach doubling of GDP is associated with a constant increase in life satisfaction" (Deaton 2008, p. 57, Figure 2). This generalization is illustrated here in Figure 5.2 using exactly the same regression relationship as that underlying Figure 5.1, but now the change in life satisfaction is measured in relation to the *proportionate,* rather than absolute change in GDP, and life satis-

faction is plotted against log GDP, not absolute GDP. The implication for change over time is more sweeping than for the first generalization. Now economic growth raises life satisfaction in rich as well as poor countries and to the same extent. Moreover, the higher the rate of economic growth, the greater the improvement in life satisfaction – doubling the rate at which GDP per capita grows doubles the improvement in happiness.

The direct quotation at the start of the paragraph above, attributable to Angus Deaton, is based on data different from those used here, 2006 Gallup World Poll data for 132 countries. As aptly illustrated in other work (Cutler, Deaton and Lleras-Muney 2006), Deaton himself is well aware that cross-sectional relationships may be a poor guide to historical experience.

Figure 5.2

"Each Doubling of GDP is Associated with a Constant Increase in Life Satisfaction"
(life satisfaction and GDP per capita (logarithmic scale) based on WVS cross-section ($n = 195$))

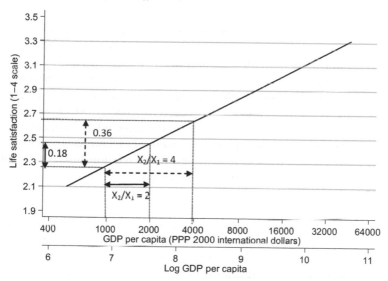

Source: See Figure 5.1. The title of this figure is from Deaton (2008, p. 57, Figure 2).

But others are less cautious. Thus, renowned educator Derek Bok in a valuable book on "The Politics of Happiness" (2010) cites Deaton's statement as contradicting time series evidence on the absence of relationship between happiness and economic growth. So too do economists Guriev and Zhuravskaya (2009, p. 152). Similarly, psychologist Daniel Kahneman's (2008) *mea culpa* on the hedonic treadmill is based on a cross-sectional relationship found in the Gallup World Poll (Kahneman 2008). No doubt it is this type of point-of-time relationship that underlies the confident assertion in the thoughtful volume on the discipline of economics by Diane Coyle (2007, p. 188): "There is no doubt that the vast majority of people in the world will be made happier by increases in GDP per capita". The paradox, of course, is that this cross-sectional relationship has not been reproduced in the limited number of time series studies done heretofore.

5.2.2. Time Series Evidence: Long Series

In turning to time series, our point of departure is the implication of Figure 5.2 that a greater increment in happiness goes with a higher rate of economic growth. Here is what we find:

1. For 17 developed countries with time series ranging from 21 to 34 years, there is no significant relationship between the rate of improvement in life satisfaction and the growth rate of GDP per capita (Figure 5.3). The countries here are most of the developed countries of Europe plus the United States, Canada, and Australia. For most countries the long term GDP growth rates are between 1.5 and 3 percent, but for two, Ireland and Luxembourg, the rates are between 3 and 5 percent. If Ireland and Luxembourg are deleted, there is still no significant relationship, as can readily be seen from a glance at Figure 5.3.

2. For 9 developing countries with time series ranging from 15 to 33 years, there is no significant relationship between the rate of improvement in happiness and the rate of economic growth (Figure 5.4). The nine countries are typically fairly populous, four in Asia, four in Latin America, and one in sub-Saharan Africa. The economic growth rates range from around zero for South Africa to almost 10 percent per year for China. If China, the outlier in the group, is omitted, the regression coefficient remains not significant.

Figure 5.3

Longer Term Relationship between Growth Rates of Life Satisfaction and GDP per Capita: 17 Developed Countries (21–34 years; mean = 29)

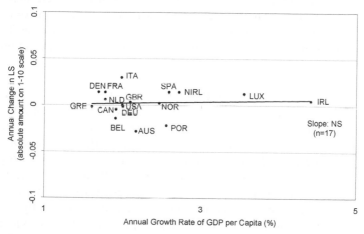

Source: See text. The fitted regression is $y = -0.001 + 0.002x$ (adjusted $R^2 = 0.006$); *t*-statistics in parentheses.
$$(-0.05) \quad (0.31)$$

Figure 5.4

Longer Term Relationship between Growth Rates of Life Satisfaction and GDP per Capita: Nine Developing Countries (15–33 years; mean = 19)

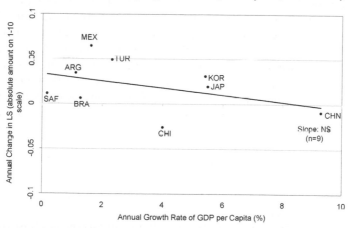

Source: See text. The fitted regression is $y = 0.033 - 0.004x$ (adjusted $R^2 = 0.168$); *t*-statistics in parentheses.
$$(2.24) \quad (-1.19)$$

3. For 11 transition countries with time series ranging from 12 to 22 years, there is no significant relationship between the improvement in life satisfaction and the rate of economic growth (Figure 5.5). The eleven countries are those for which there is a life satisfaction observation near the start of the transition (cf. Chapter 4), and range across central and eastern Europe. Their economic growth rates are from slightly negative to about 3 percent per year.

4. For all 37 countries taken together, with time series ranging from 12 to 34 years in length, there is no significant relation between the improvement in life satisfaction and the rate of economic growth (Figure 5.6). The growth rates of GDP per capita typically range from slightly negative to almost 6 percent. If the one outlier, China at almost 10 percent, is omitted, the regression coefficient is still not significant. If a higher rate of economic growth raises life satisfaction more rapidly, as the cross-section in Figure 5.2 suggests, it is hard to find evidence of it in the richer, poorer, and transitional countries included here, or in all of them taken together.

5.2.3. Time Series Evidence: Short Series

Over the short term life satisfaction and GDP per capita are positively related, moving together with macroeconomic conditions. This was first pointed out with regard to the experience of the developed countries by Di Tella, MacCulloch, and Oswald (2001). It is most readily apparent visually in simple time series plots for the transition countries, where the collapse and recovery of GDP per capita has often been on a scale much like that of the 1930s Great Depression (Figure 5.7; cf. also Chapter 4). For some transition countries, such as Slovenia, the first life satisfaction observation comes rather late in the transition and, as a result, only the recovery phase of the life satisfaction movement is observed (Figure 5.8), leading some analysts to confuse the short-term positive association of life satisfaction and GDP per capita with the long term trend relationship. Clearly, inferences about the long term trend need to be based on time series that capture both the collapse and recovery phases of the transition. This is what we have tried to do for the eleven transition countries analyzed here.

Figure 5.5

Longer Term Relationship between Growth Rates of Life Satisfaction and GDP per Capita: Eleven Transition Countries (12–22 years; mean = 15)

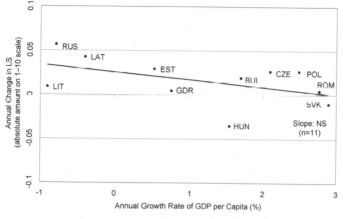

Source: See text. The fitted regression is $y = 0.025 - 0.009x$ (adjusted $R^2 = 0.229$); t-statistics in parentheses. (2.62) (-1.63)

Figure 5.6

Longer Term Relationship between Growth Rates of Life Satisfaction and GDP per Capita: 17 Developed, Eleven Transition, and Nine Developing Countries (12–34 years; mean = 22)

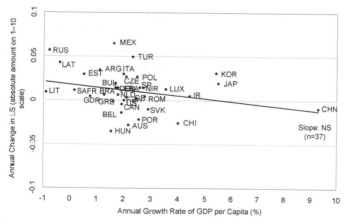

Source: See text. The fitted regression is $y = 0.018 - 0.003x$ (adjusted $R^2 = 0.069$); t-statistics in parentheses. (3.07) (-1.61)

Even for these countries, however, whose initial life satisfaction observation is around 1990, the time series may not go back far enough. As seen in Chapter 4, there is fragmentary evidence for a few transition countries that in the 1980s life satisfaction may have been higher than around 1990.

In any event, it is clear that taking contraction periods and expansion periods *separately*, with a mean time span of 7.6 years, one observes a significant positive relationship between the change in life satisfaction and the rate of economic growth (Figure 5.9). Now the GDP growth rates range from very large negative rates, approaching -20 percent, to large positive rates, almost 10 percent, and the coefficient of the regression line fitted to these data is significantly positive. In the short run a negative change in GDP per capita is associated with a negative change in life satisfaction and the recovery of GDP per capita is associated with a recovery of life satisfaction.

Figure 5.7

Life Satisfaction, c. 1990–2005, and Annual Index of Real GDP: Three Transition Countries

Former GDR

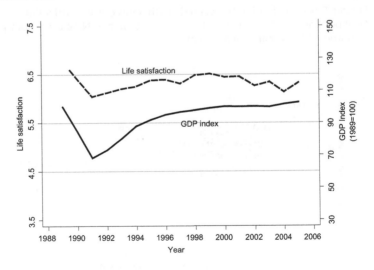

Figure 5.7 (continued)

Life Satisfaction, c. 1990–2005, and Annual Index of Real GDP:
Three Transition Countries

Estonia

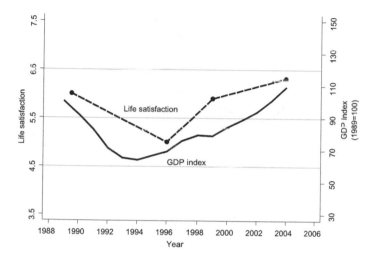

Russian Federation

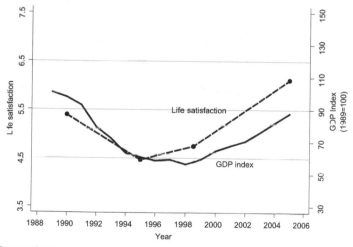

Source: Chapter 4.

Figure 5.8

Life Satisfaction, 1992–2005, and GDP per Capita, 1989–2005: Slovenia

GDP annual

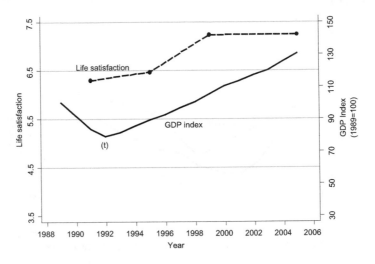

GDP for only LS dates

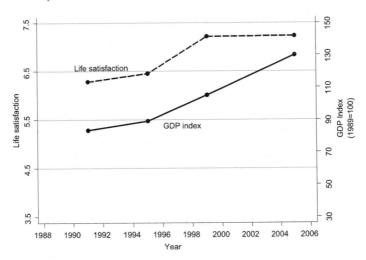

Source: Chapter 4.

Figure 5.9

Short Term Relationship between Growth Rates of Life Satisfaction and GDP per Capita: Eleven Transition Countries – Contraction and Expansion Periods Separately (mean = 7.6 years)

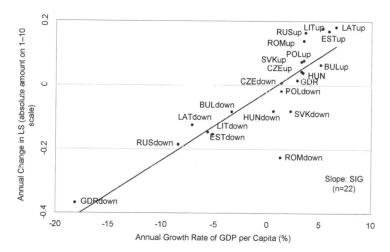

Source: See text. The fitted regression is $y = -0.020 + 0.021x$ (adjusted $R^2 = 0.741$); *t*-statistics in parentheses. $\quad (-1.22) \quad (7.57)$

5.2.4 Time Series Evidence: Mixing Short and Long Series

Over the long term there appears to be no significant relation between the improvement in happiness and the growth rate of GDP per capita; in the short run, however, the two are positively associated. If short and long series are mixed together, the short term positive relationship tends to dominate. This is most simply demonstrated by returning to the long-term series for 37 countries in Figure 5.6 and replacing the long term time trends for the eleven transition countries with the data for the contraction and expansion periods separately, used in Figure 5.9. Not surprisingly, the short-term observations dominate the long-term, and the coefficient of the regression line fitted to the data is significantly positive (Figure 5.10). The long-term economic growth rates are mainly clustered between zero and 5 percent, while the short-term rates range more widely and shape the slope of the regression line.

Figure 5.10

Mixing the Long and Short Term Relationship between Growth Rates of Life Satisfaction and GDP per Capita: Eleven Transition Countries – Contraction and Expansion Periods Separately – plus 17 Developed and Nine Developing Countries

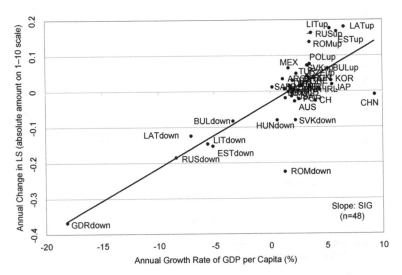

Source: See text. The fitted regression is $y = -0.030 + 0.018x$ (adjusted $R^2 = 0.634$); t-statistics in parentheses. $\quad(-3.22)\quad(8.92)$

An example of the failure to distinguish the short term from the long term relationship is the widely-publicized Stevenson and Wolfers (2008) article that seeks to establish a positive relation between life satisfaction and economic growth. (We focus on Stevenson and Wolfers' life satisfaction analysis, not happiness. As discussed in Chapter 4, there appears to be a substantial upward bias in the happiness reports in WVS Wave 3 relative to Wave 2.) In their time series analysis of World Values Survey data they estimate regression relationships like those done here between the change in life satisfaction and that in GDP per capita. They report the results of three "short first differences" and three "long first differences" regressions after eliminating countries whose data they consider noncomparable over time (Stevenson and Wolfers 2008, pp. 39-41). The time spans of the "short first differences" regressions – typically five to six years – are too brief to identify the long-term relationship between life satisfaction and

GDP per capita. Of their three "long first differences" regressions only two have a significant positive coefficient. The significant positive coefficient for the WVS waves 2 to 4 regression (based on observations for 32 countries) is due to the inclusion of eleven transition countries, whose data particularly reflect the concurrent collapse and recovery of life satisfaction and GDP per capita in these countries. If the transition countries are omitted from the regression, the slope coefficient is no longer significant.[3] The significant positive coefficient for the waves 1 to 4 analysis, based on seventeen countries, is due to the inclusion of one transition country, Hungary, with low growth in GDP per capita and a negative change in life satisfaction, and one developing country, South Korea, with very high growth in GDP per capita (it is off-scale in their diagram) and high growth of life satisfaction. Among the other 15 countries, all of which are developed, there is no significant relation between the change in life satisfaction and that in GDP per capita. Thus, the positive association between the change in life satisfaction and that in GDP per capita reported by Stevenson and Wolfers rests almost entirely on the short-term association between happiness and GDP per capita, particularly in the transition countries.

Each of the long-term time series slope coefficients estimated here in Figures 5.3 through 5.6 is not significantly different from zero. In contrast to the results reported by Stevenson and Wolfers, all of these time series coefficients are significantly different from the 0.4 satisfaction–income gradient derived by them from their cross-section within- and between-country comparisons, and considered by them to provide "a specific quantitative yardstick for assessing the importance of (even imprecisely estimated) trends in subjective well-being" (p. 41). Their comparisons with the 0.4 yardstick are, of course, based on estimated time series slope coefficients that reflect the short-term, not the long-term, relation between the change in life satisfaction and economic growth. If one estimates long-term time series trends uncontaminated by short-term relationships, then the gradients tend toward zero and differ significantly from the 0.4 cross-section "yardstick". Each of the long-term time series slope coefficients estimated here in Figures 5.3 through 5.6 is also significantly different at the 95 percent confidence level from the 0.270 [0.228, 0.312] cross-section coefficient of Figures 5.1 and 5.2.

Our discussion of the shorter-term happiness–income relation has been based on evidence from the transition countries, where the positive association is readily apparent in simple time series graphs. However, even some of the non-transition countries exhibit the short-term relationship in raw data. For example, we do not include data for Austria, Sweden, and Finland in our long series analysis of the developed countries. The Eurobarometer surveys for these countries begin quite late, in the 1990s. In all three of these countries unemployment rates in the 1990s were much worse than the long-term average; by 2006, however, unemployment rates had substantially improved in Finland and Sweden, producing a positively related recovery in life satisfaction and GDP per capita like that observed in the transition countries.

5.3. Why Do the Short- and Long-Term Relationships between Happiness and Economic Growth Differ?

A definitive answer to this question is beyond the scope of the present analysis. But a speculative answer is this: what one is observing in the disjunction between short and long-term relationships is the counterpart of the phenomenon of "loss aversion" reported in the literature of social psychology and behavioral economics. A considerable number of small group studies have found that an increase in income from an initial reference point means considerably less to people in terms of well-being than a loss of equivalent amount (the pioneering study is Tversky and Kahneman 1991; see also Rabin 1998; Kahneman 2003). The relevance of this argument here can be illustrated with a variant of the figure for the life cycle model presented in the next chapter.

Assume that at a given point in time, mean income is y_1 and happiness u_i on the utility function A_1, which illustrates the cross-sectional positive relation observed between happiness and income (Figure 5.11). If when income increases, aspirations rise commensurately, then when GDP per capita increases from y_1 to y_2, average happiness remains unchanged at u_1 (a movement from point 1 to point 2, illustrated by the heavy broken line connecting the two points). This is because the positive effect on happiness of the growth in GDP per capita (an upward movement along A_1) is undercut by a downward shift in the utility function from A_1 to A_2 as rising material aspirations shrink the happiness value of a given dollar of income. If, however, GDP per capita falls, say from y_1 to y_3, and income aspirations remain fixed at their initial level, then happiness falls from u_1 to u_2 (a downward movement along A_1 from point 1 to point 3, illustrated by the broken line connecting these points). Correspondingly, a recovery in GDP per capita from y_3

that moves people back along A_1 toward the reference level, point 1, raises happiness back toward u_1 .For illustrative purposes the diagram pictures the extreme case of complete hedonic adaptation to an income gain, and zero adaptation to an income loss.

Put simply, the argument is that people adapt hedonically to an increase in income from a given initial level, their aspirations tending to rise commensurately with income. But aspirations are much less flexible downward. Once people have attained a given level of income, they cling to this reference point – the well-known "endowment effect" (Kahneman, Knetsch and Thaler 1991). Hence, if income falls they feel deprived, and their subjective well-being declines. In turn, a recovery in income that returns them toward the reference level increases subjective well-being. Readers will note that the kink in the broken line at point 1 of Figure 5.11 is analogous to that in diagrams of loss aversion (Kahneman, Knetsch and Thaler, p. 200). The movement between points 1 and 2 illustrates the long-term happiness–income relationship; that between points 1 and 3, the short-term relationship.

Figure 5.11

Subjective Well-Being (u) as a Function of Income (y) and Aspiration Level (A)

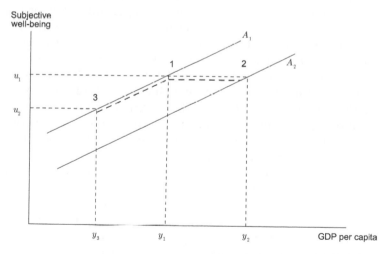

As an illustration, consider the contrasting experience of East and West Germany, sitting side by side, with a common language, history and culture. In East Germany in 1990 GDP per capita collapses and then recovers with life satisfaction following a roughly similar course. In West Germany real GDP per capita increases by 15 percent from 1990 to 2004, but life satisfaction drifts slightly downward (Easterlin and Plagnol 2008). East Germany's pattern conforms roughly to the broken line movement between points 1 and 3 in Figure 5.2; West Germany's, to that between points 1 and 2.

5.4. Conclusion

The happiness–income paradox is the contradiction between the cross-sectional relation of happiness and income (positive) and the time series relation (nil). The present time series analysis of the long-term relationship between the improvement in happiness and the rate of economic growth reveals no significant relationship in three groups of countries considered separately – 17 developed, 9 developing, and 11 transition – or when all three sets of countries are taken together.

Rejection of the paradox is based usually on two grounds. The most frequent case is where the first part of the paradox, the cross-section relationship, is cited as disproving the second, the time series relationship. This is, to say the least, a puzzling bit of logic, flying in the face of the very meaning of "paradox." More pertinent are recent time series findings seemingly at variance with the asserted absence of the happiness–income relationship. In the present analysis we demonstrate that these conflicting results arise chiefly from confusing a short-term positive happiness–income association, due to fluctuations in macroeconomic conditions, with the long-term relationship. We suggest, speculatively, that this disparity between the short- and long-term association is due to the social psychological phenomenon of "loss aversion".

When we started this analysis we had no preconceptions as to the empirical findings; with happiness data newly becoming available for many more countries in the world, we were curious to see what the data might reveal about long-term trends. To us, as to many others, it is disquieting to find no relationship between happiness and economic growth even in poorer countries. The aspiration mechanism described above may provide part of the explanation; certainly no evidence has been advanced indicating that lower-income countries are unaffected by this mechanism. Perhaps also changes in noneconomic domains of life satisfaction, such as family, social capital, and the environment, are offsetting the effect of gains in the economic domain.

It is conceivable too that as better happiness data become available for longer time spans, a significant (though perhaps slight) positive long-term relation between happiness and economic growth will emerge. Nevertheless, the fact that the surveys now available fail to pick up a positive happiness–income association in countries exhibiting such a wide disparity in economic growth rates is remarkable. Consider, for example, three countries included here with very high recent growth rates of GDP per capita – China, South Korea, and Chile. China's growth rate implies a doubling of real income in less than 10 years; South Korea's, in 13 years; and Chile's in 18 years. With the per capita amount of goods multiplying so rapidly in a fraction of a lifetime, one might think many of the people in these countries would be so happy they'd be dancing in the streets. Yet both China and Chile show mild (not statistically significant) declines in life satisfaction – China in surveys conducted by three different statistical organizations. South Korea – none of whose surveys has been faulted – shows a (not statistically significant) increase, but all of the increase results from the low value reported in the initial survey, one that was conducted a few months after the assassination of the country's president in 1980. Thereafter, in four surveys from 1990 to 2005, a period when GDP per capita continued to grow rapidly, averaging 5 percent per year, life satisfaction declines slightly. With incomes increasing so greatly in three different countries it seems extraordinary that there are no surveys that register the marked improvement in subjective well-being that one might expect to find.

One can easily imagine reasons for dismissing the present results: "The data are no good" (although to the best of our abilities we have tried to screen and test the data for comparability over time). "If perceptions (i.e., reports of happiness) and objective measures of well-being (GDP per capita) differ – well, we all know that perceptions can be faulty" (but, faulty or not, this is what people feel, and what they act on).

Alternatively, we might consider whether the data are trying to tell us something – perhaps, as Moses Abramovitz suggested a half century ago, that the casual assumption that economic growth is a sure route to greater well-being requires re-examination (see quote at the beginning of Chapter 1). Maybe there is need for broader and deeper research into the myriad ways other than the accumulation of goods that economic growth affects people's lives.

III

Life Cycle Happiness

Introduction

Do people get happier as they get older or does happiness decline? What circumstances chiefly determine the life cycle pattern of happiness? Chapters 6 through 9 of this Part reflect a continuing search to answer these questions.

As it turns out the answer differs for women and men. Women start adult life happier than men, but end up less happy (Chapter 8). In early adult life women are more likely than men to fulfill their family life and material goods aspirations; in later life, they are less likely (Chapter 9). An important reason for the shift in the attainment of aspirations and consequently in relative happiness is that women form unions – married or cohabiting – at an earlier age than men; at older ages, however, they are less likely than men at any given age to have a partner because of the higher incidence among women of marital disruption, especially widowhood. Having a partner directly contributes to greater happiness, and also raises happiness indirectly because it makes for greater financial security.

In the United States, which is the empirical focus in Part III, men's happiness increases on average over the life cycle, while women's declines, the two together forming an X-pattern over the life course. In European countries this crossover also usually occurs between women's and men's happiness, but the life cycle trajectories of each gender are not necessarily the same as in the United States. For example, life cycle happiness may decline for both genders, but more rapidly for women than for men.

As in Part II, the analysis in Part III is concerned with change over time, but now my co-authors and I follow the year-to-year experience of "birth cohorts," those born in a given year or period, using the demographers' technique of cohort analysis. Life cycle well-being does not have to follow the national population pattern of time series stability noted in Part II. Each birth cohort, for example, might have an identical pattern of increasing happiness over the life cycle, but if the starting and ending values of happiness were the same for each cohort, then the national average would be constant over time. Nor should the life cycle pattern of happiness be confused with the point-of-time association of happiness with age. As discussed in Chapter 7, this cross-sectional approach is no more likely to lead to valid conclusions about change over time than the point-of-time comparisons of countries with regard to happiness and income discussed in Part II.

Life cycle happiness is also clearly different from the U shaped regression relationship of happiness to age estimated in the economics of happiness literature. This U-shaped pattern is obtained by comparing people at different ages who have identical life circumstances – the same income, marital status, health and the like. But life circumstances change systematically with age and affect the life cycle pattern of happiness. For example, older people, in comparison with those middle-aged are, on average, more likely to have lower income, be in poorer health, and to live alone – circumstances that would affect adversely their happiness compared with those at mid-life, and that need to be taken into account in estimating the life cycle pattern of happiness.

Life cycle happiness is determined here by the net balance between aspirations and attainments. The analysis in Chapter 6 focuses on the material goods domain; the subsequent chapters extend this approach to the domains of family life, work, and health, following the domain satisfaction approach pioneered by psychologist Angus Campbell in the 1970s. In the United States, the domain satisfaction patterns typically differ from each other and from that in happiness. In combination, though, the domain patterns predict, not only life cycle happiness, but the observed stability of happiness over time, the point-of-time positive association between happiness and socio-economic status, and differences among birth cohorts (Chapter 10).

The domain satisfaction approach differs from that underlying the microeconomic equations estimated in the economics of happiness literature (Chapter 7). In the microeconomic equations, happiness is viewed as determined by objective circumstances such as family income, marital status, employment status, and the like. In the domain satisfaction analysis happiness is the result of subjective perceptions of such circumstances. The objective variable income, for example, is replaced by satisfaction with finances, which reflects how well income meets one's subjectively perceived "needs"; marital status is replaced by satisfaction with family life; and so on. Happiness is itself a subjective variable, and it is reasonable to suppose that it depends, not on objective conditions alone, but also on the subjective norms by which these objective circumstances are judged.

In recent decades psychologists have turned from Campbell's domain satisfaction approach to a "set point" theory of happiness, in which a person's happiness is thought to be constant over the life course, centering on a value given by genetics and personality. Neither the set point model, nor the traditional view of economists, that more income makes people happier, is supported by the evidence. A better theory of well-being, one that takes account of aspirations, attainments, and the multiple life domains determining happiness, would synthesize the analytical contributions of both disciplines, and provide a more meaningful guide to personal decisions and public policy (Chapter 11).

6

Income and Happiness:
Towards a Unified Theory

"Life is a progress from want to want, not from enjoyment to enjoyment."

Samuel Johnson, 1776

6.1. Introduction

The relationship between happiness and income is puzzling. At a point in time, those with more income are, on average, happier than those with less. Over the life cycle, however, the average happiness of a cohort remains constant despite substantial income growth. Moreover, even though a cohort's experienced happiness remains constant throughout the life span, people typically think that they were worse off in the past and will be better off in the future.

Can economic theory explain these paradoxical observations? Perhaps, with some amendment for systematic change in material preferences or aspirations. In what follows, after a brief discussion of the nature of these paradoxical relationships, I suggest a model to explain them, and present some supporting evidence.

This chapter is a revised version of: Easterlin, R. (2001). Income and Happiness: Towards a Unified Theory, in: The Economic Journal, 111(473), 465–484, © Royal Economic Society, 2001, reprinted with permission of Wiley Blackwell. I am grateful for the excellent assistance of Donna H. Ebata, Paul Rivera, and John Worth. For helpful suggestions I am indebted to Dennis Ahlburg, Richard H. Day, Nancy L. Easterlin, Stanley L. Engerman, Timur Kuran, Jim Martin, Bentley MacLeod, Vai-Lam Mui, Jeffrey Nugent, Andrew J. Oswald, Lynwood Pendleton, James Robinson, Alois Stutzer, participants in meetings at the California Institute of Technology, Oxford University, Penn State University, University of California Los Angeles, and the University of Southern California, and two anonymous referees. Financial support was provided by the Andrew W. Mellon Foundation and the University of Southern California.

The principal way in which subjective well-being is measured here is a direct question of the sort used since 1972 in the United States' General Social Survey (GSS): 'Taken all together, how would you say things are these days, would you say that you are very happy, pretty happy, or not too happy?' (National Opinion Research Center 1999, p. 171). As a general matter, people have little trouble answering such questions; in the GSS, for example, the average proportion of nonresponses was less than one percent in fourteen surveys conducted between 1972 and 1987. Issues such as the reliability and validity of the replies, whether respondents report their true feelings, possible biases resulting from the context in which the question is asked and comparability among persons, are discussed in the Introduction to Part II and Chapter 1.

6.2. Empirical Relationships

6.2.1. The Cross-Sectional Relationship

I start with the simple point-of-time association between happiness and income. In the 1994 GSS, the proportion reporting themselves very happy ranges from 16% in the lowest income class to 44% in the highest (Table 6.1, column 2). To avoid relying on only one happiness category, such as the percentage very happy, I have computed a mean happiness rating, which can vary from a minimum of zero to a maximum of four. By this measure, average happiness varies directly with income throughout the income range, from a low of 1.8 to a high of 2.8.

As far as I am aware, in every representative national survey ever done a statistically significant positive bivariate relationship between happiness and income has been found (Andrews 1986, p. xi; Argyle 1999, pp. 356-7; Diener 1984, p. 533). The relationship holds for household income, both adjusted for family size, and unadjusted as in Table 6.1. In recent work, there has been a tendency to discount this association between one's objective economic circumstances, as indexed by income, and subjective well-being (Diener and Lucas 1999, p. 215; Lykken and Tellegen 1996; Schwarz and Strack 1999, pp. 79-80). Partly, this is because in individual data there is a large amount of unexplained variance – the simple correlation, for example, between happiness and income in the individual data underlying Table 6.1, although highly significant, is only 0.20. Partly, it is because this modest happiness–income relationship is further weakened by the introduction of controls for other variables, such as unemployment and education (Frey and

Stutzer 1999; Oswald 1997; Veroff, Douvan and Kulka 1981). It is also sometimes argued that the happiness–income relation, such as it is, holds only in the lower part of the income range (Argyle 1999, p. 356).

Table 6.1

Percent Distribution of Population by Happiness at Various Levels of Income, United States, 1994

Total household income (1994 dollars)	(1) Mean happiness rating*	(2) Very happy	(3) Pretty happy	(4) Not too happy	(5) (Number of cases)
All income groups	2.4	28	60	12	(2,627)
75,000 and over	2.8	44	49	6	(268)
50–74,999	2.6	36	58	7	(409)
40–49,999	2.4	31	59	10	(308)
30–39,999	2.5	31	61	8	(376)
20–29,999	2.3	27	61	12	(456)
10–19,999	2.1	21	64	15	(470)
Less than 10,000	1.8	16	62	23	(340)

Source: National Opinion Research Center (1999) Question 157. 'Don't know' and 'no answer' responses are omitted.
* Based on score of 'very happy' = 4, 'pretty happy' = 2, 'not too happy' = 0.

This is not the place for detailed discussion of these arguments, but several brief comments are in order. First, the use of controls depends on one's purpose. Education and unemployment affect well-being in part through their effect on income, and if one takes income as a proxy for an interrelated set of socio-economic circumstances, then the bivariate relation is important in its own right. Second, the supposed attenuation at higher income levels of the happiness–income relation does not occur when happiness is regressed on log income, rather than absolute income. Put differently – if the same proportional rather than absolute increase in income is assumed to yield the same increase in happiness, then income change at upper income levels causes the same increase in happiness as at lower. Finally, although the high degree of variance in individual data is indisputable – a situation common in bivariate correlations of individual data – to discount the happiness–income relationship is to discount the personal testimony of individuals in country after country who mention economic circumstances most frequently as a source of happiness (Cantril 1965; Easterlin 2000 and Chapter 1). The positive happiness–income relation is consistent with this testimony.

6.2.2. The Life Cycle Pattern

When one turns to the life cycle change in happiness, however, a seeming contradiction arises to the positive happiness–income relationship. On average, income, and economic circumstances more generally, improve substantially up to the retirement ages; yet, there is no corresponding advance in subjective well-being (Figure 6.1).[1] Nor does the leveling off and decline of income in the retirement years appear to be accompanied by any change in average happiness. The lack of a life cycle trend in happiness is supported by regressions of happiness on age for each of the cohorts in Figure 6.1 – there is none with a statistically significant slope. A pooled regression with cohort dummy variables added also shows no significant coefficient.

It is possible, of course, that the seeming contradiction between the cross-sectional and life cycle relation of happiness to income is because other factors overwhelm the effect of income on happiness over the course of the life cycle. Yet, the effect of income is certainly not overwhelmed by such factors in the cross-section. Moreover, the top ranking of economic circumstances as a source of happiness persists at all points in the life cycle (Herzog, Rodgers and Woodworth 1982). Thus we are presented with a paradox: why at a point in time are happiness and income positively associated, but over the life cycle there is no relation?

Figure 6.1

Happiness and Income over the Life Cycle

Birth Cohort of 1941–50 from Ages 22–31 to 46–55

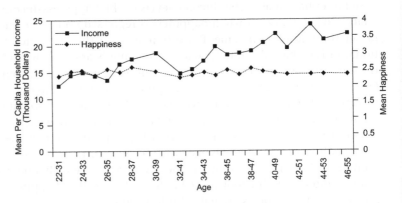

Figure 6.1 (continued)

Happiness and Income over the Life Cycle

Birth Cohort of 1931–40 from Ages 32–41 to 56–65

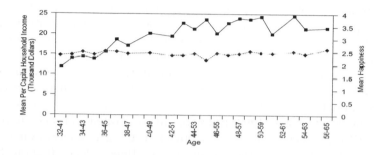

Birth Cohort of 1921–30 from Ages 42–51 to 66–75

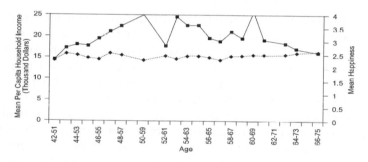

Birth Cohort of 1911–20 from Ages 52–61 to 69–78

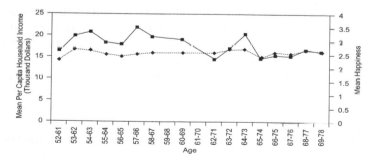

The life cycle pattern here is obtained by following each of several birth cohorts over a twenty-four year segment of its life span linking appropriate age data for successive years in what is sometimes termed a 'synthetic cohort' approach (for further detail, see Easterlin and Schaeffer 1999). This is the first time that this technique, originated by demographers a half century ago, has been used to study life cycle happiness. As noted in Chapter 7, previous generalizations about life cycle happiness are based almost entirely on cross-sectional relations between happiness and age, and give no consistent picture.

The mixed results from cross-sectional studies should come as no surprise, because they fail to consider the possibility that the cross-sectional relationship may vary over time. A survey of cross-sectional studies by George (1992) finds that in the United States before the 1970s older persons were less happy than younger; in recent surveys, however, there is no significant relation. Hence, depending on the calendar year chosen, cross-sectional studies may lead to quite different conclusions regarding the life cycle trend in happiness (cf. also Campbell 1981, Chapter 12).[2]

This is not to suggest that the present life cycle approach is without shortcomings. For one thing, it is not possible to follow the same individuals from one year to the next, as can be done with panel data. Also, the composition of a synthetic cohort, unlike that in panel data, is altered somewhat by differential mortality and international migration. In addition, there may be period as well as cohort effects in the data. But for all its shortcomings, the life cycle measurement procedure used here seems considerably better for inferring life cycle change than cross-sectional age data, because it follows essentially the same group of persons over sizeable segments of the life span.

Stability in the life cycle happiness of a cohort does not mean, of course, that at the individual level subjective well-being is simply a flat line over the life span. Significant changes in one's circumstances – life cycle events such as marriage, loss of a job, the birth of a child, retirement, and the death of a loved one – affect subjective well-being (McLanahan and Sorensen 1985; Myers 1992). If the sample size here permitted finer calibration – for example, following single year birth cohorts – one might possibly observe the imprint of such effects in the data, because some of them are age-related (see Chapter 7). For the 10 year birth cohorts and 24 year life span segments studied here, however, such effects, to the extent they exist, fail to alter the horizontal trend in happiness.

6.2.3. Past and Prospective Happiness

Based on the observed pattern of life cycle happiness, one would expect that individuals, when asked how their past and prospective happiness compares with the present, would report little change. As it turns out, this is not the case – people at any given point in the life cycle typically think that they will be better off in the future than at present, and that they are better off today than in the past. I am talking here of comparisons over periods of some length, say, five years or more, not very short intervals such as a year or less. The most comprehensive evidence of this comes from the Cantril survey discussed in Chapter 1. Respondents, after indicating their present happiness level on an integer scale from zero to ten, were asked where on the scale they were five years ago, and where they think they will be five years hence. In every country in every age group from 18-29 to 50 and over, respondents, on average, rated their prospective happiness higher, and their past happiness less, with only a few trivial exceptions (Table 6.2). Younger respondents saw, on average, greater changes than older, and future changes were envisaged to be greater than past.

Table 6.2

Past and Future Happiness Compared with Present Happiness, by Age, 14 Countries, 1965

	(1)	(2)	(3)	(4)	(5)
	Past versus present happiness			Future versus present happiness	
Age group	Number of observations	Number rating past lower	Mean difference, present minus past	Number rating future higher	Mean difference, future minus present
18-29	14	14	1.0	14	2.2
30-49	22	22	0.8	22	2.0
50+	14	12	0.6	13	1.3
65+	4	2	0.1	4	0.4

Source: Cantril (1965), pp. 365–77. An observation is the mean happiness value for an age group in a country. In some countries age groups were more detailed than those given here, hence the number of observations exceeds the number of countries. The questioning procedure is of the following nature. Respondents indicate where they currently are on a ladder with rungs from zero to ten, where ten is 'completely happy' and zero is 'unhappy'. They then indicate where on the ladder they stood five years ago and where they think they will be five years hence (Cantril 1965, p. 23). The countries included (with sample sizes) are: Brazil (2,170), Cuba (992, urban only), Dominican Republic (814), Egypt (499), India (2,366), Israel (1,170), Japan (972), Nigeria (1,200), Panama (642), Philippines (500), Poland (1,464), United States (1,549), West Germany (480), Yugoslavia (1,523).

Time series data for the United States confirm the evidence of Cantril's international cross-section. The same question as Cantril's was asked in 36 surveys in the 26-year-period from 1959 to 1985 (Lipset and Schneider 1987, pp. 130-1). In every survey respondents expected, on average, to be happier in the future, and felt that they had been worse off in the past, there being only three small exceptions in the present/past comparison. As in the international data, future changes were envisaged to be greater than past.[3] But in fact, over the entire period present happiness was, on average, constant. Thus we have another paradox to explain – why people typically think that they were worse off in the past and will be better off in the future, although their reports on present happiness remain constant over time.

6.3. Explaining the Relationships: Theory

I have noted three empirical regularities that need to be explained. At a given time those with higher incomes are happier, on average, than those with lower. Also, at a point in time respondents typically feel that they were less happy in the past and will be more happy in the future. Finally, experienced happiness is, on average, constant over the life cycle. The tentative explanation is a variant of the model in Chapter 5, and involves taking account of both income and aspirations, and how they vary at a point in time as well as over time.[4] As has been seen, the sources of happiness reported by individuals range beyond purely material concerns, but I focus in this chapter on goods aspirations.

Assume that at the start of the adult life cycle people in different socio-economic circumstances have a fairly similar set of material aspirations, say, A_1. Those with higher income will then be better able to fulfill their aspirations and, other things equal, will, on average, feel better off (Figure 6.2, compare points 1, 2, 3 on the utility function corresponding to the aspiration level, A_1). This is the point-of-time positive association between happiness and income.

If income rises and material aspirations remain constant, then individuals will move upward along the A_1 utility function in Figure 6.2, increasingly realizing their aspirations and experiencing rising levels of well-being – progressing, for example, from point 2 to point 3, with well-being rising from u_m to u_2. If, however, income remains constant and aspirations rise to, say, A_2, then the satisfaction associated with a given level of income would diminish. An individual whose income is, say, y_m, would experience a level of satisfaction u_m if she were on the utility function corresponding to aspiration level A_1 (point 2), but a lower level of satisfaction, u_1, if she were on the utility function corresponding to the higher aspiration level, A_2 (point 4).

Figure 6.2

Subjective Well-Being (u) as a Function of Income (y) and Aspiration Level (A)

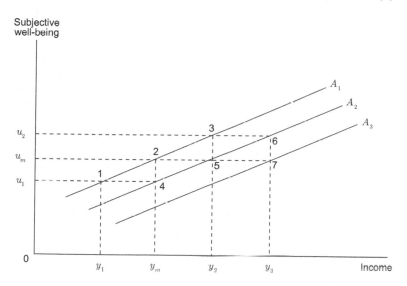

I conjecture that, in reality, material aspirations change over the life cycle roughly in proportion to income. Hence, individuals typically move from point 2, neither to point 3 nor point 4, but to point 5, because both aspirations and income rise, with roughly offsetting effects on well-being. This results in observed stability during the working ages of life cycle well-being, a product of the countervailing effects of rising income and aspirations.

How does one explain the statements on past and prospective welfare? The key is to recognise that these are point-of-time responses and are consequently based on the aspirations that people have acquired at that point in time. Consider, for example, an individual who has moved from point 2 to point 5, with income growing from y_m to y_2 and aspirations rising from A_1 to A_2. When asked at point 5 how well off he was in the past, his judgment is based on his current higher level of aspirations (A_2), not on the lower level of aspirations

(A_1) he actually had in the past. Because his aspirations have risen he evaluates his previous income, y_m, on the basis of his new utility function, A_2, and sees y_m as yielding the satisfaction level, u_1 (point 4). When he was actually at y_m, however, his material aspirations were lower, and he enjoyed the higher happiness level, u_m (point 2 on the utility function A_1).

The assessment of one's future well-being is similarly premised on one's material aspirations at the time the question is asked. A person at point 5 on the utility function A_2, who anticipates a growth in income to y_3 will envisage an improvement in welfare from u_m to u_2, that is, an upward movement along the A_2 function from point 5 to point 6. What she does not know is that when she gets to y_3 she will have, not just higher income, but higher material aspirations as well, and be on the utility function corresponding to the higher aspiration level, A_3. Thus, she will end up at point 7, not point 6, and experience about the same level of satisfaction, u_m, that she did at point 5.

The distinction drawn by psychologists between decision utility and experienced utility is illustrated clearly here (Kahneman, Wakker and Sarin 1997; Tversky and Griffin 1991). Decision utility is the perceived (ex ante) satisfaction associated with choice among several alternatives; experienced utility is the satisfaction realised (ex post) from the outcome actually chosen. When asked about well-being five years ago or five years hence, a person at point 5 with income y_2 on utility function A_2, can be thought of as telling us how she would feel today if she had the income y_m (worse off) or y_3 (better off). This is her decision utility. It explains, for example, why she says she would not want to go back to her old lower-paying job (point 4) and why she may take a new higher-paying job (point 6). However, if she does take the higher-paying job and her income goes up, her material aspirations too will rise. Hence, when asked how happy she is when she actually has income y_3, that is, what her experienced utility is, she turns out to be at point 7, not point 6.

Economists tend to assume that decision utility and experienced utility are the same. The present theory implies that there is a mechanism at work – aspirations rising in proportion to income – that makes them systematically different (see also Kahneman 1999; Rabin 1998). If one's interest is solely in the choices determining behaviour, then decision utility is enough. But if one is interested in the welfare effects of behaviour, then the effect of the income–aspiration mechanism on experienced utility needs to be taken into account.

6.4. Explaining the Relationships: Evidence

It is one thing to speculate; it is another to give supporting evidence, particularly with regard to the central feature of the theory – differences and trends in material aspirations. There is virtually no systematic empirical work on changing aspirations on which to build, but in what follows, I present a few pieces of new data that I think are consistent with the theory just presented. I also note some supporting evidence from the psychological literature.

I first divide each cohort in Figure 6.1 into two socio-economic groups whose composition remains largely the same over the life cycle – those with more than a high school education and those with a high school education or less. In effect, the educational system is seen as channeling persons into two different life cycle tracks, with the higher schooling group enjoying the benefit of higher income.[5] The analysis is necessarily more approximate than the previous one for several reasons: dividing a birth cohort by level of education results in a smaller sample size, misreporting of educational level may be a problem, and during the life cycle some individuals shift from the lower to the higher educational cohort as a result of ongoing education. In the happiness data below, I have tried to minimise these problems by using a three-year moving average, and confining the analysis to that segment of a cohort's life cycle for which the distribution by level of education remains fairly constant.[6]

The cohorts, when subdivided by level of education, present a microcosm of the cross-sectional and life cycle patterns already presented (Figure 6.3). At any given point in the life cycle, happiness varies directly with socio-economic status as measured by education; over the course of the life cycle, however, there is no change in the happiness of either socio-economic group.

The persistent differential by socio-economic status underscores the importance of objective circumstances for well-being. Essentially the same people are in each educational group throughout the life cycle, and those on the higher income track are consistently happier, on average, than those on the lower. Psychologists have sometimes pointed to the finding that over time the same individuals tend to be high (or low) on the happiness scale as evidence that personality or genetic differences are the source of differences in happiness, not 'external conditions' such as economic circumstances (Diener and Lucas 1999, p. 214). This conclusion is contradicted by the present result.

To dismiss the effect here of economic circumstances on well-being, one would have to make a very strong case that inherent genetic and personality traits are what lie behind the channeling of persons into the two educational tracks.

Figure 6.3
Life Cycle Happiness by Level of Education

Birth Cohort of 1941–50 from Ages 34–43 to 44–53

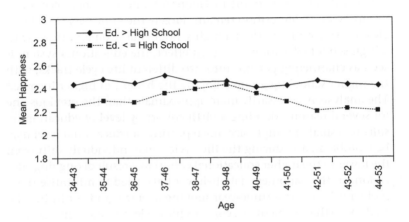

Birth Cohort of 1931–40 from Ages 33–42 to 47–56

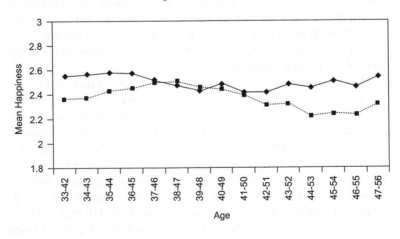

Figure 6.3 (continued)
Life Cycle Happiness by Level of Education

Birth Cohort of 1921–30 from Ages 43–52 to 59–68

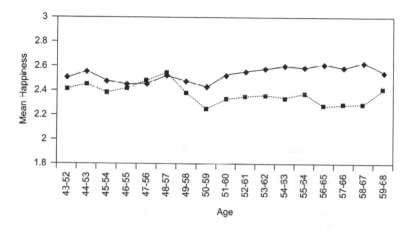

The theory I have presented makes three assumptions about material preferences: (1) early in the life cycle, preferences are fairly similar among income groups, (2) over the life cycle, preferences vary in proportion to income, and (3) in evaluating past or future happiness, people take their preferences to be the same as those held currently. Each of these will be taken up, in turn.

The desires of high school seniors (largely 18 year-olds) for big ticket consumer goods, as reported in surveys, provide striking evidence that people start out with very similar aspirations. The proportion naming each of twelve consumer goods as extremely or quite important is virtually the same for those who expect to attend a four-year college as for those who do not (Table 6.3). The average number of consumer goods named as extremely or quite important by the two groups is an identical 4.5 (see the bottom line of Table 6.3).

This does not mean that material aspirations, in general, are identical for the two groups. Although a number of important consumer goods are reported on here, the list is not exhaustive. Moreover, the responses do not indicate the specific characteristics of each good that the respondent has in mind. It is plausible to suppose that the characteristics of a 'house of my own' envisaged by those from higher status backgrounds differ systematically from those contemplated by persons from lower status backgrounds. Nevertheless, the similarity between the two lists is remarkable – who would have predicted, for example, that the proportion naming 'major labour-saving appliances' as extremely or quite important would be the same 51 percent for each group?

Table 6.3

Desires of High School Seniors for Big Ticket Consumer Goods, by Plans to Attend Four-Year College, 1976

Consumer good	(1) College plans	(2) No college plans
	(percent answering extremely or quite important)	
At least one car	76	80
A house of my own (instead of an apartment or condominium)	52	53
Lots of space around my house, a big yard	60	58
A well-kept garden and lawn	60	58
Major labor-saving appliances (washer, dryer, dishwasher, etc.)	51	51
A high quality stereo	45	44
Clothes in the latest style	41	40
A motor-powered recreational vehicle (powerboat, snowmobile)	15	16
At least two cars	14	14
A large (full-sized) car	14	13
A vacation house	12	11
A new car every 2-3 years	11	11
Mean number of goods per person extremely or quite important	4.5	4.5

Source: Bachman, Johnston and O'Malley (1980) pp. 139–41. The question asked is: Looking toward the future, how important would it be for you to have each of the following things? The number of cases in each column is about 1,400.

Given the similarity in material aspirations at the start of the life cycle, initial differences in happiness by level of schooling must be due, according to the theory, to differences in income that make it possible for those with more schooling to attain their material aspirations better than those with less. Suggestive evidence that the happiness difference early in the adult life cycle is due to differences in income comes from survey questions that were asked of a nationally representative sample of the adult population of all ages in 1978. In this survey respondents were asked whether they considered each of ten consumer goods – much like the twelve on which high school seniors reported – to be part of the 'good life', that is, 'the life you'd like to have', and also whether they actually had the items. For the youngest age group of respondents, those 18 to 29 years old, the bivariate correlation between material aspirations, measured by the number of big ticket consumer goods named as part of the good life, and income was -0.01, indicative again of the lack of difference in aspirations by socio-economic status early in the adult life cycle. The correlation between the number of big ticket consumer goods respondents actually had and income was a significant 0.21. Although there are no reports on happiness in this survey, it is noteworthy that the magnitude of the correlation with income of what one might call 'consumer wealth' is just about the same as that reported earlier for the correlation of happiness with income. These results are consistent with the view that the point-of-time positive association between happiness and income is due to the fact that higher income makes possible greater fulfillment of material aspirations.

The theory also postulates that over the life cycle material aspirations rise roughly in proportion to income. Again, the 'good life' data used above provide some support. If one follows cohorts over a roughly 15 year segment of the life span, one finds that within a cohort the increase in the number of consumer goods desired – that is, the number named as part of the good life – is greater for those with more schooling than for those with less (Table 6.4, column 1).[7] The increase in consumer wealth is also greater for the higher educational group (column 2). The greater growth in both material aspirations and consumer wealth for the higher schooling group is consistent with the hypothesis that growth in income is driving the growth in material aspirations.[8]

Table 6.4

Change between Specified Life Cycle Ages in Mean Number of Big Ticket Consumer Goods Desired and Owned for Persons With Specified Amount of Schooling

Cohort, age, and schooling	(1) Change in number of consumer goods desired	(2) Change in number of consumer goods owned
A. Cohort of 1950—64 between ages 18—29 and 30—44		
Persons with schooling greater than 12 years	1.4	1.6
Persons with schooling 12 years or less	1.0	1.1
Difference	0.4	0.5
B. Cohort of 1935—49 between ages 30—44 and 45—59		
Persons with schooling greater than 12 years	1.3	1.0
Persons with schooling 12 years or less	0.9	0.4
Difference	0.4	0.6

Source: Roper-Starch Organization (1979, 1995)

Further support for the hypothesis that income is behind the growth in aspirations comes from the changing correlation between aspirations and income over the course of the life cycle. If income is the cause of changing material aspirations, then one ought to observe the gradual emergence during the life cycle of a positive correlation between material aspirations and income, and this, in fact, is the case (Table 6.5).

Table 6.5

Correlation with Income of Number of Big Ticket Consumer Goods Desired, Specified Age in Life Cycle, Cohorts of 1950-64 and 1935-49

	(1)	(2)	(3)	(4)
	Age	Correlation coefficient	Age	Correlation coefficient
Cohort of 1950-64	18-29	-0.01	30-44	0.08*
Cohort of 1935-49	30-44	0.05	45-59	0.14*

Notes: * Significance levels are approximately as follows: 0.08 correlation is significant at 0.10 level; 0.12 at 0.01 level; and 0.15 at 0.001 level. The number of cases in the first row is 474 and 562; in the second row, 427 and 349.
Source: Same as Table 6.4

Figure 6.2 can be used to interpret these patterns by level of education. Early in the adult life cycle, those with more and less education are both on roughly the same utility function, sharing a common set of aspirations, A1. Because those with more education earn a higher average income than those with less – say, y_m compared to y_1 – their subjective well-being is correspondingly greater, the differential equalling $(u_m - u_1)$. As each group progresses through the life cycle, incomes rise more for the higher schooling group from, say, y_m to y_3, while those of the lower schooling group rise from y_1 to y_m. But the greater growth of income of the higher schooling group causes their aspirations also to rise more – from, say, A_1 to A_3, compared to a growth in aspirations for the lower schooling group from A_1 to A_2. Hence, the higher schooling group moves from point 2 to point 7 while the lower schooling group moves from point 1 to point 4. As a result, the happiness differential enjoyed by the higher schooling group remains constant at $(u_m - u_1)$.

The psychological mechanism implicit in the view here of the determinants of material aspirations is suggested by the well-known ring toss experiment in which individuals – given free choice of how close to stand to the peg – are found to set their aspirations in proportion to their abilities. Then, as they get better at the ring toss, they tend to move farther away. Increasing skill is thus matched by increasing aspirations, in much the same way that increasing ability to get goods is matched by increasing material aspirations.

The third assumption about preferences is that people base their past or prospective happiness evaluations on their current preferences. The social science literature provides some support for this hypothesis. A cohort study of political attitudes by Markus (1986) found that respondents whose attitudes actually had changed tended to report that their past attitudes were the same as those currently held. Social psychologists Kahneman and Snell (1992), based on small group experiments, report that 'the dominant heuristic [to predict future tastes] is to consult current desires' and that 'there was little or no correlation between the predictions of hedonic change that individuals made and the changes they actually experienced' (pp. 187, 189). Rabin (1998), generalising from a survey of the social psychology literature, observes that 'we don't always accurately predict our own future preferences, nor even accurately assess our experienced well-being from past choices' (p. 12). Such statements, though not providing as specific support as one might like, are consistent with the current hypothesis.

The present model, however, leaves unanswered an important question – how does one explain the similarity in material aspirations among those of different socio-economic status at the start of the life cycle? Those with more schooling typically come from more affluent backgrounds; hence, one would suppose that they would start out with higher material aspirations as well.

I believe that the explanation for the initial similarity and then growing divergence in aspirations by socio-economic status lies in the changing role over the life cycle of two factors determining aspirations – one's own past experience and social comparison. The importance of peer influences – that is, social comparison – in shaping the aspirations of the young is widely recognized. These peer influences, I believe, typically make for a commonality in the aspirations of young persons from different socio-economic origins. In the pre-adult ages, those from different backgrounds intermingle to a fair extent – at school, in sports, in recreational activities such as rock concerts, and at work, where they may hold the same jobs, such as fast food vendors. They see much the same television programmes, movies, and advertisements. These common experiences and social contacts make for more similar aspirations by socio-economic status than if family background were the only factor. However, once people enter the working ages, the experiences and contacts shared by those of different socio-economic status diminishes. Those who go on to college are embarked on a different career trajectory, and have limited contact in the workplace with those who do not share the same educational background. Their higher income also makes for residential segregation by socio-economic status. Although the experiences of others continue to influence aspirations, it seems likely that throughout the socio-economic spectrum, reference groups, over the course of the life cycle, become increasingly narrower than in the pre-adult years, and more confined to those of like status. As a result, the factors making in the pre-adult years for similarity in aspirations among those from different socio-economic backgrounds become progressively less salient over the course of the life cycle.

This reasoning can be tied to the more general theoretical literature in psychology and economics on the formation of preferences. In psychology, the two sets of factors identified here as influencing aspirations – one's past personal experience and the experience of others – correspond roughly to what is known as adaptation level theory and social comparison theory (Brickman and Campbell 1971; Frederick and Loewenstein 1999; Helson 1964; Myers 1992; Olson, Herman and Zanna 1986).[9] The counterparts in economics of these two theories are habit formation models and theories of interdependent preferences (Day 1986; Duesenberry 1949; Frank 1985b, 1997; Modigliani 1949; Pollak 1970, 1976; Tomes 1986). Both the psychological and economic theories stress that judgments are formed by comparison – in the first case with one's past experience; in the second, with the experience of others.

I am suggesting that while both influences are at work in shaping material aspirations and hence judgments of well-being, their relative importance shifts over the course of the life cycle. In the pre-adult years social comparison over a wide socio-economic spectrum plays a relatively larger part than personal background in shaping aspirations. In the adult years, as individuals with different educational backgrounds embark on relatively segregated socio-economic tracks, past personal experience becomes more important and social comparison influences are increasingly confined to a reference group comprised of those of one's own socio-economic status. Hence, material aspirations start out much more alike among those from different socio-economic backgrounds than is true later in the life cycle, when one's personal income experience and that of others on the same track becomes the major driving force behind material aspirations.

6.5. Summary

The pattern of change in material aspirations over the life cycle explains some of the paradoxical relationships between subjective well-being and income. At the start of the adult life cycle material aspirations are fairly similar throughout the population, but over the life cycle, aspirations increase in proportion to income. Utility functions shift inversely with material aspirations.

As a general matter, subjective well-being varies directly with income and inversely with material aspirations. At the start of the life cycle those with higher income are happier, because material aspirations are fairly similar throughout the population, and those with more income are better able to fulfill their aspirations. Income growth does not, however, cause well-being to rise, either for higher or lower income persons, because it generates equivalent growth in material aspirations, and the negative effect of the latter on subjective well-being undercuts the positive effect of the former. Even though rising income means that people can have more goods, the favourable effect of this on welfare is erased by the fact that people want more as they progress through the life cycle. It seems as though Ralph Waldo Emerson (1860) had it right when he said 'Want is a growing giant whom the coat of Have was never large enough to cover.'

Because the educational system channels people into two different life cycle tracks characterised by higher and lower income trajectories, those with more education are, on average, happier throughout the life cycle than those with less. Some psychologists have claimed that persistent interpersonal differentials in well-being over the life cycle are evidence that personality or genetic traits primarily determine relative well-being, not 'external' factors such as income. The present analysis makes clear that external factors are important, because the educational tracking of persons leads to persistent differences in well-being via its effect on relative incomes.

Judgments of well-being at any particular point in time are based on the material aspirations prevailing at that time. As a result, people tend to evaluate past lower incomes less favourably than they did when they were actually in that situation and had lower aspirations. Similarly, they judge prospective higher income situations more favourably than when they actually are in those situations, because they fail to anticipate the rise in material aspirations that will come with the growth in income. Choice among alternatives – decision utility – is based on the aspirations prevailing at the time of choice. The actual welfare effect of such choice – experienced utility – differs systematically from decision utility, because of unforeseen changes in aspirations. Thus, movement to a higher income situation is envisaged by a decision-maker as increasing happiness, because it is based on a projection of income growth with aspirations unchanged. But the increase in income itself engenders a corresponding rise in material aspirations, and experienced utility does not rise as expected.

7

Life Cycle Happiness and Its Sources: Intersections of Psychology, Economics, and Demography

At what stage of life are people happiest – when they are on the threshold of their adult lives, at mid-life when families are complete and many are close to the peak of their working careers, or in the "golden years" of retirement? What are the factors responsible for the life cycle pattern of happiness? These are the issues of interest here – the nature and causes of life cycle happiness. In answering them, this chapter, which continues the discussion in Chapter 6, draws on theoretical and empirical work in economics and psychology and the methodology of demography.

7.1. Psychology and Economics

7.1.1. The Nature of Life Cycle Happiness

Surprisingly, there is little agreement on how happiness varies, on average, over the life course. Consider four recent surveys of research on subjective well-being (SWB), three in psychology and one in economics, published almost contemporaneously. David G. Myers (2000, p. 58), in a special issue of the "American Psychologist" that surveys

This chapter is a revised version of: Easterlin, R. (2006). Life Cycle Happiness and Its Sources: Intersections of Psychology, Economics and Demography, in: Journal of Economic Psychology, 27(4), 463–482, reprinted with permission from Elsevier. This chapter has benefited from exceptional research assistance and comments by Olga Shemyakina, Anke C. Plagnol, and Pouyan Mashayekh-Ahangarani. Helpful ideas were suggested by David Cutler, Daniel T. Gilbert, Enrico Marcelli, Bob Osborne, and Steven J. Sherman. Financial support was provided by the University of Southern California.

work in the new field of positive psychology states: "Although many people believe there are unhappy times of life – times of adolescent stress, midlife crisis, or old age decline – repeated surveys across the industrialized world reveal that no time in life is notably happiest and most satisfying".

In contrast, Michael Argyle, writing in the encyclopedic volume on "hedonic psychology" edited by Kahneman, Diener, and Schwarz (1999) concludes that studies both of life satisfaction and positive and negative affect imply that well-being increases with age (p. 354, cf. also Argyle 2001). A survey by Diener et al. (1999, p. 291) blends these two results, stating that "recent studies converge to show that life satisfaction often increases, or at least does not drop, with age". But Bruno S. Frey and Alois Stutzer in a book synthesizing the recent economics literature argue that "much care should be taken when claiming that old age leads to unhappiness, or that the old are happier than the young ... [T]he economic studies just referred to reach a more differentiated conclusion – namely, that the young and the old are happier than the middle-aged" (2002a, p. 54).

All of these surveys appear to be addressing the straightforward question of life cycle well-being: as people progress from young adulthood through midlife to older age, experiencing life's various joys and vicissitudes, do they become, on average, happier, less happy, or does happiness remain unchanged? But the economic studies on which the Frey and Stutzer statement is based are, in fact, considering a quite different question. The U-shaped generalization derives from multivariate regressions of happiness on age controlling for a number of life circumstances that vary systematically over the life cycle. Hence, these studies are in effect asking, if one compares young, midlife, and older persons who are in the same circumstances with regard to income, employment, marital status, and health, how does their happiness differ? Although Frey and Stutzer imply that this economic research contradicts assertions that "the old are happier than the young", in fact it does not, because this research abstracts from numerous economic, family, and health conditions that differentiate older persons from younger. Clearly if one wants to know whether a person is likely to be happier in his or her golden years than when forming families, one would not want to set aside the fact that older people are likely to have lower income, be less healthy, and are more likely to be living alone. The conclusion of the economic studies – that the happiness–age relationship is U-shaped when many age-related differences in life circumstances are controlled – is, no doubt, of interest, but it is misleading to suggest that it says anything about how the happiness of young or old persons compares with those at midlife.

All of the generalizations just cited are based on research consisting almost wholly of point-of-time comparisons of happiness with age. This is true even of those studies that pool data for more than one year, because these studies typically include survey year as a control, and, in effect, derive the average of a succession of cross-sections over the years included (cf. e.g. Blanchflower and Oswald 2004). Point-of-time studies are an uncertain basis for generalizing about life cycle experience, because the young and old in such comparisons are persons from different birth cohorts with different life histories. When data, say, for the year 2000 for happiness classified by age are used to infer change over the life cycle, the implicit assumption is that those born in 1980 (who are 20 years old in 2000) will follow the same life course trajectory as did those born fifty years earlier (and are 70 years old in 2000). The unease created by this assumption is compounded when one realizes that cross-sectional data for the United States in the 1950s reveal a negative association of happiness with age, while current cross-sections show a zero relation (Campbell 1981, pp. 175, 245). The difference between these point-of-time comparisons very likely reflects a shift over the period, not in the relation of happiness to age, but in the happiness of older compared with younger birth cohorts as the relative circumstances of different cohorts changed over the past half century (Easterlin 1987).

If the life cycle pattern of happiness is to be better established, then what is needed are longitudinal studies that follow the happiness of a given birth cohort – those born in the same year or group of years – as it ages. The problem here is that there are very few studies that span many years of the life cycle of a birth cohort. The one perhaps most frequently cited is that by Costa et al. (1987); this, for example, is the only longitudinal study of the relation of SWB to age cited in the article by Diener and his collaborators that summarizes the results of three decades of psychological research on subjective well-being (1999, pp. 291–292). The Costa et al. article concludes (p. 54) that "the present data provide compelling evidence for the stability of levels of well-being in adulthood." This conclusion is based on the net balance of observations of positive and negative affect for 9-year segments of the life cycle of five different 10-year birth cohorts, some younger, some older. The same result is reached here in Chapter 6 and in a "synthetic panel" study by Easterlin and Schaeffer (1999), which examines ten 5-year birth cohorts with segments of experience ranging from 13 to 21 years in length. Two newer studies by psychologists, however, each offer different results. Charles, Reynolds and Gatz (2001) examine linear trends in positive and negative affect for three "generations" of adults (younger, middle-aged, and older) for segments of the life cycle up to 23 years in length. They conclude that "positive affect remains fairly stable" while "negative affect decreases across the adult life span" (p. 149). This result implies that, on balance, subjective well-being increases over the life cycle. But the latest panel study of some length, that by Mroczek and Spiro (2005), following 1900 men for 22 years, reports an overall trajectory in well-being that is hill-shaped with a peak at age 65. Thus, even the few fairly lengthy longitudinal studies that have been done do not agree on the pattern of life cycle happiness.

7.1.2. Determinants of Life Cycle Happiness

If one turns to explanations of life cycle well-being, the literature is equally mixed. For purposes of contrast it is useful to distinguish two extreme views, one common in economics, the other sometimes found in psychology.

Economists typically adopt the view that well-being depends on actual life circumstances, and that one can safely infer well-being simply from observing these circumstances. At the extreme this view reduces to using real GDP per capita as a measure of well-being, and asserting that if people have more goods and services they must be better off. Economists recognize, of course, that well-being is influenced by other conditions than just the amount of goods and services people have, but typically they assume that if this amount increases substantially, then overall well-being will move in the same direction (cf. Chapter 1).

In contrast, psychologists typically view the effect on well-being of objective conditions as being mediated by psychological processes in which people adjust to the ups and downs in their life circumstances. At the extreme, this adjustment process, sometimes termed "hedonic adaptation", has led to the notion that people are on a hedonic treadmill (Brickman and Campbell 1971; Kahneman, Diener and Schwarz 1999, p. 13–15). This view is often formulated as a "setpoint model", and "[t]he assumption that happiness set points exist has guided much of the current theory and research on SWB" (Lucas et al. 2004, p. 8). In this approach individual happiness tends to a setpoint level established by personality and genetic heritage. Life events, such as marriage, loss of a job, and serious injury or disease, may deflect a person above or below this setpoint, but hedonic adaptation will fairly quickly return an individual to the setpoint. In this "strong" setpoint model hedonic adaptation to life events is rapid and complete. This view is exemplified by recent statements such as the following by David G. Myers (2000, p. 60): "Our human capacity for adaptation [...] helps explain a major conclusion of subjective well-being research, as expressed by the late Richard Kammann (1983): 'Objective life circumstances have a negligible role to play in a theory of happiness'" (cf. also Cziksmentmihalyi and Hunter 2003, pp. 185–186; Lykken and Tellegen 1996, p. 189).

Psychologists support this view empirically by pointing to the results of multivariate analyses of SWB, including those by economists, that typically find that objective life circumstances account for only a small part of individual differences in happiness – perhaps only 15 percent, at best (Diener 2000, p. 37). What this reasoning overlooks, however, is that the factors that are most important in determining *individual differences* in happiness are not necessarily the same as those most important in explaining the average life cycle pattern of happiness. This distinction is not generally recognized in the psychological literature where the role of a variable in explaining individual differences is typically taken as the sole criterion of that variable's explanatory importance. However, a variable that is important in explaining differences among persons at a point in time is not necessarily equally important in accounting for a change over time common to these persons as a group. As an example, consider the marked upswing and subsequent collapse in the United States rate of childbearing in the three decades after World War II – the great baby boom and bust. Among the various factors explaining individual differences in childbearing at any given time, both religion and economic circumstances are important. In explaining the baby boom and bust, however, economic considerations are of overriding significance, and religion, which changes very little over time, is unimportant (Easterlin 1987). Similarly, it is possible that in explaining the average trend of life cycle happiness, the relative importance of life circumstances is greater than it is in explaining differences among persons, because life circumstances tend to change more over the life cycle than do factors such as personality and genetic heritage.

The sharp contrast between the mainstream economics view and the strong setpoint model is illustrated by the distinction drawn by psychologists between a "top down" and "bottom up" explanation of well-being (Diener 1984; Diener et al. 1999; Headey, Veenhoven and Wearing 1991). The economics model would fall in the bottom up category where overall happiness is seem as the outcome of experiences, good and bad, in various life domains. The setpoint model exemplifies the top down view in which global happiness is a personality trait and hedonic adaptation in different life domains overrides the impact of life events. Thus a top down advocate would see people as adapting fairly quickly to an event like the death of a spouse and returning to the happiness setpoint given by personality and genetic make-up, while bottom up proponents would expect such an adverse occurrence to depress happiness significantly.

Not all psychologists subscribe to the setpoint model nor do all economists view well-being as depending solely on actual life circumstances. As mentioned in earlier chapters, in economics there is a line of work, some of it extending back over 50 years, that brings into consideration the effect on well-being of psychological processes such as social comparison and habituation. Economists engaged in the recent upsurge of research on happiness uniformly acknowledge the importance of psychological factors in the explanation of well-being (Clark, Frijters and Shields 2008; Di Tella and MacCulloch 2006; Frey and Stutzer 2002a; Graham 2005, 2008; Layard 2005; Stutzer 2003; van Praag and Frijters 1999; van Praag and Ferrer-i-Carbonell 2005). Indeed, to the extent any explanation has been offered by economists of their finding of a U-shaped relation of happiness to age controlling for life circumstances, it is in terms of a psychological factor, aspirations. Thus, Blanchflower and Oswald speculate about the source of the U-shape as follows: "One tentative possibility is that this decline and then rise in well-being through the years may reflect a process of adaptation to circumstances; perhaps by the middle of their lives, *people relinquish some of their aspirations and thereby come to enjoy life more*" (2004, p. 1375, emphasis added). Frey and Stutzer (2002a, p. 54) say virtually the same thing.[1]

In psychology there has been a retreat from the strong setpoint model. At a minimum, allowance is usually made for the possibility of individuals being able to improve their well-being through various psychological measures (Seligman 2002). Beyond this, there is often recognition that at least some life circumstances may have lasting effects on happiness. Myers (1992, 2000), for example, makes a specific exception to the hedonic treadmill in the case of family and social relationships. Lucas et al. (2003) report that while adaptation to marriage is, on average, rapid and complete, adaptation to widowhood may take, on average, eight years (but on adaptation to marriage, see Zimmermann and Easterlin 2006). Elsewhere, they conclude that the effect on well-being of unemployment is even more enduring, changing the "happiness setpoint" (Lucas et al. 2004). A clear implication of this work is that life circumstances, rather than being lumped together in a portmanteau generalization, need to be considered separately with regard to their effects on well-being, as is done by Diener and Seligman (2004) in their thoughtful proposal for a national well-being index.[2] Recent research by Kahneman and others (2004), making clear that all life circumstances are not hedonically equal, underscores the importance of looking separately at different life circumstances (see Robinson and Godbey 1997, Chapter 17 for a similar analysis based on a broader population sample). Thus, there is evidence of some convergence of the disciplines toward a view that in explaining happiness both life circumstances and psychological factors matter. Nevertheless, there persists an important difference in emphasis, with economics stressing objective life circumstances and psychology, subjective factors.

7.1.3. Policy

The mainstream economic theory of well-being and the strong setpoint model have quite different implications for public policy. The economic model implies that programs that improve people's life circumstances can improve subjective well-being. In contrast, the strong setpoint model amounts virtually to an "iron law of happiness" – any measure taken to improve people's economic and social conditions can have only a transient effect on well-being, because each individual will, in time, revert to his or her given setpoint of happiness.[3] Lykken and Tellegen (1996) were at one time outspoken exponents of this view, and it is made quite explicit with regard to policy by Ed Diener and Richard E. Lucas: "The influence of genetics and personality suggests a limit on the degree to which policy can increase SWB ... Changes in the environment, although important for short-term well-being, lose salience over time through processes of adaptation, and have small effects on long-term SWB" (Diener and Lucas 1999, p. 227).

As I have mentioned, in recent years psychologists have increasingly backed away from the strong setpoint model. Lykken's (1999) book explicitly renounces the view in his earlier article with Tellegen, and the article by Diener and Seligman (2004) advocating governmental participation in the measurement of SWB, specifies a number of ways through which improvements in economic and social conditions might be expected to raise SWB. Nevertheless, the sharp contrast between the two disciplinary views highlights a major policy issue – the potential for public programs to improve well-being is less, the more people are found to adapt psychologically to changing life circumstances. Hence, a crucial policy issue is the relative weight in determining well-being of actual life events versus hedonic adaptation.

7.2. Conceptual Framework

This chapter adopts the life domain approach to explaining happiness pioneered by psychologist Angus Campbell and his collaborators (Campbell, Converse and Rodgers 1976; Campbell 1981).[4] In this view responses on global happiness are seen as the net outcome of reported satisfaction with various domains of life – material living conditions, family life, health, work, and so on. Statements about satisfaction in each domain are, in turn, viewed as reflecting the extent to which objective outcomes in that domain match the respondent's aspirations, goals, or needs in that area (cf. Chapter 6). In the domain of family life, for example, one's goals, simply put, might be a happy marriage with two children and warm family relationships. Satisfaction with family life would reflect the extent to which objective circumstances match these goals – the greater the shortfall, the less the satisfaction with family life. Over time, subjective goals, objective circumstances, or both may change, and thereby alter judgments on domain satisfaction. Given objective conditions, goals may be adjusted to accord more closely with actual circumstances, in line with the process of hedonic adaptation emphasized by psychologists. Given goals, objective circumstances may shift closer to or farther from goals, altering satisfaction along the lines stressed by economists.

An advantage of this approach is that judgments on domain satisfaction that are central to determining happiness reflect both subjective factors of the type emphasized in psychology and objective circumstances stressed by economics. Another advantage is that it classifies into a tractable set of life domains the everyday circumstances to which people refer when asked about the factors affecting their happiness. Of course, there is not complete agreement on what domains of life are conceptually preferable, and the classification of life domains remains a subject of continuing research. Virtually all life domain studies, however, agree that economic condition, family circumstances, health, and work are important domains determining happiness. These four, for example, with slightly different labels, are at the head of Cummins's (1996) meta-analysis of the domains of life satisfaction, and all figure prominently in recent empirical studies using the life domain approach (Rojas 2007; Salvatore and Muñoz Sastre 2001; Saris, Veenhoven, Scherpenzeel and Bunting 1995; van Praag and Ferrer-i-Carbonell 2004; van Praag, Frijters and Ferrer-i-Carbonell 2003). It is these four domains – economic, family, health, and work – that are studied here.

7.3. Data and Methods

The data are from the United States General Social Survey (GSS) conducted by the National Opinion Research Center (Davis and Smith 2002). This is a nationally representative survey conducted annually from 1972 to 1993 (with a few exceptions) and biannually from 1994 to 2002. The present analysis is based on data for 1973-1994, because two of the variables of interest, family and health satisfaction, are included in the GSS only during this time span. The GSS is a survey of households, and weighted responses are used here to represent more accurately the population of persons (Davis and Smith 2002, pp. 1392-1393 of Codebook). For happiness there are 3 response options; financial satisfaction, 3 options; job satisfaction, 4 options; family satisfaction, 7 options; and health satisfaction, 7 options. The specific question for each variable is given in Appendix A. In the present analysis the response of an individual to each question is assigned an integer value, with a range from least satisfied (or happy) equal to 1, up to the total number of response options (e.g. 3 for happiness, 7 for health satisfaction).

The average trend of happiness from ages 18 to 89 is established by regressing happiness on age controlling for year of birth (birth cohort), gender, race, and education. The same technique is used to estimate the life cycle pattern for each domain satisfaction variable. The technique is essentially a statistically refined variant of demographers' birth cohort analysis. The control for birth cohort means, in effect, that segments of life cycle experience for numerous closely overlapping birth cohorts are combined to infer the typical life cycle pattern. In any given year the individuals actually surveyed differ from the previous year – the surveys provide a random sample year after year of persons from the same birth cohort, but not the responses of exactly the same members of the cohort; thus it is a "synthetic" panel. One of the benefits of a synthetic panel is that the data are a random sample of the entire population, thus avoiding the problem of possible bias due to sample selectivity. But because a synthetic panel does not follow exactly the same individuals as they age, it is not possible to study variability in individual life course patterns as is done by Fujita and Diener (2005) and Mroczek and Spiro (2005); hence, the present study is confined to the average pattern.

The total number of birth cohorts included in the analysis is 93. The 51 cohorts born in successive years from 1905 to 1955 are each followed over 21 years of the life cycle (those born in 1955 starting at age 18; those in 1905, at age 68). For the other 42 cohorts the time span covered ranges from 20 years (for the cohorts of 1956 and 1904) down to 1 year (for the cohorts of 1976 and 1884), with a mean time span for these 42 cohorts of 10.5 years.

Gender, race, and education are characteristics that are either fixed throughout the adult life cycle, or, in the case of education, fixed early on for almost all persons. The controls for these characteristics are because older persons and older cohorts differ somewhat in their demographic composition from younger, having somewhat larger proportions of females, nonblacks, and less educated persons. If cohort patterns were analyzed without controls, generalizations about happiness over the entire life course would be distorted because happiness or domain satisfaction varies by gender, race, and education (Argyle 1999; Blanchflower and Oswald 2004; Frey and Stutzer 2002a).

A dichotomous variable for education is used here – 12 years or less or 13 years or more, but the results would be virtually the same if, instead, highest grade completed were the variable. A dichotomous variable is used because education is viewed as dividing the population in much the same way as the gender and race variables – into two distinctive social groups, in this case, those who go to college and those who do not. Each of these subdivisions – gender, race, and education - may be thought of as identifying classes of the population whose average trend in life cycle happiness may differ from that for the total population. Differences among these subgroups is an important research issue, and Chapters 8 and 9 specifically address differences by gender. In the present analysis the focus is on the pattern typical of the population as a whole, and gender, race, and education are treated only as control variables. Descriptive statistics for all variables are presented in Appendix B.

The regression technique used throughout is ordered logit, because responses to the several variables are categorical and number three or more. Ordinary least squares regressions yield virtually identical results, suggesting that the findings are robust with regard to methodology. In the regression analysis to determine the life cycle pattern for happiness and each domain satisfaction variable various linear and quadratic combinations have been tried for both the age and cohort variables. The combination yielding the best fit for happiness or domain satisfaction is used here, because there is no reason to suppose that life cycle and cohort patterns would be the same from one domain to another or for global happiness. The average trend in life cycle happiness and in each domain satisfaction variable is the estimated value at each age 18 to 89 when mean values for all independent variables other than age are entered in the regression equation.[5] The estimated value for a given age differs from the raw mean of individual responses at that age, because it is adjusted for compositional differences across ages in cohort, gender, race, and education.

7.4. Results
7.4.1. The Average Trend in Life Cycle Happiness

Happiness is greatest at midlife, but not by very much. On average, it rises somewhat, as people progress from age 18 to 51 and declines thereafter (Figure 7.1; see Appendix C, column 1, for the underlying equation). On the three-option happiness scale – very happy, pretty happy, not too happy – the increase from age 18 to 51 is equivalent to an upward shift over the first 33 years of the adult life cycle of 7 percent of the population by one response category, say from "pretty happy" to "very happy." Subsequently, happiness drops at about the same rate as it previously rose, and by age 89 it is below the level at age 51 by an amount equivalent to a downward shift of one response category for about 9 percent of the population. Panel studies (Fujita and Diener 2005) make clear that many more individual shifts in SWB are actually occurring – the 7 and 9 percent changes reported here are the net balance of a much larger number of individual movements.

Figure 7.1

Life Cycle Happiness

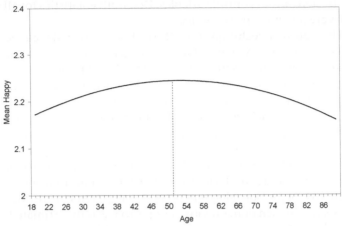

Source: Appendix C, column 1.

The mild hill-shape found here for life cycle happiness differs from the constancy in happiness reported in Chapter 6 and Easterlin and Schaeffer (1999), and is due to the use here of a more sensitive statistical technique. As mentioned, Mroczek and Spiro (2005) also find a hill-shaped trajectory for life cycle satisfaction. The amplitude of movement that they report is difficult to compare with that in Figure 7.1, because they use a different measure and scale for SWB – life satisfaction, ranging in value from 0 to 11. Their peak occurs somewhat later in life at age 65. Their difference from the peak here may be due to the fact that their sample comprises relatively healthy men from around age 40 onward (Mroczek and Spiro 2005, p. 192) whereas the present results are for the total population from age 18 on. It is likely too that the peak for all males would occur earlier than that for healthy males.

It was noted previously that Costa et al. (1987) in a panel study following respondents for nine years report a constant level of affect balance over the life cycle. Their data, however, do not clearly contradict the present findings or those of Mroczek and Spiro (2005). If one plots against age the mean level of affect balance from their study (with or without the "health concerns" component) for the five successive life cycle segments represented by the cohorts they analyze, there is, in fact, a pattern suggesting that the overall trend in mean level peaks around age 65.

A closer look at the positive trend in life cycle happiness suggested by Charles, Reynolds and Gatz (2001) also yields a result consistent with the present pattern. If one differences at each age the mean values of positive and negative affect estimated in their study, one finds that affect balance rises to age 55 and falls thereafter (pp. 144–145, Figures 2 and 3).

All panels, synthetic or not, lose members of a cohort through mortality. (A synthetic panel, however, does not have the additional problem of attrition due to inability to locate the original panel members.) Over the life cycle selection occurs in favor of happier persons, because persons in poor health are both less happy and more likely to die (Idler and Benyami 1997; Mehnert et al. 1990; Smith, Taylor and Sloan 2001). Such selection is not very great up to age 70, when three-fourths of the cohort alive at age 18 are still living. By age 80, however, the proportion surviving drops to one-half and by 89, to little more than a fifth.[6]

Mortality causes an upward bias at older ages of the curve in Figure 7.1, because the average is increasingly based on persons in better health. Mroczek's and Spiro's valuable analysis (2005, pp. 194–5 and Table 4) provides an idea of the magnitude of this bias, because they estimate separate life satisfaction trajectories for those who died and those who remained alive, an analysis possible only with data following the same individuals as they age. Their statistical results imply that at age 85 the mean life satisfaction of those who died would have been about 8 percent less than those who remained in the sample. Those who died comprise about one-third of the original sample; hence in the absence of attrition due to mortality mean satisfaction would have been about 3 percent less (1/3 x 8). In the synthetic panel analyzed here attrition due to mortality reaches one-third when people are in their mid-seventies. If the Mroczek-Spiro estimates are applicable here, then the bias due to mortality in Figure 7.1 is probably small up to about age 75. Nevertheless, this selection bias plus the fact that observations for persons over age 75 become increasingly scarce suggest that the present results for ages over 75 be viewed as rather tentative.

On the face of it, the life cycle pattern for overall happiness in Figure 7.1 appears fairly consistent with the strong setpoint model – that happiness, on average, is fairly stable and not much affected by life circumstances. True, there is some evidence of change, but it is fairly mild and hardly contradicts the model seriously. The domain patterns, however, are a rather different story.

Figure 7.2

Life Cycle Happiness and Domain Satisfaction

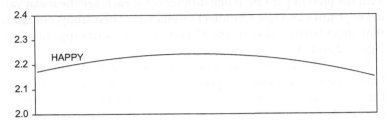

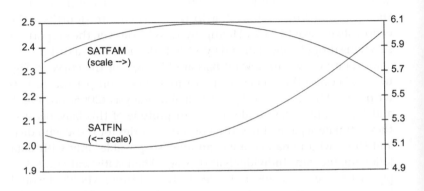

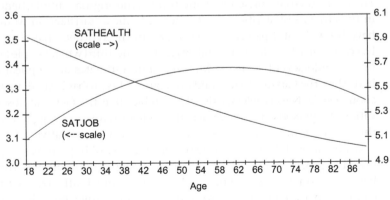

Source: Appendix C, columns 1–5.

7.4.2. Average Trends in Domain Satisfaction

Satisfaction in the individual domains typically varies considerably more over the life cycle than does happiness (Figure 7.2; see Appendix C, columns 2–5, for the underlying equations). The exception is satisfaction with family life whose life cycle movement is very similar to that in happiness in that it peaks around age 50 and has only a slightly greater amplitude. Satisfaction with one's financial situation, however, has a strikingly different pattern; it declines very slightly through age 36, but thereafter rises considerably, with the biggest increase late in life. The pattern for satisfaction with health too is distinctive, falling throughout the life course. Finally, satisfaction with one's work rises to age 60, and then drops. For all of the domain satisfaction variables, mortality probably causes a selection effect in favor of those in better health that leads to an upward bias at the oldest ages like that for happiness just mentioned. For satisfaction with health this bias is probably the reason for the slowing of the rate of decline as people move into their seventies and eighties, where this selection bias becomes increasingly important.

The amplitude of the changes in satisfaction with particular aspects of life are, on average, considerably greater than that for happiness, even after allowing for the fact that, except for financial satisfaction, the number of response categories for the domain variables is greater than for happiness. The scales for domain satisfaction in Figure 7.2 are adjusted for differences in number of response categories; for example, health and family situation, which have a response range of 6 compared with a range of 2 for happiness, are drawn to a scale one-third as great as that for happiness. As can be seen, even after adjustment, the amplitude of life cycle change for each of the domain satisfaction variables is greater than that for happiness. So while the life cycle pattern of happiness in Figure 7.1 seemingly gives some credence to the strong setpoint model, the domain satisfaction patterns in Figure 7.2 are typically counter to what one would expect if adaptation were rapid and complete within each domain.

An analysis of the specific factors determining each of the domain satisfaction variables is beyond the scope of this paper. But the patterns here of domain satisfaction do seem to say something about the importance of objective life circumstances relative to subjective goals in determining satisfaction in each domain. The pattern for satisfaction with family life, for example, can be seen to parallel roughly life cycle trends in objective circumstances in the family domain (cf. Waite 1995; Delbes and Gaymu 2002). As unions are formed and families built, satisfaction with family life rises; then, in midlife and beyond, as children leave home, and divorce and widowhood take their toll on partnerships, satisfaction turns downward. Satisfaction with health also appears dominated by actual life circumstances, declining throughout the life course as the incidence of disability and disease rises (Reynolds, Crimmins and Saito 1998). Satisfaction with work rises as people move up the career ladder, but drops off as work careers come to their end. If, in each of these domains people were adapting rapidly and completely to changing life circumstances, then satisfaction would not follow the general pattern of actual events. This is not to say that no adaptation is occurring, but clearly adaptation is not enough in each domain to offset the similarity of life cycle satisfaction to the actual course of life events.

But actual life circumstances do not dominate in every domain. In contrast to the others, satisfaction with one's financial situation does not follow the life course pattern of people's actual economic condition. Income rises throughout most of the working years and then levels off and declines, but satisfaction with one's financial situation moves almost inversely, starting to rise noticeably in midlife, and increasing most in late life when income, if anything, is typically declining. The upswing in satisfaction with one's financial situation in midlife and beyond suggests that an economic model relying on objective circumstances alone as determining well-being is mistaken, for the upturn in later life clearly cannot be due to rising income. A clue to the explanation may come from modifying the aspirations hypothesis presented in Chapter 6. Early in adult life material aspirations may rise faster than income and households incur a growing burden of debt to income that creates financial worries. These emotional strains undercut the rise in financial satisfaction that income growth in itself would engender. Then later in life aspirations may level off and decline, and the pressure of debt payments on income diminish. As financial worries recede, satisfaction with one's financial situation rises (for empirical support see Zimmermann 2007; Hansen, Slagsvold and Moum 2008). If this reasoning is right, it points to the important effect in the financial domain of subjective influences such as material aspirations.

The domain results contradict a top-down interpretation of the determinants of life cycle well-being. A top-down advocate, who sees happiness as a reflection of stable traits like personality and genetic make-up, would expect that the fairly constant life cycle pattern of happiness in Figure 7.1 would be replicated in each of the various domains. But this does not happen: as Figure 7.2 demonstrates, most of the domain patterns differ markedly from the happiness pattern and they differ also among themselves. The considerable variability in the domain patterns thus belies the top-down view, and calls into question the idea that personality and genetic make-up principally determine the average life course pattern of happiness. The next section addresses the bottom-up view.

7.4.3. Domain Satisfaction and Happiness

Do the domains studied here play an important role in shaping the life cycle pattern of overall happiness? To answer this, the relation of happiness to satisfaction in the individual domains is first examined; then, based on this result, an attempt is made to predict the average trend in life cycle happiness from the life cycle patterns in the four domains taken together.

Table 7.1

Regression of Happiness on Specified Domain Satisfaction Variables: Ordered Logit Statistics[a]

Independent variable	Model			
	(1)	(2)	(3)	(4)
Satfam	0.578	0.542	0.527	0.461
Satfin	–	0.705	0.599	0.573
Satjob	–	–	0.518	0.498
Sathealth	–	–	–	0.242
Cut1	1.132	2.266	3.519	4.299
Cut2	4.166	5.448	6.899	7.744
n	23,119	23,035	18,470	18,440
Chi^2	2168	3232	2920	3200
Log likelihood	-20,334	-19,526	-15,099	-14,852
Pseudo R^2	0.065	0.099	0.121	0.133

[a] For all coefficients, $P > |z| = 0.000$

One would expect that if satisfaction in a particular domain had an important effect on happiness, then overall happiness would increase if satisfaction in that domain rises and no change takes place in any other domain. Is this, in fact, the case? The answer is yes. On average, happiness varies directly and significantly with each dimension of people's lives included here: with one's financial situation, family life, health, and work. This is the lesson of a multivariate ordered logit regression on the domain satisfaction variables (Table 7.1, column 4). Thus, the greater is satisfaction with each of these life situations, the greater, on average, is overall happiness.

The domain satisfaction variables array as follows from high to low with regard to magnitude of effect on happiness: family life, financial situation, job, and health. When the effect on happiness of each domain variable is considered singly, family satisfaction has the highest pseudo-R^2. After family satisfaction, the pseudo-R^2 increases most with the addition of financial situation, then with job satisfaction, and finally with health satisfaction (Table 7.1, columns 1–4).

Figure 7.3

Life Cycle Happiness, Actual and Predicted

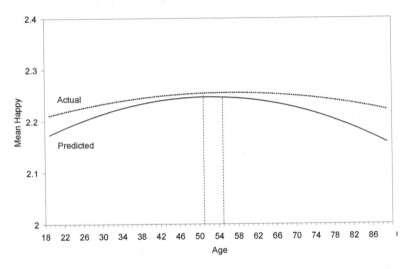

Source: Actual, same as Figure 7.1. Predicted happiness at each age is obtained by entering the Figure 7.2 values for that age in the regression of Table 7.1, column 4.

Can the life cycle patterns for the domain satisfaction variables taken together actually explain the observed life cycle pattern of happiness? To answer this, predicted life cycle happiness at each year of age from 18 to 89 is estimated here by substituting in the regression equation in column 4 of Table 7.1 the value for each domain satisfaction variable for each year of age shown in Figure 7.2. The outcome is that the four domain satisfaction variables predict fairly closely the actual pattern of life cycle happiness (Figure 7.3). The amplitude of the predicted movement is somewhat greater than in actual happiness, and the peak, a little later, at 55 years of age, compared with 51.

The correspondence between predicted and actual life cycle happiness supports the bottom-up view of the determinants of happiness. The similarity further implies that the considerable stability observed in overall happiness in Figure 7.1 is due, not to rapid and complete adaptation to life events within domains, but to offsetting changes in people's satisfaction with different domains of life.[7] The mild rise in happiness through midlife that occurs in the population as a whole is due, on average, chiefly to growing satisfaction with family life and work, which in combination more than counteract diminishing satisfaction with health. Beyond midlife happiness decreases, because the continuing decline in satisfaction with health is joined by diminishing satisfaction with family life and work. However, these negative influences on happiness beyond midlife are offset to a considerable degree by a progressive improvement in people's satisfaction with their financial situation.

7.5. Summary and Implications

Bearing in mind that one is dealing here with averages for the total population and that this is a study only of the United States in the period 1973–1994, the following tentative conclusions may be drawn.

In the population as a whole the tendency, on average, is for the happiness of a birth cohort to rise mildly from age 18 to midlife, and to decline somewhat thereafter. This is the net result of disparate movements in satisfaction within major life domains – family life, financial situation, work, and health. Until people are around age 50 increased satisfaction with family life and work outweigh diminished satisfaction with health and contribute, on average, to a mild rise in happiness. From midlife onward, decreasing satisfaction with family, life, and work join that in health in causing a decline in happiness. This negative impact is considerably offset, however, by increasing satisfaction of people with their financial situation.

The average trends in satisfaction with family life, work, and health appear to reflect the dominance, on balance, of actual life circumstances in determining satisfaction in those domains, although some adaptation is probably occurring. This is consistent with economists' emphasis on the importance of objective conditions in determining well-being, but not necessarily with the strong economic model in which no adaptation occurs. On the other hand, the movement in people's satisfaction with their financial situation runs counter to the economists' emphasis on objective conditions, and points to the importance in determining happiness that psychologists place on subjective variables such as aspirations.

In general, the results consistently support neither the mainstream economic model, in which objective conditions alone determine well-being, nor the strong setpoint model or its close ally, the top-down model, that see life cycle happiness as the highly stable product of personality and genetic make-up. Rather the results point to a bottom-up approach, in which the pattern of life cycle happiness is the net outcome of satisfaction in the principal life domains, and satisfaction in each domain is the product of both objective conditions and goals or aspirations in that domain.

The finding that life cycle happiness is the net outcome of disparate movements in the four life domains implies that there is nothing inevitable about the average trend reported here in life cycle happiness – there is no "iron law of happiness". For example, policies reducing the incidence of disability and disease would moderate the downtrend in satisfaction with health, where actual health circumstances seem to dominate over adaptation. Such policies, by reducing mortality and morbidity, would also reduce the dissolution of marriages and the consequent decline at older ages of satisfaction with family life. In turn, milder declines in satisfaction with health and family life would, other things constant, raise the average trend of life cycle happiness, especially in later life. In this way, public policy might raise overall happiness.

Appendix A

Questions and Response Categories for Happiness and Satisfaction Variables

HAPPY: Taken all together, how would you say things are these days – would you say that you are very happy, pretty happy, or not too happy? (Coded 3, 2, 1 respectively)

SATFIN: We are interested in how people are getting along financially these days. So far as you and your family are concerned, would you say that you are pretty well satisfied with your present financial situation, more or less satisfied, or not satisfied at all? (Coded 3, 2, 1 respectively)

SATJOB: (Asked of persons currently working, temporarily not at work, or keeping house.) On the whole, how satisfied are you with the work you do – would you say you are very satisfied, moderately satisfied, a little dissatisfied, or very dissatisfied? (Coded from 4 down to 1)

SATFAM: For each area of life I am going to name, tell me the number that shows how much satisfaction you get from that area.

Your family life

> 1. A very great deal
> 2. A great deal
> 3. Quite a bit
> 4. A fair amount
> 5. Some
> 6. A little
> 7. None

(Reverse coded here)

SATHEALTH: Same as SATFAM, except "Your family life" is replaced by "Your health and physical condition."

Appendix B

Descriptive Statistics

Variable	Number of observations	Mean	Standard deviation	Minimum	Maximum
Happy	29,651	2.21	0.63	1	3
Age	29,651	45.1	17.65	18	89
Birth cohort (1890=0)	29,651	48.9	18.68	-6	86
Male	29,651	0.44	0.5	0	1
Black	29,651	0.11	0.32	0	1
Educ ≤ 12 yrs.	29,651	0.61	0.49	0	1
Satfin	29,710	2.04	0.74	1	3
Satjob	23,816	3.29	0.82	1	4
Satfam	23,189	5.91	1.36	1	7
Sathealth	23,235	5.43	1.49	1	7

Appendix C

Regression of Happiness and Each Domain Satisfaction Variable on Specified Independent Variables: Ordered Logit Statistics (in paren. $P > |z|$)

Independent Variable	Dependent Variable				
	Happy (1)	Satfin (2)	Satjob (3)	Satfam (4)	Sathealth (5)
Age	0.020686	-0.030693	0.046965	0.044662	-0.032047
	[-0.001]	[0]	[0]	[0]	[0]
Age^2	-0.000203	0.000432	-0.000394	-0.000453	0.000142
	[-0.001]	[0]	[0]	[0]	[-0.042]
Cohort	-0.017975	-0.010219	-0.022615	–	0.028104
	[-0.001]	[0]	[-0.002]		[0]
Cohort^2	0.000129	–	0.000114	–	-0.000336
	[-0.014]		[-0.091]		[0]
Male	-0.101324	0.016625	0.023647	-0.180871	0.121271
	[0]	[-0.483]	[-0.381]	[0]	[0]
Black	-0.735731	-0.671642	-0.461883	-0.480112	-0.238758
	[0]	[0]	[0]	[0]	[0]
Ed ≤ 12	-0.260456	-0.392832	-0.216605	-0.097925	-0.238501
	[0]	[0]	[0]	[0]	[0]
Cut1	-2.510397	-2.360142	-3.027477	-3.68573	-4.751097
Cut2	0.316674	-0.32067	-1.678026	-2.780609	-3.637703
Cut3	–	–	0.272434	-2.12574	-2.99655
Cut4	–	–	–	-1.244581	-1.881087
Cut5	–	–	–	-0.4823342	-1.16334
Cut6	–	–	–	1.035689	-0.279621
n	29,651	29,728	23,808	23,207	23,252
Chi^2	508	1492	812	279	802
LR	-27,395	-30,852	-25,397	-31,446	-37,218
Pseudo-R^2	0.0119	0.027	0.0187	0.0055	0.0117

8

The Cross-Over in the Life Cycle Happiness of American Women and Men

Women and men are about equally happy – or so several surveys on subjective well-being say (Diener et al. 1999, p. 292b; Layard 2005, p. 254; Myers 2000, p. 58).[1] But is the gender relationship the same throughout the life course? Data for the United States say, no, the gender relation reverses around midlife. Women start adult life happier than men, but the difference narrows with age, the happiness of women declining and that of men rising. After midlife, the differential turns around, with men the happier of the two. The overall similarity in the happiness of women and men reported in the literature is the outcome of averaging younger ages, in which women have the advantage, with older ages, at which men are happier. This chapter presents evidence of the cross-over in the life cycle happiness of American women and men and its proximate causes.

As in the preceding chapter, the happiness measure is from the United States General Social Survey (GSS): "Taken all together, how would you say things are these days would you say you are very happy, pretty happy, or not too happy?" – and the conceptual framework is the domain satisfaction model. Descriptive statistics are given in Appendix A. The detailed regressions are given in Appendix B.

This chapter was co-authored by Enrico A. Marcelli (San Diego State University). I would like to express my gratitude for his invaluable contributions. For excellent research assistance, we are grateful to Laura Angelescu, Onnicha Sawangfa, and Olga Shemyakina. Financial support was provided by the University of Southern California.

8.1. Results

Life cycle happiness – At young adult ages females are happier than men (Figure 8.1). Over the life course, however, female happiness trends steadily downward and male happiness, upward. Around midlife the two genders are about equally happy, and thereafter male happiness increasingly exceeds that of females.

Figure 8.1

Happiness by Gender and Age

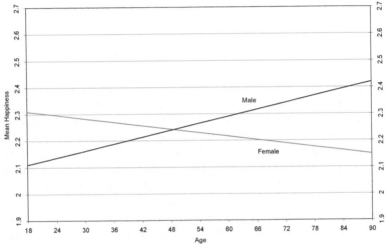

Note: In Figures 8.1–8.5 and 8.7 differences by age in birth cohort, race, and education are controlled for.

The magnitude of the turnaround between ages 18 and 89 is equivalent to about 15 percent of females shifting downward from "very" to "pretty" happy, while 30 percent of males shift upward from "pretty" to "very" happy. The precise age at which the happiness cross-over takes place, as estimated here, is 47.5 years. For the population as a whole these disparate patterns by gender result in the mild hill-shaped pattern of happiness analyzed in Chapter 7.

As discussed in Chapter 7, mortality causes an upward bias at older ages of the curves in Figure 8.1, because the average is increasingly based on persons in better health. Our impression, however, is that there is probably not much effect on the female-male differences up to around age 75; thereafter the gender differential may be somewhat overstated.[2]

Figure 8.2

Satisfaction With Family Life, by Gender and Age

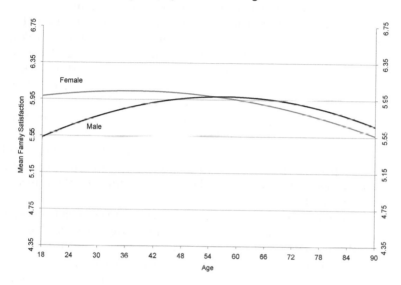

Figure 8.3

Financial Satisfaction, by Gender and Age

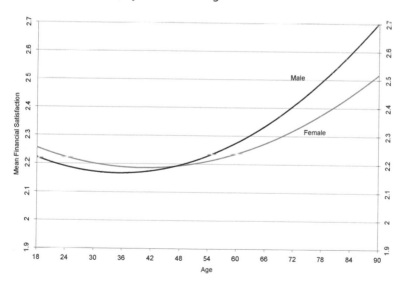

Domain satisfaction – Is the gender cross-over in life cycle happiness reproduced in the individual life domains? The answer is yes for the family and financial domains, no for the health domain.

For both women and men satisfaction with family life is hill-shaped, rising to midlife and then declining, with women peaking earlier than men, at age 42 compared with 55 (Figure 8.2). However, at the start of adult life, females are more satisfied with their family life than males, while beyond midlife they are less satisfied, the cross-over occurring at age 53. In contrast to the life cycle pattern for happiness, the gender differential in family satisfaction at the oldest ages is less than at the youngest.

The pattern for financial satisfaction is virtually the opposite of the hill pattern of satisfaction with family life. For both women and men satisfaction with finances declines to midlife and then rises – a U-shaped pattern (Figure 8.3).

The curve for men bottoms out first, at age 32; the trough for women is at age 39. As in the case of the family life pattern, females start out slightly higher than males in financial satisfaction, but end up lower, the cross-over in this case taking place around age 44.5. For financial satisfaction, however, the gender differential is greater at the oldest ages than at the youngest, in keeping with the pattern for life cycle happiness.

Figure 8.4

Satisfaction With Health, by Gender and Age

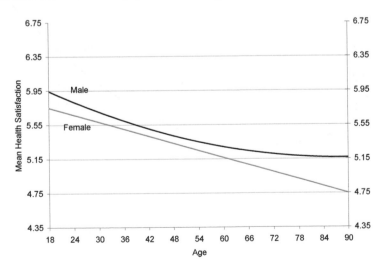

Satisfaction with health presents yet a third pattern, trending downward over the life course for both women and men (Figure 8.4). In contrast to the family and financial domains, however, there is no cross-over – throughout the life cycle men are more satisfied with their health than women.

This result for health satisfaction is similar to that found for self-reported health. The seeming contradiction with the gender difference in mortality – higher for males than females – is explained by the higher prevalence among females at all ages of non-lethal diseases such as arthritis and asthma. The excess of male over female satisfaction decreases slightly to about age 48; thereafter it progressively increases and at age 89 is about twice as great as at age 18.

The sources of the life cycle differences in happiness between women and men are suggested by comparing the life cycle differentials in domain satisfaction with that in happiness. Men start out less happy than women because they are less satisfied with their family life and finances, even though more satisfied with their health (Figure 8.5).[3] In both the family life and financial domains, the trends in the differentials are very similar to those for happiness, with men starting to exceed women in midlife. In the health domain, before midlife the advantage of men declines slightly, and this somewhat offsets their increasing advantage in satisfaction with family life and finances. Beyond midlife, however, the advantage of men in health satisfaction widens, and the health domain joins family and finances in contributing to the increasing advantage of men over women in overall happiness.

It is reasonable to speculate that the life cycle trends in the family and financial domains are linked to the life cycle differential in part nership status of women and men. At younger ages women are more likely than men to be in unions; at older ages, the opposite is true. The differential in marital unions illustrates this reversal (Figure 8.6). The GSS data used in Figure 8.6 do not allow us to include cohabitation in the figure, but if it were included, the differentials at both the youngest and oldest ages would probably increase (Casper and Cohen 2000, Table 8.4).

One of the principal findings of research on subjective well-being is that, other things constant, persons in unions, marital or cohabitating, are happier than those who are not (see Zimmermann and Easterlin 2006 and the references therein). Other things equal, the differential in partnership status at younger ages would tend to make women, on average, happier than men.

Figure 8.5

Excess of Male over Female Happiness and Domain Satisfaction at Each Age

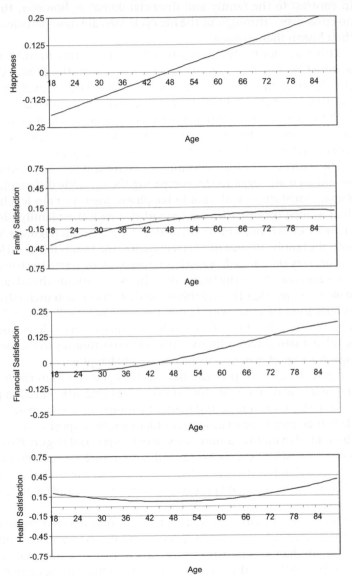

Figure 8.6

Excess of Male over Female Percentage Married, by Age Group

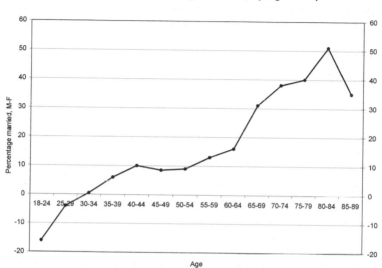

The financial position of persons in unions is likely also to be more secure than those dependent solely or largely on their own resources (Schmidt and Sevak 2006; Waite 1995; Waite et al. 2002; Waite and Luo 2009). Hence the fact that at younger ages women are more likely to be in unions would raise their relative financial satisfaction and additionally contribute to their greater happiness.

At older ages, however, the effect of differential partnership status shifts to the advantage of men. Male mortality is greater than female; hence those men who survive to older age are likely to be in unions, while women are more likely to be single (Easterlin 2003a). Older women are likely to suffer therefore, not only from the lack of a partner (cf. Delhes and Gaymu 2002), but also from the lack of greater financial security accompanying a union. Hence for older women satisfaction with both family life and finances tends to be less than for men, and happiness correspondingly lower. Thus the shifting circumstances of men and women over the life course with regard to partnership status is most likely an important source of the cross-over in happiness.

Predicting happiness – The foregoing comparison of the trends in life cycle differentials in domain satisfaction with that in happiness is suggestive of the causes of the cross-over, but an important question remains. If family life, finances, and health are, indeed, circumstances that play a large part in determining life cycle happiness, then is it possible to predict the cross-over in happiness from the gender patterns of satisfaction with these domains?

Table 8.1

Regression of Happiness on Domain Satisfaction for Each Gender: Ordered Logit Statistics

Independent variable	Female			Male		
	Coefficient	95% Confidence interval		Coefficient	95% Confidence interval	
Satfin	0.654577**	0.600023	0.709130	0.687157**	0.625756	0.748559
Satfam	0.517919**	0.481769	0.554068	0.419772**	0.383990	0.455553
Sathealth	0.263978**	0.234839	0.293116	0.235251**	0.200798	0.269704
cut1:Constant	3.372090**	3.138573	3.605607	2.763294**	2.516358	3.010229
cut2:Constant	6.621184**	0.234839	0.293116	6.037174**	5.754897	6.319450
Observations	12959			10032		
Pseudo R^2	0.123			0.105		
Chi^2	2115.2			1540.3		
Log Likelihood	-10733.5			-8394.3		

Note: ** significant at 1%

To answer this, a procedure is followed like that in the previous chapter. First, for each gender we estimate the average relation of happiness to each domain. This is of interest in itself, because it seems plausible that the individual domains are not of equal importance to the happiness of women and men. The relationship is estimated here from the individual data for each gender with an ordered logit regression of happiness on the three domain satisfaction variables (Table 8.1). There is, indeed, some difference between women and men in the importance of the three domains in determining happiness, but also considerable similarity. For women, family life is more important than for men. With regard to the importance of finances and health, there is no significant difference between the two genders. This is shown by the 95% probability range for each coefficient. Only with regard to family life do the two gender coefficients fall outside the 95% probability range.

The next step is to predict the pattern of life cycle happiness for each gender. To do this, the domain values for each gender in Figures 8.2–8.4 at, for example, age 18 are entered in that gender's regression in Table 8.1 to see what the value of happiness would be at that age if only these three domain satisfaction values were known. This procedure is repeated for each year of age up to age 89 to obtain a predicted value of happiness at each age for each gender.

Predicted happiness for women and men, estimated from the three life cycle domain patterns, does indeed, have a cross-over (Figure 8.7). The overall pattern is flatter, and the cross-over occurs later in life, around age 59.5, compared with age 47.5 in the actual happiness patterns of Figure 8.1. The finding of a flatter pattern suggests, reasonably enough, that life circumstances other than in the financial, family, and health realms are also involved in the gender differences by age. However, the three domains analyzed here are clearly a substantial part of the story.

The cross-over is very largely due, not to the fact that women and men differ somewhat in the relative importance of the three domains in determining happiness, but to gender differences in the life cycle domain patterns themselves shown in Figure 8.5. To test for the effect of the gender difference in the relative importance of domains, we replaced the female coefficients of Table 8.1 with those for men to predict life cycle happiness for women and found little change in the predicted life cycle pattern of female happiness. We reversed the procedure and obtained the same result for men. Thus, the fact that family life is more important in determining happiness for women than for men does not play much of a role in generating the overall pattern of gender differences by age.

Figure 8.7

Predicted Happiness by Gender and Age

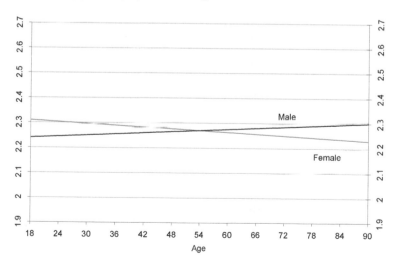

183

Controlling for gender differences in domain satisfaction – Happiness differences between women and men over the life course depend to a considerable extent on gender differences in satisfaction with family, finances, and health. But what about women and men who are in the same situation with regard to the three domains – is there then a gender difference? To answer this, we pooled the data for women and men and ran an ordered logit regression of happiness on gender, age, birth cohort, and race, controlling, in addition, for family satisfaction, financial satisfaction, and health satisfaction. For females and males in the same states of domain satisfaction, it turns out that females are, on average, happier (Table 8.2).

Table 8.2

Regression of Happiness on Specified Variables for Both Genders Combined: Ordered Logit Statistics
(robust p-value in parentheses)

Independent variable	Statistic
Female (=1)	0.107425
	(0.000)**
Age	0.034435
	(0.000)**
Agesq	-0.00026
	(0.001)**
Coh	-0.02894
	(0.000)**
Cohsq	0.000283
	(0.000)**
Black (=1)	-0.52098
	(0.000)**
Educ ≤ 12 (=1)	-0.10842
	(0.000)**
Satfin	0.611703
	(0.000)**
Satfam	0.460212
	(0.000)**
Sathealth	0.275031
	(0.000)**
cut1:Constant	3.250576
	(0.000)**
cut2:Constant	6.542992
	(0.000)**
Observations	22941
Pseudo R^2	0.121
Chi^2	3849.2
Log Likelihood	-18955.8

Note: ** significant at 1%

This finding is similar to that of SWB regressions reported in the economics literature where, when women and men in the same objective life circumstances are compared, women are, on average, happier than men (Blanchflower and Oswald 2004; Di Tella, MacCulloch and Oswald 2001). The difference here is that it is satisfaction with life circumstances that is controlled, and thus subjective perceptions of these circumstances rather than the objective circumstances alone that are taken into account.

8.2. Summary and Discussion

American women start adult life happier than men, being more satisfied, on average, with both their family life and financial situation. But the advantage they enjoy over men in their family and financial satisfaction progressively diminishes as they get older. In older age men are more satisfied with their family and financial circumstances, and, in consequence, are the happier of the two. Beyond midlife, the happiness advantage of men is enhanced by an increasing advantage of men in satisfaction with their health.

The reversal in the relative satisfaction of women and men with family life and finances is, to a substantial extent, probably due to the turnaround over the life course in the gender differential in partnership status. Early on women are more likely to be in unions; in older age, men are. Having a partner raises satisfaction with family life, and also increases financial satisfaction because of greater security. Hence, the life course reversal in the gender differential in partnership status makes for a happiness turnaround through its effects on family and financial satisfaction.

Our analysis is for the United States. But if we are right that the life course reversal in the relative happiness of women and men is due to an important extent to the life cycle differential in partnership status of women and men, then one would expect a similar cross-over might be found in other places where women typically form unions at younger ages than men. In fact, aggregate data for nineteen of the European Union countries spanning 1970–1999 also reveal a cross-over.[4] Women are happier than men at younger ages, but men are happier in later life. As in the United States, the happiness of women, controlling for birth cohort, trends downward with age. The happiness of men differs somewhat from the American pattern, declining noticeably from ages 15–19 to 20–24, then only mildly to about age 60, after which it turns upward and starts to surpass that of women beyond age 60.

Our primary interest here is how differences in life circumstances affect the relative happiness of women and men over the life course. If, however, we abstract from these differences, and compare women and men in the same circumstances with regard to satisfaction with family life, finances, and health, a significant gender difference in favor of women is found.

Appendix A

Descriptive Statistics

	Female				
Variable	Number of Observations	Mean	Standard Deviation	Minimum	Maximum
Happy	16699	2.23	0.63	1	3
Satfam	13076	4.70	1.60	1	7
Satfin	16743	2.04	0.74	1	3
Sathealth	13098	4.20	1.69	1	7
Age	16817	44.22	17.28	18	89
Birth Cohort (1880=0)	16817	59.90	18.32	5	96
Educ ≤ 12 = 1	16817	0.64	0.48	0	1
Black = 1	16817	0.12	0.32	0	1

	Male				
Variable	Number of Observations	Mean	Standard Deviation	Minimum	Maximum
Happy	12952	2.21	0.62	1	3
Satfam	10131	4.61	1.64	1	7
Satfin	12985	2.05	0.74	1	3
Sathealth	10154	4.30	1.67	1	7
Age	13036	43.51	17.06	18	89
Birth Cohort (1880=0)	13036	60.32	18.38	4	96
Educ ≤ 12 = 1	13036	0.58	0.49	0	1
Black = 1	13036	0.10	0.30	0	1

Appendix B

Regression of Happiness and Each Domain Satisfaction Variable on Specified Independent Variables: Ordered Logit Statistics (robust p-values in parentheses)

	Female			
	Happy (1)	Satfam (2)	Satfin (3)	Sathealth (4)
Age	-0.007072 (0.006)**	0.030427 (0.000)**	-0.028984 (0.000)**	-0.02234 (0.011)*
Agesq		-0.000363 (0.000)**	0.00037 (0.000)**	0.000045 (-0.623)
Coh	-0.010723 (0.000)**		-0.013436 (0.000)**	0.037321 (0.000)**
Cohsq				-0.000348 (0.000)**
Educ ≤ 12 = 1	-0.327075 (0.000)**	-0.168742 (0.000)**	-0.375303 (0.000)**	-0.349112 (0.000)**
Black = 1	-0.888046 (0.000)**	-0.583881 (0.000)**	-0.684715 (0.000)**	-0.349026 (0.000)**
cut1:Constant	-3.429734 (0.000)**	-4.382019 (0.000)**	-2.715487 (0.000)**	-4.265868 (0.000)**
cut2:Constant	-0.625672 (0.017)*	-3.374939 (0.000)**	-0.660671 (0.017)*	-3.089597 (0.000)**
cut3:Constant		-2.711797 (0.000)**		-2.45737 (0.000)**
cut4:Constant		-1.736876 (0.000)**		-1.323811 (0.000)**
cut5:Constant		-0.95623 (0.000)**		-0.610975 (0.065)+
cut6:Constant		0.551997 (0.000)**		0.796927 (0.016)*
Observations	16699	13076	16743	13098
Pseudo R^2	0.015	0.007	0.026	0.015
Chi^2	373.767	201.495	836.921	579.646
Log Likelihood	-15439.4	-17264.5	-17371.1	-21214.7

Notes: + significant at 10% * significant at 5% ** significant at 1%

Appendix B (continued)

	Male			
	Happy (1)	Satfam (2)	Satfin (3)	Sathealth (4)
Age	0.013931 (0.000)**	0.059565 (0.000)**	-0.03407 (0.000)**	-0.045404 (0.000)**
Agesq		-0.00054 (0.000)**	0.000524 (0.000)**	0.000279 (0.010)**
Coh	0.001584 (-0.56)		-0.006132 (0.019)*	0.034331 (0.002)**
Cohsq				-0.000344 (0.000)**
Educ ≤ 12 = 1	-0.20227 (0.000)**	-0.018539 (-0.639)	-0.417667 (0.000)**	-0.12347 (0.002)**
Black = 1	-0.528542 (0.000)**	-0.352074 (0.000)**	-0.649071 (0.000)**	-0.085443 (-0.209)
cut1:Constant	-1.605211 (0.000)**	-2.820869 (0.000)**	-2.179728 (0.000)**	-4.750309 (0.000)**
cut2:Constant	1.261175 (0.000)**	-1.992359 (0.000)**	-0.157679 (-0.606)	-3.721804 (0.000)**
cut3:Constant		-1.34231 (0.000)**		-3.066656 (0.000)**
cut4:Constant		-0.549498 (0.000)**		-1.973723 (0.000)**
cut5:Constant		0.197177 (-0.179)		-1.246789 (0.001)**
cut6:Constant		1.73827 (0.000)**		0.24279 (-0.528)
Observations	12952	10131	12985	10154
Pseudo R^2	0.011	0.006	0.029	0.008
Chi^2	201.257	139.794	658.129	229.884
Log Likelihood	-11918.3	-14094.4	-13474	-15988.3

Notes: + significant at 10% * significant at 5% ** significant at 1%

9

Aspirations, Attainments, and Satisfaction: Life Cycle Differences between American Women and Men

9.1. Aims

As seen in Chapter 8, women start adult life happier than men, but end up less happy. This reversal is largely due to a similar turnaround in the relative satisfaction of women and men in each of two life domains – finances and family. At the beginning of the adult life course women are more satisfied than men with both their financial situation and family life; at the end, they are less satisfied.

As originally construed by Angus Campbell (1981) satisfaction in a given domain depends on the net balance between aspirations and attainments. Empirical tests of this hypothesis have been limited, however, because of a lack of data on aspirations. Indeed, in life course studies there are, to our knowledge, no empirical studies linking domain satisfaction to the net balance of aspirations and attainments. In this chapter we demonstrate that the life course differentials observed in the GSS data in Chapter 8 between women and men in satisfaction with both family life and finances are consistent with the life course differentials observed in another data set

This chapter is a slightly revised version of: Plagnol, A., Easterlin, R. (2008). Aspirations, Attainments, and Satisfaction: Life Cycle Differences between American Women and Men, in: Journal of Happiness Studies, 9(4), 601–619, reprinted with permission of Springer Science & Business Media. We are grateful for financial support to the University of Southern California in the net balance of aspirations and attainments. The aim is to provide new empirical support for the aspirations/attainments model of domain satisfaction.

9.2. Data

Data on aspirations and attainments are from nine nationally representative surveys conducted by the Roper-Starch Organization about every three years from 1978 to 2003 that include questions on the "good life" (Roper Reports from 1997 to 2003 were generously made available by NopWorld, www.nopworld.com; earlier reports, by the Roper Center for Public Opinion Research at the University of Connecticut.). In these surveys the questioning procedure is as follows (see Appendix A for the full survey question):

1. We often hear people talk about what they want out of life. Here are a number of different things. [The respondent is handed a card with a list of about 25 items.] When you think of the good life – the life you'd like to have, which of the things on this list, if any, are part of that good life as far as you personally are concerned?

2. Now would you go down that list and call off all the things you now have?

The answers to question 1 tell us about an individual's aspirations; those to question 2, their attainments. The excess of aspirations over attainments – which we define here as the "shortfall" – is the extent to which aspirations are unfulfilled.

In response to open-ended questions on the sources of personal well-being the things typically cited by people are matters of everyday life, those that consume most people's time and energy, and over which they feel they have some control (Chapter 1). The good life questions are not open-ended, but the list of items presented to respondents overlaps substantially with the kind of things most frequently mentioned – especially matters relating to material goods and family life. In regard to family life the Roper item that we principally use here is that asking about a "happy marriage" – whether the respondent considers it part of the "good life" and whether the respondent has a happy marriage. In the family domain we also touch briefly on desires for children. In the material goods domain, our analysis is based on responses regarding each of ten "big-ticket" consumer goods – ranging from a home of your own, TV, and car, to "nice clothes", travel abroad, a swimming pool, and vacation home. We construct for each respondent a measure of the total number of these ten goods that the respondent considers part of the good life, and, among those considered part of the good life, how many the respondent actually has. Unfortunately, no question on health was included until the 2003 survey.

As mentioned, to gauge how respondents differ in regard to the fulfillment of their aspirations, we compute their "shortfall", the excess of aspirations over attainments. At the individual level, the shortfall with regard to a "happy marriage" is either zero or one – a person either does or does not have a happy marriage. In the goods domain, the shortfall at the individual level could in principal range from zero (the respondent has every one of the big-ticket consumer goods named as part of the good life) up to ten (the respondent considers every big-ticket consumer good part of the good life but has none of them). In the analysis that follows we present the mean for all respondents of a given gender. For example, if at a given age six-tenths of women who consider a happy marriage part of the good life actually have a happy marriage (so that the shortfall value for each is zero) while four-tenths who desire a happy marriage do not have one (so that each has a shortfall value of one) then the proportion of women with a shortfall is 0.4. Because individual shortfall responses can range from zero to ten in the goods domain, the mean shortfall value for respondents is the average number of big-ticket consumer goods that respondents want but do not have.

In the Roper data age is reported mainly in five-year age groups, and we assign age to individual respondents based on the midpoint age of the group in which they fall, e.g. an individual in the 45–49 age group is assigned a value of 47. The exception is the oldest age group. This is usually 65+, for which we assign age 73; for recent surveys it is 70+, and we assign age 78. Because of the lumping together of the older age population, the life cycle patterns of these later ages are not well-defined, but because this problem applies equally to both females and males, we believe the gender difference at older age is roughly representative.

As in Chapters 7 and 8, the satisfaction and happiness data are from the GSS. Descriptive statistics for the GSS variables and the Roper variables on aspirations and attainments are given in Appendix B. Both data sets are representative of the non-institutionalized US adult population.

9.3. Methods

As in previous chapters the average life cycle pattern of a variable – aspirations, attainments, satisfaction, and happiness – is estimated for each gender by regressing that variable on age, controlling for year of birth (birth cohort), race, and education. In addition, we also add now a control for period effects, namely, survey year in dummy form.[1] The life cycle pattern of the variable is the estimated value at each age when mean values for all independent variables other than age are entered in this regression equation. The value of the variable, so estimated, differs from the raw mean of the variable at each age in that it controls for differences by age in the composition of persons by essentially fixed characteristics – birth cohort, race, and education – as well as period effects. The regression technique used throughout is logit or ordered logit, because responses to the several variables are categorical and are either binary or number three or more. Ordinary least squares regressions yield virtually identical results.

Table 9.1

Comparison of Roper and GSS Sample Characteristics, by Gender

	Male		Female	
	Roper 1978-2003	GSS 1973-1994	Roper 1978-2003	GSS 1973-1994
Total n	8,463	12,512	9,377	16,148
Mean age	43.3	44.2	44.6	45.8
Percent distribution:				
Less than 30 years	26.4	24.3	25	22.8
30-39	20.8	22.5	19.9	21.9
40-49	19.7	17.2	19.1	16.1
50-59	12.8	14	12.6	13.6
60 and over	20.2	22	23.3	25.7
Percent black	11.3	9.6	11.6	11.9
Percent high school education or less	52.9	57.1	58.7	64
Percent married	63.2	64.3	58.3	55
Mean birth year	1947.2	1939.4	1945.8	1938.2
Percent distribution:				
Born 1990 or earlier	0	2.1	0	2.3
1901-1920	10.6	16.6	12.3	19.1
1921-1940	21.8	27	22.9	27.3
1941-1960	39.9	42.8	39.1	40.6
1961 or later	27.7	11.4	25.6	10.7

Data source: Roper and GSS.

It is again worth emphasizing that in any analysis that seeks to generalize about life course patterns, it is essential to control for birth cohort. Inferences about life course change are often made from associations with age observed at a single point of time. In terms of the present analysis, one might find, for example, that in 1990 material goods aspirations of those age 65 are less than those at age 25, and conclude from this that material goods aspirations decline with age. But those age 65 in 1990 were born in 1925 and raised in the economically depressed period from 1930 to 1945, while those age 25 in 1990 were born in 1965 and raised in a much more affluent period. Hence, the 1990 difference in material goods aspirations between 65 and 25 year-olds might be due to a difference in material aspirations arising from their different life histories, rather than a difference in age.

The sample characteristics of each gender by age, race, education, and marital status are, in general, quite similar in the Roper and GSS surveys included here (Table 9.1). The characteristic on which the two data sets differ most is birth cohort, with the Roper survey including a somewhat larger proportion of recent cohorts and fewer early cohorts. This difference is because the Roper surveys start and end several years later than the GSS surveys. We could reduce the birth cohort disparity by eliminating the three Roper surveys taken after 1994, but to do so would reduce the Roper sample size by one-third. It would also shorten the maximum life cycle segment observed for a birth cohort from 25 to 16 years, thus weakening our ability to trace the life cycle pattern of each cohort. We decided, therefore, to retain the complete Roper data set, in effect assuming that life cycle patterns are the same across all cohorts included in the present analysis.

9.4. Results: Gender Differences in Aspirations, Attainments, Satisfaction, and Happiness

9.4.1. Family Life

Throughout most of the life cycle the desire for a happy marriage is high among both women and men (Figure 9.1a; the regressions on which the figure is based are given in Table 9.2, columns 1 and 2). At the start women's aspirations are slightly higher than those of men. Then, for both genders aspirations decline gradually with age but somewhat more rapidly for women. Beyond age 42 the proportion of women desiring a happy marriage is less than that of men and the gap continues to widen slightly into older age.

Table 9.2

Logit Regression of Aspirations for and Attainments of a Happy Marriage on Specified Independent Variables, by Gender (p-values in parentheses)

	Aspirations		Attainments	
	(1)	(2)	(3)	(4)
	Male	Female	Male	Female
Age, centered	-0.0263	-0.0409	0.0016	-0.0346
	(0.00)	(0.00)	(0.84)	(0.00)
Age cent., squared	-0.0002	0.0000	-0.0015	-0.0012
	(0.18)	(0.71)	(0.00)	(0.00)
Birth cohort, cent.	-0.0337	-0.0311	-0.0401	-0.0459
	(0.00)	(0.00)	(0.00)	(0.00)
Coh. c., squared	-0.0001	-0.0003	0.0000	-0.0003
	(0.45)	(0.00)	(0.72)	(0.00)
Black	-0.4329	-0.5428	-0.8836	-1.2845
	(0.00)	(0.00)	(0.00)	(0.00)
Education > 12	0.4120	0.3560	0.2543	0.2612
	(0.00)	(0.00)	(0.00)	(0.00)
Survey year dummies included	yes	yes	yes	yes
Constant	1.1828	1.2652	0.3290	0.2886
	(0.00)	(0.00)	(0.00)	(0.00)
Observations	8,372	9,280	8,371	9,281
Pseudo R^2	0.0184	0.0243	0.0923	0.0663
Chi^2	158	233	1071	848
LR	-4228	-4691	-5266	-5975

Data source: Roper.

This gender difference in the pattern of life cycle marriage aspirations would in itself make for less satisfaction among women than men at younger ages and more at older ages. But in young adulthood women are more likely than men actually to have a happy marriage, while late in life the opposite is true (Figure 9.1b; Table 9.2, columns 3 and 4). Moreover, the gender gap with regard to having a happy marriage is greater than that with regard to desires at both the youngest and oldest ages. Consequently, for women the shortfall – or failure to attain aspirations – is less early in the life cycle, and greater later on (Figure 9.1c).

Figure 9.1

Happy Marriage: Aspirations, Attainments, and Shortfall, by Gender and Age

a. Aspirations

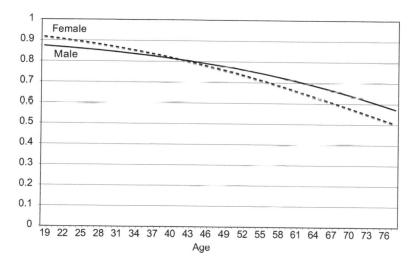

b. Attainments

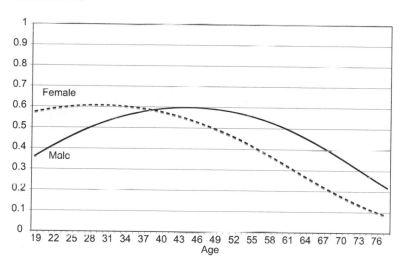

Figure 9.1 (continued)

Happy Marriage: Aspirations, Attainments, and Shortfall, by Gender and Age

c. Shortfall

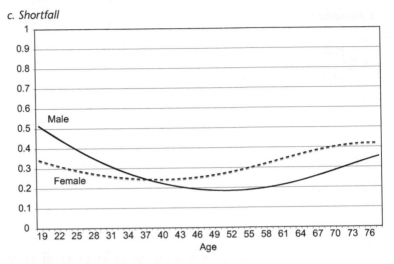

Source: Table 9.2. Data: Roper.

Figure 9.2

Satisfaction with Family Life by Gender and Age

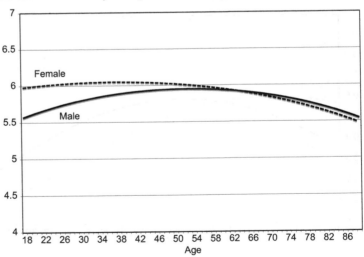

Source: Table 9.3, columns 1 and 2. Data: GSS.

Thus, as far as a happy marriage is concerned, the early life advantage and late life disadvantage of women implies that at the start of the life cycle women would be more satisfied with family life than men, and at the end less satisfied. Turning to the GSS data set, we observe as in Chapter 8 that this, in fact, is the case (Figure 9.2; Table 9.3, columns 1 and 2). The gender cross-over in fulfilling desires for a happy marriage occurs earlier, however (at age 39) than that in satisfaction with family life. But family life consists of more than a happy marriage, and it is especially likely that children help sustain beyond age 39 the family life satisfaction of women relative to men. In our data women and men are virtually the same throughout the life cycle in terms of fulfilling their desires for number of children. However, family life is a more important ingredient of happiness for women (Chapter 8). Thus, it is likely that children help sustain the family life satisfaction of women relative to men beyond the age when, on average, women's attainment of a happy marriage starts to fall short of that of men.

9.4.2. Big-Ticket Consumer Goods

In the material goods domain a turnaround in the attainment of aspirations occurs similar to that in family life. At young adult ages the shortfall in attainment of material goods aspirations is greater for men than for women; in later life the shortfall is greater for women (Figure 9.3c). The greater shortfall for men at younger ages is chiefly due to men having greater material goods aspirations (Figure 9.3a). The greater shortfall for women in later life is largely because they actually have somewhat fewer big-ticket consumer goods than men (Figure 9.3b). Table 9.4 presents the regression results on which Figure 9.3 is based.

The shortfall reversal in Figure 9.3c is for all ten big-ticket consumer goods taken together, but each of the individual material goods shows a similar reversal except for one. The exception is the fulfillment of aspirations for "nice clothes", for which women's shortfall is always greater than men's and increases over the life course.

The gender difference in satisfaction with finances observed in Chapter 8 conforms quite closely to what one would expect based on that in the attainment of aspirations for big-ticket consumer goods (Figures 9.3c and 9.4). Early in adult life men have a greater shortfall than women in fulfilling their material goods aspirations and are correspondingly less satisfied with their finances; later in life, women

Figure 9.3

Big-Ticket Consumer Goods: Aspirations, Attainments, and Shortfall, by Gender and Age

a. Aspirations

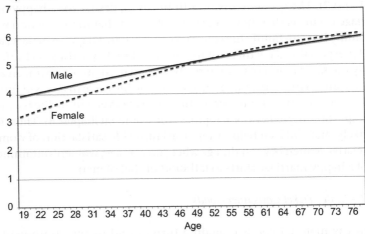

b. Attainments

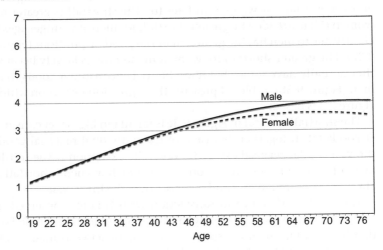

Figure 9.3 (continued)

Big-Ticket Consumer Goods: Aspirations, Attainments, and Shortfall, by Gender and Age

c. *Shortfall*

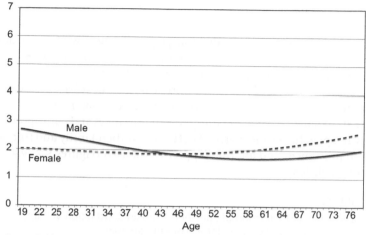

Source: Table 9.4. Data: Roper.

Figure 9.4

Satisfaction With Finances by Gender and Age

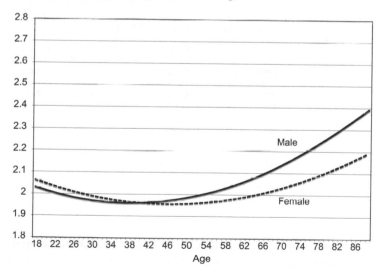

Source: Table 9.3, columns 3 and 4. Data: GSS.

have a greater shortfall and are the less satisfied gender. The cross-over age for the shortfall in attainment of big-ticket goods aspirations (45) is quite close to that in satisfaction with finances.

9.4.3. Happiness

Personal happiness depends in large part on how well one is doing with regard to family life and finances. As seen in Chapter 8, differences between women and men in the life cycle pattern of overall happiness are very largely what one would expect based on the domain satisfaction patterns. Early in adult life women are more satisfied than men with their family life and finances and correspondingly happier. In late life men feel better about their family and financial circumstances and are the happier of the two (Figures 9.2, 9.4, and 9.5; Table 9.3).

Table 9.3

Ordered Logit Regression of Specified Domain Satisfaction Variable and Happiness on Specified Independent Variables, by Gender (p-values in parentheses)

	Satfam		Satfin		Happy	
	(1) Male	(2) Female	(3) Male	(4) Female	(5) Male	(6) Female
Age centered	0.0076	-0.0042	0.0052	-0.0016	0.0033	-0.0086
	(0.00)	(0.00)	(0.31)	(0.73)	(0.53)	(0.08)
Age centered,	-0.0004	-0.0003	0.0004	0.0003		
squared	(0.00)	(0.00)	(0.00)	(0.00)		
Birth cohort			-0.0138	-0.0205	-0.0066	-0.0107
centered			(0.01)	(0.00)	(0.20)	(0.03)
Education	-0.0058	0.1242	0.4338	0.4013	0.1972	0.3489
> 12 years	(0.88)	(0.00)	(0.00)	(0.00)	(0.00)	(0.00)
Black	-0.3695	-0.5673	-0.7089	-0.6811	-0.5564	-0.8448
	(0.00)	(0.00)	(0.00)	(0.00)	(0.00)	(0.00)
Year dummies included	yes	yes	yes	yes	yes	yes
Observations	9,518	12,297	12,368	15,963	12,341	15,926
Pseudo R^2	0.0047	0.0085	0.0309	0.0326	0.0096	0.0161
Chi^2	129	284	763	1073	206	480
LR	-13820	-16709	-12832	-16533	-11428	-14873

Data source: GSS.

As one might expect, the cross-over in happiness falls between those in family and financial satisfaction, at age 48. This chapter shows that these gender differences in domain satisfaction very largely reflect life cycle differences between women and men in fulfillment of their family and material goods desires. Thus, when the life course gender differentials in the two data sets – Roper and GSS – are compared, we find patterns consistent with the theory that reversals in the net balance of aspirations and attainments cause corresponding gender shifts in domain satisfaction, and the shifts in domain satisfaction, in turn, lead to a reversal in the relative happiness of women and men.

Figure 9.5

Happiness by Gender and Age

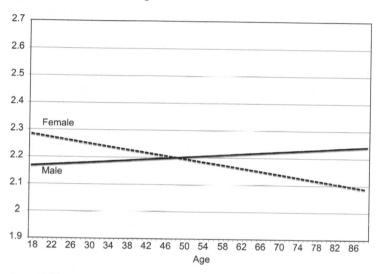

Source: Table 9.3, columns 5 and 6. Data: GSS.

9.5. Differences by Race, Education, and Birth Cohort

Happiness differences by race, education and birth cohort are also largely consistent with differences in the fulfillment of aspirations. Although these differences are not the primary concern of this chapter the regression results reported here provide new evidence on aspirations and attainment differentials for each of these characteristics. It is useful to note them briefly, therefore, because they provide additional support for the relevance of the aspirations/attainments model to explaining well-being.

9.5.1. Race

Blacks have lower marriage aspirations than whites, are less likely to have a happy marriage, and – despite their lower marriage aspirations – are less likely to achieve a happy marriage (Table 9.2). With regard to big-ticket consumer items, blacks tend to want more than whites (although for women the difference is not statistically significant), have considerably less, and, in consequence, fall much shorter than whites in fulfilling their desires for these big-ticket goods (Table 9.4). These greater shortfalls for blacks than whites in achieving their family life and material goods aspirations are consistent with numerous findings that blacks are less happy than whites (Blanchflower and Oswald 2004; Easterlin 2001b; Frey and Stutzer 2002a).

Table 9.4

Ordered Logit Regression of Aspirations for and Attainment of Ten Big Ticket Consumer Goods on Specified Independent Variables, by Gender (p-values in parentheses)

	Aspirations		Attainments	
	(1)	(2)	(3)	(4)
	Male	Female	Male	Female
Age, centered	0.0251	0.038	0.0517	0.0471
	(0.00)	(0.00)	(0.00)	(0.00)
Age cent., squared	-0.0001	-0.0003	-0.0008	-0.001
	(0.26)	(0.00)	(0.00)	(0.00)
Birth cohort, cent.	0.0323	0.0452	0.0233	0.0219
	(0.00)	(0.00)	(0.00)	(0.00)
Coh. c., squared	0.0000	0.0001	0.0000	0.0000
	(0.76)	(0.32)	(0.59)	(0.88)
Black	0.2963	0.0826	-0.4358	-0.6715
	(0.00)	(0.15)	(0.00)	(0.00)
Education > 12	0.1673	0.1855	0.413	0.4947
	(0.00)	(0.00)	(0.00)	(0.00)
Survey year dummies included	yes	yes	yes	yes
Observations	8372	9280	8372	9281
Pseudo R^2	0.0100	0.0122	0.0249	0.0247
Chi^2	389	522	852	928
LR	-19298	-21220	-16726	-18318

Data source: Roper.

9.5.2. Education

Setting aside differences in gender, age, race, and birth cohort, those with more education are happier than those with less (Chapter 10).

This happiness difference corresponds to what one would expect based on educational differences in success in fulfilling aspirations for material goods. Although better educated persons have slightly higher material goods aspirations than those less educated, the amount of goods they have is even greater, and the result is that they come closer to fulfilling their material goods aspirations (Table 9.4). In the family domain those with more education are more likely both to want and to have a happy marriage (Table 9.2). These family life differences in aspirations and attainments balance out so that there is no statistically significant difference by level of education in the shortfall in achieving a happy marriage. So far as the data go, therefore, they suggest that happiness differences in education are linked chiefly to the greater success of the more educated in achieving their material goods aspirations.

9.5.3. Birth Cohort

Cohort differences in the fulfillment of both family life and material goods aspirations are consistent with cohort differences in global happiness. At a given age recent cohorts are less likely than their predecessors to want a happy marriage, less likely to have one, and more likely to fall short of achieving their marriage aspirations (Table 9.2). Also, as one would expect, recent cohorts have more big-ticket items than earlier cohorts (Table 9.4). But their aspirations for such goods are even higher. As a result, success in attaining aspirations for these goods is less for recent cohorts than earlier. These greater shortfalls in the marriage and material goods domains for recent cohorts are consistent with their typically lower levels of happiness reported in the next chapter.

9.6. Summary

Early in adult life women are more likely than men to fulfill their material goods and family life aspirations; their satisfaction in these domains is correspondingly higher; and so too is their overall happiness. In later life these gender differences turn around. Men come closer than women to fulfilling their material goods and family life aspirations, are more satisfied with their financial situation and family life, and are the happier of the two. As seen in Chapter 8, an important factor probably underlying the turnaround in fulfillment of aspirations for material goods and family life is the shift over the course of the life cycle in the proportion of women and men in unions. In early adult life women are more likely than men to be in unions, and this makes for greater fulfillment of both family life and material goods aspirations. In later life women are less likely to be in unions, and correspondingly have a greater shortfall in the fulfillment of aspirations.

These conclusions are based on comparing two nationally representative data sets – one providing information on gender differences in aspirations and attainments; the other, on gender differences in domain satisfaction and happiness. What is noteworthy is that the gender differentials and cross-overs in these two quite separate surveys provide mutually consistent support for the aspirations/attainments model of domain satisfaction and happiness.

The research implications of this analysis are clear – the need for work on the nature and determinants of aspirations. The Roper surveys used here provide some guidance on the empirical study of aspirations, but there is need for new inquiries that will flesh out more comprehensively people's aspirations, especially in the family life and material goods domains so central to determining subjective well-being. There is need too for incorporating questions on these aspirations in surveys of domain satisfaction and subjective well-being.

With regard to the determinants of aspirations, there is little more in the social science literature than conceptual recognition of the importance of one's childhood socialization experience in the shaping of early adult-life aspirations, and the reshaping of aspirations during adulthood by on-going experience. We can see some evidence here of this shaping and reshaping of aspirations in regard to desires for a happy marriage. In keeping with the social norms instilled in the course of their upbringing, about nine out of ten young people reach adulthood wanting a happy marriage (Figure 9.1a). But over the life course the proportion who actually have a happy marriage barely ever exceeds six in ten (Figure 9.1b). It is likely that the disappointment for those who fail to reach the goal of a happy marriage gradually erodes marriage aspirations and contributes to the observed life course decline in those aspirations. Much more research is needed on the way in which aspirations such as these are shaped over the life course.

Appendix A

Good Life Questions from Roper Surveys

1. We often hear people talk about what they want out of life. Here are a number of different things. (HAND RESPONDENT CARD) When you think of the good life – the life you'd like to have, which of the things on this list, if any, are part of that good life as far as you personally are concerned?
2. Now would you go down that list and call off all the things you now have? Just call off the letter of the items. (RECORD BELOW)

	1. Part of the Good Life	2. Now have
a. A home you own		
b. A yard and lawn		
c. A car		
d. A second car		
e. A vacation home		
f. A swimming pool (except 1996, 1999)		
g. A happy marriage (except 2003)		
h. No children (except 2003)		
i. One child (except 2003)		
k. Three children (except 2003)		
l. Four or more children (except 2003)		
m. A job that pays much more than average		
n. A job that is interesting		
o. A job that contributes to the welfare of society		
p. A college education for myself		
q. A college education for my children		
r. Travel abroad		
s. A color TV set (except 2003)		
t. A second color TV set (except 2003)		
u. Really nice clothes		
v. A lot of money		

Appendix B

Table B-1
Descriptive Statistics, Roper Data on Aspirations and Attainments

Variable	n	Mean	Std. Dev.	Min	Max
Males					
Happy marriage					
Want	8,440	0.7895	0.4077	0	1
Have	8,439	0.4949	0.5	0	1
Shortfall	8,440	0.2947	0.4559	0	1
Big ticket goods					
Want	8,440	4.8624	2.6327	0	10
Have	8,440	2.7221	2.1167	0	10
Shortfall	8,440	2.1403	2.115	0	10
Females					
Happy marriage					
Want	9,383	0.786	0.4101	0	1
Have	9,384	0.4564	0.4981	0	1
Shortfall	9,383	0.3297	0.4701	0	1
Big ticket goods					
Want	9,383	4.7065	2.5811	0	10
Have	9,384	2.6533	2.0597	0	10
Shortfall	9,383	2.0533	2.0306	0	10

Table B-2
Descriptive Statistics, GSS Data on Happiness and Domain Satisfaction

Variable	n	Mean	Std. Dev.	Min	Max
Males					
Global happiness	12,341	2.2052	0.6262	1	3
Satisfaction with one's finances	12,368	2.0513	0.745	1	3
Satisfaction with family life	9,518	5.8275	1.4358	1	7
Females					
Global happiness	15,926	2.2174	0.6376	1	3
Satisfaction with one's finances	15,963	2.0297	0.7439	1	3
Satisfaction with family life	12,297	5.9805	1.2893	1	7

10

Happiness and Domain Satisfaction: New Directions for the Economics of Happiness

The purpose of this chapter is to see to what extent the domain satisfaction model of psychology explains four different patterns of happiness in the United States, (1) the positive cross-sectional relation of happiness to socio-economic status, (2) the nearly horizontal time series trend, (3) the hill pattern of life cycle happiness, and (4) the decline across generations. The domain model sees each of these happiness patterns as the net result of the corresponding patterns of satisfaction that people have in each of several realms of life – in the present analysis, finances, family life, work, and health. These domain satisfaction patterns do not simply replicate the happiness pattern – with regard to age, for example, happiness may go up through midlife, but satisfaction with finances, down. Thus, given that the domain satisfaction patterns may differ from that for happiness, and also among themselves, the questions of interest here are specifically the following. Do the patterns by socio-economic status of satisfaction with each of the following – finances, family life, work, and health – come together in a way that predicts the positive cross-sectional relation of happiness to socio-economic status? Do the life cycle patterns of satisfaction in each of these four domains account

This chapter is a revised version of: Sawangfa, O., Easterlin, R. (2009). Happiness and Domain Satisfaction: New Directions for the Economics of Happiness, in: Dutt, A. K., Radcliff, B. (Eds.), Happiness, Economics, and Politics: Towards a Multi-Disciplinary Approach, Edward Elgar, Cheltenham. For valuable comments we are grateful to Andrew Clark, Andrew J. Oswald, John Strauss, Anke C. Plagnol, and participants in the Conference on New Directions in the Study of Happiness: United States and International Perspectives, University of Notre Dame, Oct. 22-24, 2006. Laura Angelescu provided excellent research assistance; financial help was provided by the University of Southern California.

for the hill pattern of life cycle happiness? Do the time series trends in satisfaction with finances, family life, work, and health explain the nearly horizontal time series trend in happiness? Finally, is the decline in happiness across cohorts the net outcome of the cohort patterns of satisfaction in each of the four domains?

10.1. Prior Work

Economic research on domain satisfaction has heretofore been quite limited, and much of what has been done focuses on explaining, not overall happiness, but satisfaction with specific economic circumstances, e.g. job satisfaction, housing satisfaction, financial satisfaction, satisfaction with income, satisfaction with standard of living, and so on (Diaz-Serrano 2006; Hayo and Seifert 2003; Hsieh 2003; Solberg et al. 2002; Vera-Toscano, Ateca-Amestoy and Serrano-del-Rosal 2006; Warr 1999). Few studies explore the relation of global happiness to the different domains. An important exception is the work of van Praag and Ferrer-i-Carbonell (2004), which examines the extent to which differences among individuals in overall satisfaction are related to satisfaction with a variety of life domains, several of which correspond to those studied here (see Chapters 3 and 4; also van Praag, Frijters and Ferrer-i-Carbonell 2003). Their results, based on data for the United Kingdom and Germany, support the importance of the domains studied here, and suggest that domain satisfaction variables provide a better statistical explanation of happiness than objective conditions (for a similar result with regard to wages and hours of work, see Clark 2005). In another interesting study Rojas (2007) uses the domain satisfaction approach to study individual happiness in Mexico, focusing on domains deriving from the philosophical rather than social science literature.

Outside of economics, work relating happiness to domain satisfaction is more extensive (see, for example, the bibliography in Veenhoven 2005, section 12-a). One of the most ambitious projects brings together studies of individual data for twelve European countries of both domain satisfaction and satisfaction with life in general (Saris et al. 1996). The domains included vary somewhat among countries, but one result common to all countries is that two domains are consistently positively related to overall life satisfaction – material living conditions (captured in satisfaction with housing and satisfaction with finances) and "social contacts", reflecting the importance to well-being of personal relationships (ibid, p. 227). The counterparts of these two in the present study are financial satisfaction and satisfaction with family life.

All of these earlier studies, both within and outside of economics, focus on explaining how happiness varies in relation to one particular variable, usually among individuals at a point in time. In contrast, the aim here is to test how well the domain satisfaction approach explains mean happiness within the United States population in relation to each of four different variables – by socio-economic status (education), over time (year), over the life cycle (age), and across generations (birth cohort). In effect, it extends the life cycle analysis of Chapters 7 through 9 to the variation in happiness by socio-economic status, time, and birth cohort. For each variable the test is the same, to see how well the actual relation of happiness to that variable can be predicted from the corresponding patterns for the four domain satisfaction variables – financial situation, family life, work, and health.

10.2. Data and Methods

As before, the data are from the United States General Social Survey (GSS). Socio-economic status is measured by years of schooling, ranging from zero to 20. The age range is from 18 to 89; birth cohort, from 1884 to 1976. Survey year is in terms of time dummies with 1973 being the reference year. As in Chapter 9, the use of time dummies enables us to separate period from age and cohort effects (cf. also Blanchflower and Oswald 2007). Descriptive statistics are given in Appendix A.

The procedure consists of the following steps:

1. A regression of happiness on age, cohort, education, gender, race, and survey year (in dummy form) is estimated from the individual data for 1973–1994 (see Appendix B column 1). Both linear and quadratic forms are tried for the age, cohort, and education variables, and the form yielding the best fit in terms of significant t-statistics is selected. This single regression is then used to estimate how happiness varies in relation to each of the four variables (age, cohort, education and year) controlling for the other three. We call these estimated values "actual happiness". Actual happiness differs from the raw mean of happiness in relation to any

given variable, such as education, in that it controls for other, essentially fixed, characteristics of individuals. Thus, in the case of education, the estimated happiness–education pattern controls for differences from one level of education to another in the composition of the population by age, cohort, gender, and race, and also in period effects.

Formally, we have:

$$\text{Happy} = B^{(1)} \text{ (age, cohort, education, gender, race, year dummy),}$$

where $B^{(1)}$ denotes equation (1) in Appendix B. The typical pattern of variation of happiness in regard to a given variable, say, years of schooling, is then estimated by entering in this regression the mean values given in Appendix A of the other variables (age, cohort, gender, race, and year), while allowing that variable to range from its minimum to maximum value as given in Appendix A (for education, from zero to 20 years of schooling).

Thus,

$$\text{Happy for the } i^{th} \text{ year of schooling}$$
$$= B^{(1)} \text{ (} \overline{\text{age}}, \overline{\text{cohort}}, \overline{\text{male}}, \overline{\text{black}}, \overline{\text{education}}, \overline{\text{t1973}}, \overline{\text{t1974}}, \dots \overline{\text{t1994}})$$

where $\overline{\text{age}}$ is the mean age, $\overline{\text{cohort}}$ is the mean birth cohort, and so on. Since years of schooling range from 0 to 20, following the above procedure for each level of education results in a series:

$$\text{Happy\_Ed(0), Happy\_Ed(1), } \dots, \text{Happy\_Ed(20),}$$

where Happy_Ed(j) is actual happiness of a person with j years of schooling. This series is plotted in Figures 10.1a and 10.2a as actual happiness, the happiness pattern that is to be predicted.

2. A similar procedure is followed to derive the typical pattern of variation of satisfaction in each of the four domains. First, a regression is estimated of satisfaction in a given domain in relation to age, cohort, education, gender, race, and year (in dummy form) as presented in Appendix B, columns 2–5. Then, the typical pattern of variation of satisfaction in that domain in regard to a given variable, say, education, is estimated by entering in the regression the mean values of all other variables, while allowing

210

that variable to range from its lowest to highest value as given in Appendix A.

Thus, as in the computation of actual happiness by level of education, the series of actual domain satisfaction by education can be obtained from $B^{(2)}$, $B^{(3)}$, $B^{(4)}$, and $B^{(5)}$, respectively:

(i) Satfin_Ed(0), Satfin_Ed(1), ... , Satfin_Ed(20);
(ii) Satfam_Ed(0), Satfam_Ed(1), ... , Satfam_Ed(20);
(iii) Satjob_Ed(0), Satjob_Ed(1), ..., Satjob_Ed(20); and
(iv) Sathealth_Ed(0), Sathealth_Ed(1), ... , Sathealth_Educ(20).

These series are plotted in Figure 10.3a.

3. A regression is estimated from the individual data of the relation of happiness to the four domain satisfaction variables – financial satisfaction (Satfin), family satisfaction (Satfam), work satisfaction (Satjob), and health satisfaction (Sathealth) – to establish the relative impact of each domain on happiness (Appendix C).
Formally,

Happy = C(Satfin, Satfam, Satjob, Sathealth).

All domains turn out to have a significant positive effect on happiness, as one might expect. Although there is some variation in the domain weight by demographic characteristics, such as sex and age, they are not sizeable enough to alter the basic results obtained here.

4. A prediction of the variation of happiness with regard to each variable (education, time, age, and cohort) is obtained by substituting in the step 3 regression equation the domain satisfaction values estimated in step 2. For the cross-section analysis, for example, predicted happiness for a given education level is estimated by entering in the step 3 regression equation the four domain satisfaction values for that level of education derived in step 2. Thus, mean predicted happiness for zero years of schooling, controlling for age, cohort, gender, race, and year, is computed as:

PredHappy_Ed(0)
= D(Satfin_Ed(0), Satfam_Ed(0), Satjob_Ed(0), Sathealth_Ed(0)).

Similarly,

PredHappy_Ed(1)
= D(Satfin_Ed(1), Satfam_Ed(1), Satjob_Ed(1), Sathealth_Ed(1)).

This procedure is repeated for all other levels of education to obtain the predicted pattern of happiness in relation to education. The series

PredHappy_Ed(0), PredHappy_Ed(1), ... , PredHappy_Ed(20)

is then plotted as predicted happiness in Figure 10.2a.

The regression technique used is ordered logit, because responses to the several variables are categorical and number three or more. Ordinary least squares regressions yield virtually identical results.

In step 3, in estimating the relation of happiness to domain satisfaction from individual data, a question arises about possible bias in reports on satisfaction (cf. Diener and Lucas 1999, p. 215; van Praag and Ferrer-i-Carbonell 2004, Chapter 4). Responses on satisfaction – whether with life in general or an individual domain – are known to be influenced by personality traits. Consider two persons with identical objective conditions and subjective goals. If one of them is neurotic, then it is likely that this person's responses on satisfaction with both life in general and the various domains of life will be lower than the other person's, because a neurotic tends to assess his or her circumstances more negatively than others. However, a purpose of the step 3 regression is to establish the relative weights in determining happiness of the four domain satisfaction variables. Because the happiness and domain satisfaction responses for any given individual would be similarly biased by personality, the estimate of relative weights for that individual, and correspondingly for the population as a whole, should be free of personality bias.

Another purpose of the step 3 regression is to predict actual happiness from domain satisfaction. If personality bias exists in an individual's report on happiness, then actual happiness, which is based on this report, is biased by personality. Similarly, personality bias in an individual's report on domain satisfaction leads to personality bias in actual domain satisfaction. Predicted happiness, derived from actual domain satisfaction, is then also biased by personality.

But since the personality bias in actual happiness is the same as that in actual domain satisfaction and, thus, in predicted happiness, the predictive power of the domain model judged by comparing actual happiness with predicted happiness should not be influenced by personality bias.

10.3. Results

Actual happiness – The happiness patterns to be explained are both familiar and unfamiliar. Most familiar, perhaps, is the positive cross-sectional association of happiness to socio-economic status (Figure 10.1a). Also well-known is the fairly flat relation of happiness to time (Figure 10.1b).

Less familiar are the patterns in relation to age and cohort. As seen in Chapter 7, over the life cycle happiness rises slightly to midlife and declines slowly thereafter (Figure 10.1c). Although the swing in happiness is mild, it is statistically significant. The pattern differs from the usual U-shaped relation to age reported in the economics literature, because the U-shaped happiness–age relation is the result of a multivariate regression in which controls are included, not only for the variables used here (education, time, cohort, gender, race), but also for life circumstances (income, work status, marital status, health) (Blanchflower and Oswald 2004, 2007). Controls for life circumstances would be inappropriate here and also in regard to the happiness patterns for education, time, and cohort, because the specific purpose of the analysis is to test whether satisfaction with life circumstances in various domains, reflecting both objective life circumstances and subjective norms, explains the happiness patterns observed.

Least studied is how happiness varies by cohort.[1] For cohorts born between the late nineteenth century and the 1970s, the relation of happiness to cohort is negative and curvilinear, with the lowest happiness levels found in the cohorts born in the mid-1950s (Figure 10.1d). Thus, the happiness of younger cohorts is, on average, significantly less than older, except that among the most recent cohorts there is a slight upturn in happiness. The magnitude of the happiness differences among cohorts is not very great, but it is somewhat larger than the changes found in the time series and life cycle patterns.

Figure 10.1

Mean Actual Happiness by Years of Schooling, Year, Age, and Birth Cohort, 1973–1994

(a) By Years of Schooling

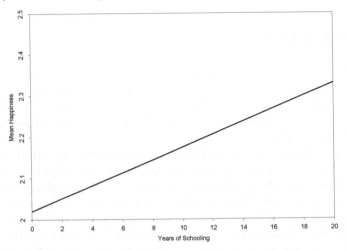

(b) By Year

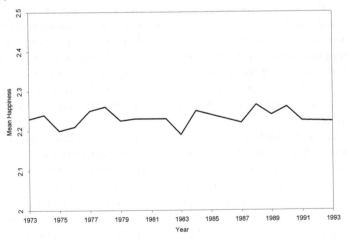

Figure 10.1 (continued)

Mean Actual Happiness by Years of Schooling, Year, Age, and Birth Cohort, 1973–1994

(c) By Age

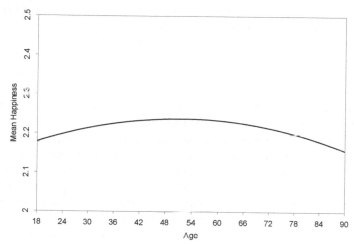

(d) By Birth Cohort

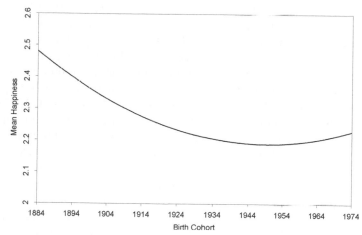

Note: Values in each panel are after controlling for the three variables heading the other panels, and also gender and race. See Appendix C.

The difference among cohorts found here is after controlling for cohort differences in age, education, period influences, gender, and race. If data were available for a single year only, then it would be impossible to distinguish the cohort pattern from that for age. If, for example, in the survey year 1980 mean happiness were to increase from age 20 (i.e., persons born in 1960) to age 80 (persons born in 1900), then the cohort pattern would be negative, the reverse of that for age, with happiness declining from the cohort of 1900 to that of 1960. (If the age pattern were hill-shaped moving from left to right on the x-axis, the cohort pattern would be hill-shaped too – in effect, the cohort pattern traverses the same hill in reverse fashion.) With data for only one year, there would be no way of deciding whether one is observing the relation of happiness to age or to cohort.

Our data, however, span 21 years, and thus in deriving cohort effects we compare the happiness of 21 different cohorts at a given age, and, correspondingly, in deriving age effects the happiness at 21 different ages of a given cohort. The fact that our age and cohort patterns of happiness are not simply the reverse of each other (as is true also of the age and cohort patterns for the individual domains) indicates that we are successfully differentiating between age and cohort influences.

Predicted happiness – There are four fairly disparate patterns of happiness to be explained – a positive cross-sectional relation to education, a fairly flat relation to time, the "hill" pattern of the life cycle, and a negative curvilinear relation across cohorts. How well do the domain satisfaction patterns predict these patterns of happiness?

The answer, based on the procedures outlined in steps 2–4 above is, reasonably well. The cross-sectional relation of happiness to education is closely predicted by the cross-sectional patterns of happiness to education derived from the domain model (Figure 10.2a). The predicted time series pattern of happiness based on the time series patterns of satisfaction in each domain corresponds closely to the actual horizontal time series pattern (Figure 10.2b). Life-cycle happiness as predicted by the life-cycle patterns of domain satisfaction, follows the hill pattern of actual happiness, although the predicted movement peaks slightly earlier, at age 43 compared with 52, and the amplitude is slightly less than the actual (Figure 10.2c). Least satisfactory is the prediction of the cohort pattern. Although happiness of younger cohorts is correctly predicted to be less than older, the predicted curve is virtually linear rather than concave upward, so that the upturn among the youngest cohorts is missed (Figure 10.2d).

Figure 10.2

Mean Predicted and Actual Happiness by Years of Schooling, Year, Age, and Birth Cohort

(a) By Years of Schooling

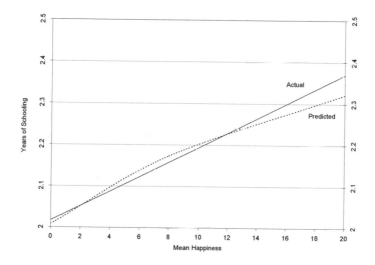

(b) By Year

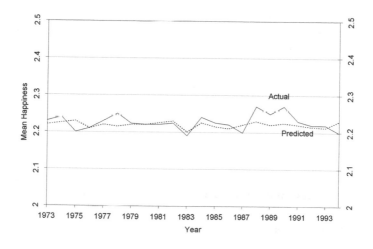

Figure 10.2 (continued)

Mean Predicted and Actual Happiness by Years of Schooling, Year, Age, and Birth Cohort

(c) By Age

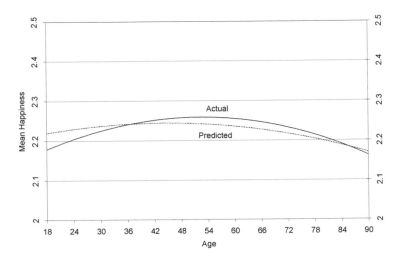

(d) By Cohort

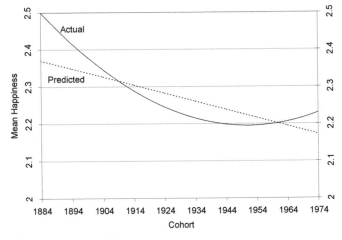

Note: See note to Figure 10.1.

Table 10.1 compares the mean squared error of the prediction of happiness by education, year, age, and cohort. The most satisfactory prediction is that for life cycle happiness. It is closely followed by the predictions for years of schooling and the time series pattern of happiness. Confirming the visual observation of Figure 10.2, the least satisfactory is the prediction of the cohort pattern, with a mean squared error more than five times that of the life-cycle prediction.

Table 10.1

Mean Squared Error of the Prediction of Happiness

Variable	Mean Squared Error
Years of Schooling	0.00033
Year	0.00054
Age	0.00028
Birth Cohort	0.00152

Domain satisfaction – As a general matter, the four domain patterns for any one variable typically differ from each other, and the domains dominating the prediction of happiness are not the same for all four variables. This is brought out in Figure 10.3, which presents for each variable the actual domain patterns and, for comparison, that for actual happiness. The top panel presents the patterns for the domains of family life and financial satisfaction; the bottom panel, the patterns for satisfaction with work and health. By comparing the actual domain patterns with that for actual happiness, one is able to form a tentative impression of which domains are chiefly responsible for the happiness pattern for any given variable.

Perhaps most striking is that more educated persons are happier because they enjoy greater satisfaction in all four realms of life. For family life, finances, work, and health, satisfaction increases with the level of education (Figure 10.3, panels a.1 and a.2). The rate of change, however, varies among the domains. Satisfaction with family life and health increases at a decreasing rate, while satisfaction with finances grows at an increasing rate. Only for satisfaction with work is the trend linear like that for actual happiness.

The fairly flat relation of happiness to time appears from the figure to reflect similar patterns in the four domains (panels b.1 and b.2). However, if one fits ordinary least squares trend lines to the fluctuating lines in the figures, some subtle differences emerge. All of the patterns have very slight, but significant trends. Actual happiness has a small uptrend, amounting to a total increase for the period of .013 on the happiness scale of one to three. This is the equivalent of a net upward shift by one response category – say, from "pretty happy" to "very happy" – of 1.3 percent of respondents over the entire twenty-one year period. This is not very much of a shift, although it is statistically significant. Based on the fitted trends, the corresponding shift for each domain (all of them significant) are for financial satisfaction +3.2 percent, work satisfaction +2.3 percent, family life satisfaction -0.5 percent, and health satisfaction +1.4 percent. Thus, the very slight uptrend for actual happiness is the net outcome of the slight positive trends in satisfaction with finances, work, and health outweighing the slight negative trend in satisfaction with family life. The very slight but statistically significant uptrend in happiness found here differs from the results for the United States reported in Chapter 5 because it reflects the use of controls for age, education, and birth cohort, and is for a considerably shorter period.

Turning to the age patterns, one finds, as in Chapter 7, that the increase to midlife of life cycle happiness is due to increasing satisfaction with family life and work outweighing negative changes in satisfaction with finances and health (panels c.1 and c.2). The decline of happiness beyond midlife occurs because declines in satisfaction with family life and work join the downtrend in satisfaction with health. The adverse impact on happiness of these negative trends is moderated, however, by increasing satisfaction that people express with their financial situation as they move into older age.

Finally, the lower happiness of younger compared with older cohorts is due to downtrends in satisfaction in three domains – finances, work, and health (panels d.1 and d.2). Satisfaction with family life does not differ between older and younger cohorts, despite the striking differences in family life between today's cohorts and those of their parents and grandparents. The slight upturn in actual happiness among the youngest cohorts cannot be explained by the domains studied here, because none of the domains shows an improvement of younger relative to older cohorts.

One important conclusion that emerges from surveying the domain patterns is that no single domain is the key to happiness. Rather, happiness is the net outcome of satisfaction with all of the major life domains, and the domain patterns frequently differ from each other. Moreover, the importance of any given domain varies depending on the happiness relationship being studied – cross-sectionally by education, over time, through the life cycle, or across generations.

Figure 10.3

Mean Domain Satisfaction and Actual Happiness by Years of Schooling, Year, Age, and Birth Cohort, 1973–1994

(a.1) By Years of Schooling

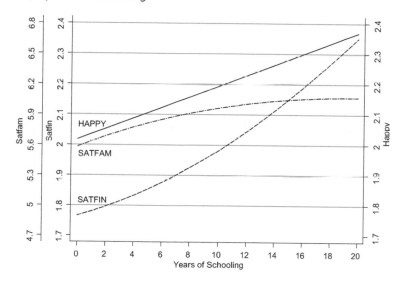

(a.2) By Years of Schooling

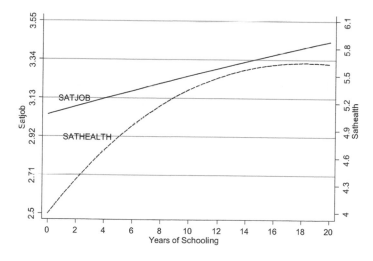

Figure 10.3 (continued)

Mean Domain Satisfaction and Actual Happiness by Years of Schooling, Year, Age, and Birth Cohort, 1973–1994

(b.1) By Year

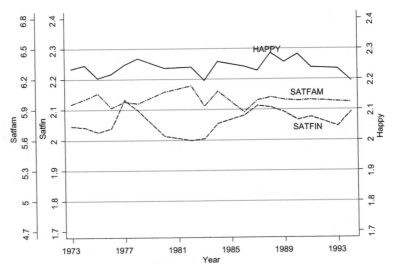

(b.2) By Year

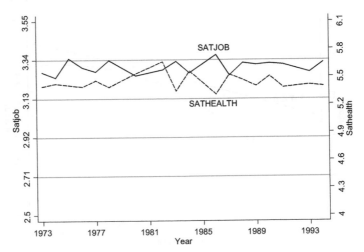

Figure 10.3 (continued)

Mean Domain Satisfaction and Actual Happiness by Years of Schooling, Year, Age, and Birth Cohort, 1973–1994

(c.1) By Age

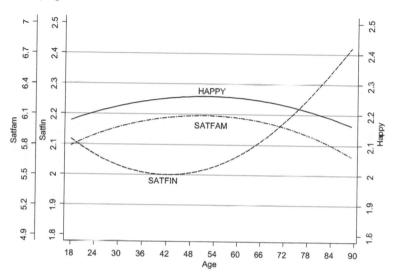

(c.2) By Age

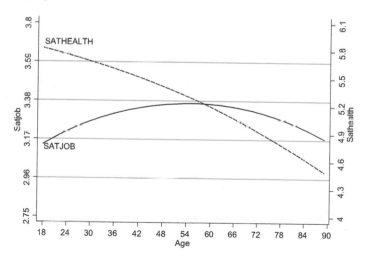

223

Figure 10.3 (continued)

Mean Domain Satisfaction and Actual Happiness by Years of Schooling, Year, Age, and Birth Cohort, 1973–1994

(d.1) By Birth Cohort

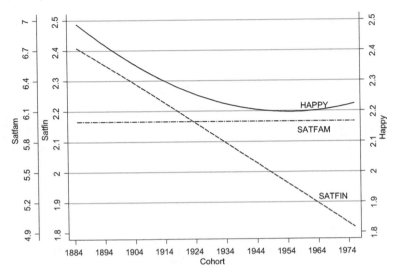

(d.2) By Birth Cohort

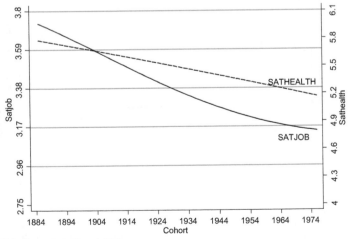

Note: See note to Figure 10.1.

10.4. Conclusions

How well does the domain satisfaction model predict the way in which mean happiness varies by socio-economic status, year, age, and birth cohort? The answer is quite well for the first three – education, year, and age – and not too badly for the fourth, birth cohort.

Some skeptics might say the success of the predictions is no great surprise – due to the common influence of personality, reports of happiness and satisfaction with finances, family life, work, and health all are highly correlated in data for individuals. But we are analyzing here the relations among group means, not individuals, and as can readily be seen from Figure 10.3 the patterns of the domain means often differ from that for happiness and among themselves. The observation that the happiness and domain satisfaction variables are highly positively correlated among individuals does not imply, for example, that the mean values by age of happiness and the four domain satisfaction variables will also be positively correlated. Personality tends to be stable from one age to another while the means for happiness and domain satisfaction follow different and sometimes contrary paths with regard to age. Similarly, unless one believes that personality varies systematically by socio-economic status, birth cohort, and over time, there is no reason to suppose that the individual-based correlation among the happiness and domain satisfaction variables would result in corresponding correlations among the group means for these categories. Put differently, the point is, not whether personality varies among individuals in a way that would explain individual differences in happiness, but whether, on average, it varies by age, level of education, year, and cohort in ways that would generate the prediction of happiness by these characteristics. To our knowledge there is no research demonstrating that personality varies by age, level of education, year, and cohort in the same way as happiness.

Some might contend that because actual happiness is derived from the same explanatory variables as are the domain means (Appendix B), it is inevitable that actual happiness and happiness as predicted by these domain means would come together well. An argument similar to that just given applies here. There is no reason to suppose that a weighted average of the four domain means at, say, a certain age should equal actual happiness at that age. Different life-cycle patterns among the four domains need not together produce a life-cycle pattern of happiness that fits nicely with the life-cycle pattern of actual happiness.

It would be interesting to see if happiness regressions of the type found in the economics literature, based only on objective variables, do as well in predicting the happiness patterns as the domain satisfaction variables used here. If, for example, one estimates the life cycle pattern of such "objective" variables as income, marital status, employment status, and health, would one be able to predict from these patterns the actual life cycle pattern of happiness? We venture that the answer is no – that Angus Campbell is right when he says that subjective well-being depends not on objective conditions alone, but on the psychological processing of objective circumstances, as captured in reports on satisfaction with these conditions.

The fact that the domain patterns studied here come together reasonably well to predict actual happiness provides new support for the meaningfulness of subjective data on well-being and its components. Thus, while a skeptic of the present analysis might point to the startling contrast between the life cycle pattern for happiness and that for satisfaction with finances – almost diametrical opposites – it turns out that when the movements in the other domains are accounted for, along with that for financial satisfaction, the hill pattern observed for actual happiness is predicted fairly closely by the domain patterns. This close prediction would be unlikely to occur if no credence could be given to what people say about their feelings.

In addition, the similarity between the present patterns of predicted and actual happiness supports the conclusion that the four domains studied here are important in determining happiness, a result consistent with the literature on domain satisfaction. But these four domains do not tell the whole story of happiness movements, as is made especially clear here by the disparity between the predicted and actual happiness patterns by birth cohort.

Finally, depending on the happiness relationship being studied – by socio-economic status, time, age, or cohort – the role played by different domains in determining happiness tends to vary. Happiness is the net outcome of satisfaction with all of the major domains of life, and no single domain is sufficient to explain the various patterns of overall happiness.

This is in many ways a first pass at testing fairly comprehensively Campbell's domain satisfaction model, and while the model performs reasonably well, the results raise a number of questions for further research. For example, would increasing the number of life domains improve the predictions? What chiefly determines the domain satisfaction patterns – objective conditions like those emphasized in economics or subjective factors stressed in psychology? To what extent are there interrelations among the various domains themselves? The domain satisfaction model provides a new and reasonable start on unraveling the mysteries of happiness – a new direction, perhaps, for research on the economics of happiness. But it is only a start.

Appendix A

Descriptive Statistics

Variable	Number of Observations	Mean	Standard Deviation	Minimum	Maximum
Happy	29651	2.22	0.63	1	3
Satfin	29728	2.04	0.74	1	3
Satjob	23808	2.66	0.92	1	4
Satfam	23207	4.66	1.62	1	7
Sathealth	23252	4.24	1.68	1	7
Age	29853	43.89	17.18	18	89
Birth Cohort (1880=0)	29853	60.1	18.34	4	96
Years of Schooling	29853	12.35	3.12	0	20
Male	29853	0.45	0.50	0	1
Black	29853	0.11	0.31	0	1
t1973	29853	0.05	0.22	0	1
t1974	29853	0.05	0.22	0	1
t1975	29853	0.05	0.22	0	1
t1976	29853	0.05	0.21	0	1
t1977	29853	0.05	0.22	0	1
t1978	29853	0.05	0.22	0	1
t1980	29853	0.05	0.22	0	1
t1982	29853	0.05	0.22	0	1
t1983	29853	0.05	0.22	0	1
t1984	29853	0.05	0.22	0	1
t1985	29853	0.05	0.22	0	1
t1986	29853	0.05	0.22	0	1
t1987	29853	0.05	0.22	0	1
t1988	29853	0.05	0.22	0	1
t1989	29853	0.05	0.22	0	1
t1990	29853	0.05	0.21	0	1
t1991	29853	0.05	0.22	0	1
t1993	29853	0.05	0.23	0	1
t1994	29853	0.10	0.30	0	1

Appendix B

Steps 1 and 2 Equations
Regression of Happiness and Each Domain Satisfaction Variable
on Specified Independent Variables: Ordered Logit Statistics
(robust p-value in parentheses)

Independent Variable	Dependent Variable				
	Happy (1)	Satfin (2)	Satfam (3)	Satjob (4)	Sathealth (5)
Age	0.022772	-0.04344	0.044079	0.043668	-0.01198
	[0.001]**	[0.000]**	[0.000]**	[0.000]**	[0.060]+
Agesq	-0.00022	0.000514	-0.00043	-0.0004	-0.0001
	[0.001]**	[0.000]**	[0.000]**	[0.000]**	[0.018]*
Coh	-0.02851	-0.01713		-0.03556	-0.0089
	[0.000]**	[0.000]**		[0.000]**	[0.064]+
Cohsq	0.00019			0.000164	
	[0.000]**			[0.018]*	
Educ	0.055533	0.035612	0.075085	0.047991	0.210914
	[0.000]**	[0.050]+	[0.000]**	[0.000]**	[0.000]**
Educsq		0.002054	-0.00192		-0.00579
		[0.005]**	[0.023]*		[0.000]**
Male	-0.09836	0.012652	-0.17479	0.021695	0.138811
	[0.000]**	[-0.596]	[0.000]**	[-0.423]	[0.000]**
Black	-0.69836	-0.61869	-0.45077	-0.43641	-0.16603
	[0.000]**	[0.000]**	[0.000]**	[0.000]**	[0.000]**
t1973	--------------	--------------	Reference Year	--------------	--------------
t1974	0.035135	-0.00994	0.077578	-0.07021	0.038031
	[-0.648]	[-0.886]	[-0.281]	[-0.373]	[-0.583]
t1975	-0.09603	-0.05083	0.171288	0.187315	0.014605
	[-0.199]	[-0.466]	[0.019]*	[0.021]*	[-0.826]
t1976	-0.05226	-0.01693	-0.05673	0.060301	-0.00767
	[-0.471]	[-0.8]	[-0.419]	[-0.441]	[-0.906]
t1977	0.043856	0.224268	0.039493	0.00468	0.079327
	[-0.538]	[0.001]**	[-0.584]	[-0.949]	[-0.254]
t1978	0.10802	0.133804	0.007053	0.159489	-0.01189
	[-0.11]	[0.051]+	[-0.922]	[0.034]*	[-0.856]
t1980	0.006386	-0.08415	0.199211	-0.04797	0.177236
	[-0.927]	[-0.197]	[0.007]**	[-0.52]	[0.009]**
t1982	0.017871	-0.1206	0.303385	0.02714	0.352281
	[-0.793]	[0.054]+	[0.000]**	[-0.707]	[0.000]**

Appendix B (continued)

Independent Variable	Dependent Variable				
	Happy (1)	Satfin (2)	Satfam (3)	Satjob (4)	Sathealth (5)
t1983	-0.12173	-0.1065	-0.03378	0.141839	-0.0688
	[0.062]+	[0.099]+	[0.637]	[0.045]*	[0.319]
t1984	0.07414	0.021233	0.208851	-0.01138	0.212522
	[0.281]	[0.737]	[0.005]**	[0.881]	[0.003]**
t1985	-0.14544	0.024798		0.073894	
	[0.024]*	[0.697]		[0.302]	
t1986	0.022754	0.090113	-0.12431	0.231755	-0.11249
	[0.732]	[0.178]	[0.085]+	[0.002]**	[0.141]
t1987	-0.02126	0.172639	0.06154	-0.04379	0.163291
	[0.759]	[0.006]**	[0.410]	[0.554]	[0.039]*
t1988	0.162877	0.158673	0.107415	0.121667	0.087871
	[0.016]*	[0.015]*	[0.196]	[0.107]	[0.309]
t1989	0.068958	0.119368	0.066921	0.09812	0.001555
	[0.307]	[0.076]+	[0.407]	[0.194]	[0.986]
t1990	0.15064	0.051672	0.052268	0.115772	0.141139
	[0.032]*	[0.473]	[0.526]	[0.145]	[0.136]
t1991	0.013087	0.077566	0.065499	0.100156	-0.01768
	[0.852]	[0.252]	[0.420]	[0.200]	[0.855]
t1993			0.0394		0.019645
			[0.621]		[0.845]
t1994	-0.12405	0.120657	0.028085	0.12954	
	[0.059]+	[0.060]+	[0.780]	[0.074]+	
cut1:Constant	-2.03755	-2.19873	-2.92248	-3.07068	-3.54667
	[0.000]**	[0.000]**	[0.000]**	[0.000]**	[0.000]**
cut2:Constant	0.79881	-0.14451	-2.0171	-1.72014	-2.42659
	[0.052]+	[0.713]	[0.000]**	[0.000]**	[0.000]**
cut3:Constant			-1.36141	0.234316	-1.77893
			[0.000]**	[0.608]	[0.000]**
cut4:Constant			-0.47882		-0.65057
			[0.006]**		[0.189]
cut5:Constant			0.285209		0.075143
			[0.102]		[0.879]
cut6:Constant			1.808822		1.529096
			[0.000]**		[0.002]**
Observations	29651	29728	23207	23808	23252
Pseudo R^2	0.014	0.031	0.007	0.02	0.016
Chi^2	607.512	1734.832	371.977	879.21	1052.814
Log Likelihood	-27328.6	-30710.4	-31389.3	-25354	-37052.7

Notes: + significant at 10% * significant at 5% ** significant at 1%

Appendix C

Step 3 Equation
Regression of Happiness on Domain Satisfaction Variables:
Ordered Logit Statistics
(robust p-value in parentheses)

Independent Variable	Happy
Satfin	0.573019
	[0.000]**
Satjob	0.498200
	[0.000]**
Satfam	0.460422
	[0.000]**
Sathealt	0.242419
	[0.000]**
cut1:Constant	4.299545
	[0.000]**
cut2:Constant	7.743151
	[0.000]**
Observations	18440
Pseudo R^2	0.133
Chi^2	3200.648
Log Likelihood	-14855.8

Notes: + significant at 10% * significant at 5% ** significant at 1%

11

Explaining Happiness

In Chapter 7, I noted the differing views of economists and psychologists regarding the determinants of happiness. In this chapter, I return to this refrain with a view to developing its implications for a theory of happiness. My point of departure is the prevailing theories of well-being in psychology and economics. In referring to the dominant theory in each discipline, I do not want to suggest that there is unanimity in either field. Rather, these theories are what might be viewed as the central tendency in each subject.

In psychology, the inclination is towards "setpoint theory" (Chapter 7). Each individual is thought to have a setpoint of happiness given by genetics and personality. Life events such as marriage, loss of a job, and serious injury or disease may deflect a person above or below this setpoint, but hedonic adaptation will fairly quickly return an individual to the initial level.

In contrast, in economics, life circumstances, and particularly growth of income, are believed to have lasting effects on happiness. The prevailing theory might be termed "more is better." As a general matter economists prefer not to theorize about subjective states

This chapter is a revised version of: Easterlin, R. (2003). Explaining Happiness, in: Proceedings of the National Academy of Sciences 100(19), 11176–11183. I have benefitted especially from the work of psychologists Paul T. Costa, Ed Diener, Robert R. McCrae, David G. Myers, and the contributors to the path-breaking volume on well-being assembled by Daniel Kahneman, Ed Diener, and Norbert Schwarz. In economics I am indebted particularly to the research of Robert H. Frank, Andrew J. Oswald, Tibor Scitovsky, and Bernard M.S. van Praag. Without the invaluable data collections of James A. Davis, Tom W. Smith, and Ruut Veenhoven, the present research would not have been possible. This article is a shorter revised version of "Building a Better Theory of Well-being," in: Bruni, L., Porta, P.L. (Eds.). Economics & Happiness: Framing the Analysis, Oxford: Oxford University Press, and available as a discussion paper at www.iza.org. My thanks for comments to Luigino Bruni, Eileen M. Crimmins, Ronald D. Lee, and Linda J. Waite. I am grateful for the excellent assistance of Donna Hokoda Ebata, Pouyan Mashayekh-Ahangarani, and Paul Rivera. Financial support was provided by the University of Southern California.

of mind and to deal only with observed behavior. Their argument, termed "revealed preference," is that if an individual is observed to buy a certain combination of goods, say x_2, y_2, when an alternative combination, x_1, y_1, is affordable with that person's given income and the prevailing prices, then (based on certain axioms) the individual is deemed to prefer x_2, y_2 to x_1, y_1 and hence, to be better off (Samuleson 1947, Varian 1987). A major implication of this theory is that one can improve well-being by increasing one's own income, and that policy measures aimed at increasing the income of society as a whole lead to greater well-being. Economists recognize that happiness depends on a variety of circumstances besides material conditions, but they have long assumed that if income increases substantially, then overall well-being will move in the same direction (Pigou 1932, p. 3).

In what follows, I note survey evidence on happiness – some new, some touched on previously – inconsistent with these theories, and based on this analysis, I try to outline the directions a better theory would take. As in other chapters in this Part, the empirical work takes chiefly a life cycle approach, applying the demographers' technique of cohort analysis to survey data. I sometimes use three or five year averages in order to minimize the problem of small sample size that arises when one subdivides the total sample by characteristics such as age, gender, health, and marital or work status. The three-option happiness question is scaled from 3 = very happy to 1 = not too happy, to compute mean happiness for various population subgroups.

11.1. Is there a Setpoint of Happiness?

Let me start with the psychological theory. The critical issue here is not whether *any* adaptation to life events occurs, but whether adaptation is *complete*, that is, whether individuals return to their initial level of happiness, and, if so, how quickly. There are psychological studies that make clear that with respect to experiences such as loud noise and cosmetic surgery hedonic adaptation is typically less than complete, and that these experiences have a lasting effect on people's well-being (Frederick and Lowenstein 1999). The survey evidence presented below suggests, in addition, that individuals do not fully adapt to changes in either health or marital circumstances. Needless to say, I am speaking of average effects; there is considerable dispersion about the mean.

Health and happiness. The seminal article repeatedly cited in the psychology literature as demonstrating complete adaptation to adverse changes in health is a study by Brickman and Coates (1978) which reports that serious accident victims (paraplegics and quadriplegics), numbering 29, when compared with a group of controls, numbering 22, "did not appear nearly as unhappy as might have been expected" (p. 921). The sample size in this study is very small, but in any event, the study does *not* find that accident victims are as happy as controls. On the contrary, accident victims, compared with controls, "rated themselves significantly *less* happy" (p. 924, italics added). Setpoint (or "adaptation level") theory is saved in this study only by introducing a quite different comparison, one between accident victims and an unspecified "what might have been expected."

There have been a number of studies since, some supporting the notion of complete adaptation, others contradicting it. To my knowledge the most comprehensive investigation is, like the one above, a point-of-time study (Mehnert et al. 1990). It examines the life satisfaction (on a 5 point scale) of a *national* sample of 675 persons reporting disabling conditions and compares them with a *national* sample of over 1,000 nondisabled persons. This study finds that the life satisfaction of those with disabilities is, on average, significantly less than those who report no disabilities (ibid., p. 13). Moreover, persons with disabilities are classified in various ways – according to the severity of the disability, whether the respondent suffers from one or multiple conditions, to what extent the respondent is limited in daily activities, and whether close others are thought to perceive the respondent as disabled. On every one of these dimensions, happiness is less for those with more serious problems (ibid., pp. 10–12).

A question is sometimes raised as to which way the causal arrow runs – from health to life satisfaction or life satisfaction to health? If health is conceived unidimensionally, a plausible a priori argument can be made that life satisfaction affects health, as well as vice-versa. But when health is characterized multidimensionally, as in this study, the plausible inference is that greater health problems result systematically in less happiness.

These results suggest that, on average, an adverse change in health reduces life satisfaction, and the worse the change in health, the greater the reduction in life satisfaction. The results do not mean that no adaptation to disability occurs. The initial impact on happiness, say, of an accident or serious disease, is no doubt greater than its long-term impact. Adjustment to a disabling condition may be facilitated by health devices such as hearing aids, medications, or wheelchairs, and by a support network of friends and relatives. Moreover, the extent of adaptation may vary depending on the personality or other characteristics of the individual affected. But the evidence does suggest that even with adaptation, there is, on average, a lasting negative effect on happiness of an adverse change in health.

Let me turn from health at a point in time to some life cycle evidence. There is no question that among adults real health problems increase as people age. But what do persons say about their health? If adaptation were complete to adverse changes in health, then the life course trend in self-reported health should be flat. It would also be flat if persons implicitly evaluate their health only by comparison with others of their age. Is it true that self-reported health doesn't change?

The answer is no, self-reported health declines throughout the life course. Since 1972, the GSS has asked the following question: "Would you say your own health, in general, is excellent, good, fair, or poor?" (National Opinion Research Center 1999, p. 172). If one follows successively older ten-year birth cohorts for 28-year segments of the life span, one finds for each cohort a clear (and statistically significant) downtrend in mean self-reported health (Figure 11.1). (The mean health rating is obtained by scaling the responses from excellent = 4 down to poor = 1.) In the two oldest cohorts – those in their sixties and seventies – the apparent leveling off of self-reported health is due to the truncation of the sample caused by mortality; those reporting poorer health do, in fact, die more rapidly (Idler and Benyami 1997; Smith, Taylor and Sloan 2001). The conclusion suggested by the data on self-reported health is the same as that for the preceding data on disability. There is not complete hedonic adaptation to adverse changes in health.

This life course analysis, of course, assesses adaptation in terms of self-reported health, not well-being, as in the disability analysis. Perhaps health might get worse, but people do not feel unhappy about it. Throughout the life cycle, however, those who report they are less healthy also say they are less happy. In cohorts spanning ages from the twenties through the seventies happiness is systematically less, on average, the poorer the state of self-reported health (Table 11.1). This is consistent with the results above on how life satisfaction is related to various disabling conditions and with numerous multivariate studies that find significant positive associations between happiness and self-reported health (Argyle 1999; Blanchflower and Oswald 2004; Frey and Stutzer 2002a,b; Michalos, Zumbo and Hubley 2000). These studies, which, among other things, control for income, make clear that the negative impact of poorer health on happiness is due to nonpecuniary effects as well as loss of income due to poor health. The conclusion to which all of these findings consistently lead is that adverse health changes have a lasting and negative effect on happiness, and that there is less than complete adaptation to deteriorating health.

Figure 11.1

Mean Self-Reported Health, Cohorts of 1911–20 to 1951–60, by Age
Five Year Average Centered at Each Age

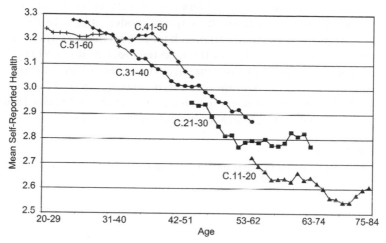

Source: Davis and Smith 2002.

Table 11.1

Mean Happiness by Self-Reported Health Status,
Birth Cohorts over Indicated Age Spans, 1972–2000

(1)	(2)	(3)	(4)	(5)	(6)
			Mean happiness		
Birth cohort	Age span	Excell. health	Good health	Fair health	Poor health
1951-60	23 to 45	2.36	2.12	1.85	1.63
1941-50	27 to 55	2.37	2.17	1.92	1.74
1931-40	37 to 65	2.43	2.23	1.98	1.74
1921-30	47 to 75	2.48	2.24	2.06	1.83
1911-20	57 to 85	2.52	2.27	2.12	1.96

Source: Davis and Smith 2002.

Marital status and happiness. Despite claims by setpoint theory proponents that life circumstances have virtually no lasting effect on
well-being, little evidence on marital formation or dissolution has
been advanced supporting setpoint theory. There is, however, one
important recent study, using German longitudinal data, that examines the effects on well-being of marriage and widowhood (Lucas et
al. 2003). Although presented as a critique of the setpoint model, it is
actually supportive, especially as regards marriage, for it concludes:
"[O]n average, people adapt quickly and completely to marriage, and
they adapt more slowly to widowhood (though even in this case, adaptation is close to complete after about 8 years)" (ibid., p. 538).

Study of the life cycle experience of cohorts, however, suggests a
substantial departure from the setpoint model. At ages 18-19 when
most women and virtually all men have not yet married, their mean
happiness is around 2.1; over the next ten years, as up to 50 percent
or more of a cohort becomes married, those who are married report
significantly higher happiness levels, on average, around 2.2 to 2.3,
while those who have never married remain at about 2.1. (See Figure
11.2 for females; the pattern for males is quite similar.)

Figure 11.2
Mean Happiness of Females by Marital Status, Birth Cohort of 1953–72
from Ages 18–19 to 28–29

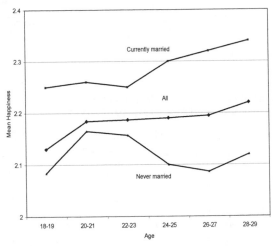

Source: Davis and Smith 2002.

Figure 11.3

Mean Happiness of Currently Married and Unmarried Females in Specified Birth Cohort, by Age. Five-Year Average Centered at Each Age

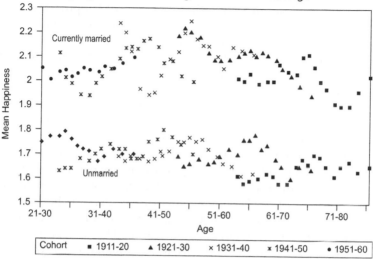

Source: Davis and Smith 2002.

These results cannot be due to selection effects. Persons who marry in the first decade of the adult life cycle could not have been happier than others, on average, before they got married. If this were true, then as these persons married and left the never-married group, the average happiness of the remaining never-married would fall. In fact, the happiness of those never-married remains constant as more and more persons marry and exit the group (Figure 11.2). As a result, the mean happiness of the cohort as a whole increases as the proportion married increases; note in Figure 11.2 that the curve for all persons starts close to 2.1 and ends above 2.2.

Beyond age 30 the proportion of a cohort currently married tends to level off and then decline as the effect of marital dissolution due to divorce, separation, and widowhood gradually outweighs that due to the formation of unions through marriage and remarriage. Throughout the adult life cycle, however, the gap in average happiness persists between those who are currently married and those who are not. (See Figure 11.3 for females; the pattern for males is similar.)

Remarriage has the same positive effect on happiness as a first marriage. When the cohort data for married persons in Figure 11.3 are divided between those who are still in their first marriage and those who are remarried, there is no significant difference in happiness between the two groups. If respondents are asked specifically about their marital satisfaction, rather than overall happiness, it is again true that those who are remarried are, on average, as satisfied with their marriage as those still in their first marriage.

Comparisons across cohorts suggest that happiness does not decline with duration of marriage. For those still in their first marriage the average length of marriage ranges from around 10 years or less in the cohort of 1951–60 to over 35 years in the cohort of 1921–30. The mean level of both overall happiness and marital happiness for these two cohorts is virtually the same despite their much different marriage durations, and is significantly greater than that of unmarried persons in their cohorts.

None of these life cycle marriage patterns squares easily with the notion that married persons are reverting "quickly and completely" to their average level of happiness prior to marriage. As a cohort enters into marriage, the happiness of married persons is significantly greater than the unmarried and, if anything, increasing. Throughout the life cycle the happiness of married persons, whether remarried or continuously married, remains significantly higher than others. Moreover, even after 35 years of marriage, the happiness of those still in their first marriage remains significantly greater than that of their unmarried counterparts.

Just as marriage affects happiness positively, the dissolution of marriage has a negative impact. As has been seen, the mean happiness of women not currently married is significantly below that of their married counterparts. Within the unmarried group, however, those with broken marriages, that is, the divorced, separated, or widowed, are significantly less happy than those who never married (Table 11.2). One might speculate that personality has sorted out those who are divorced or separated, but there is no significant happiness difference between them and those who are widowed. The widowed are unlikely to have been selected on the basis of personality, and the fact that their mean happiness and that of the divorced or separated group is virtually the same suggests that one is observing here the effect of marital dissolution on happiness, not the selective effect of personality differences.

Results supporting these findings from cohort analysis can be found in a panel study by sociologists that follows a group of 5,000 married Americans over a five-year period (Waite et al. 2002). At the end of the period there is no significant change in the happiness of those who remained married. The happiness of persons who remarried after becoming divorced is not significantly different from those who stayed married. In contrast, mean happiness among those who separated or divorced and did not remarry, is significantly less than that of the married.

Table 11.2

Mean Happiness of Unmarried Women by
Marital Status, Specified Birth Cohort, 1972–2000

(1)	(2)	(3)	(4)
	Mean happiness		
Birth cohort	Widowed	Divorced or separated	Never married
1951-60	1.98	1.96	2.07
1941-50	1.95	2.01	2.05
1931-40	2.00	1.97	2.11
1921-30	1.97	2.00	2.15

Source: Davis and Smith 2002.

These life cycle results on marital status and happiness from both cohort analysis and panel data are consistent with cross-sectional regression analyses of the marriage–happiness relationship in which controls are introduced for a variety of socio-economic circumstances (Argyle 1999; Blanchflower and Oswald 2004; Frey and Stutzer 2002a,b), and with other studies that focus on specific marital conditions such as divorce or widowhood (Johnson and Wu 2002; Wortman, Silver and Kessler 1993). The study of German data cited at the beginning of this section that concludes that people adapt to marriage "quickly and completely" is at variance with this sizeable body of evidence (Lucas et al. 2003). The results of the German study arise from the peculiar treatment of the age variable in that analysis. Age is assumed not to change over time, an assumption that eliminates the effect on happiness of circumstances that are age-related other than one's partnership status. When age is allowed to vary with time, as it necessarily does, the conclusion of complete adaptation no longer holds and the usual effects of marital status prevail (Zimmermann and Easterlin 2006).

In sum, the bulk of evidence suggests that the formation of unions has a lasting positive effect on happiness, while dissolution has a permanently negative effect. This does not mean that no adaptation occurs after unions are formed or dissolved, but the adaptation that occurs is less than complete. If the setpoint model of happiness is correct, it is hard to see how one can reconcile it with the survey evidence on marriage, as well as health.

Note should be made of other evidence on happiness that is difficult to square with the setpoint model. Throughout the life cycle blacks are consistently less happy than whites (Easterlin 2001b). It seems doubtful that this difference by race is a result simply of different average setpoints resulting from genetic and personality differences. Also, at older ages, the life cycle excess of female over male happiness is reversed; it is hard to explain this without reference to differences by gender in the incidence at older age of life events, especially widowhood (Chapter 8).

11.2. Is More Better?

To turn to economic theory, a basic problem with the revealed preference approach is that the judgment on a person's happiness is made, not by the individual concerned, but by an outsider who is observing the person's consumption choices (Hollander 2001). If one takes the view that the only one who can make authoritative judgments on a person's feelings of well-being is the person concerned, then one is led to look at self-reports on well-being.

Does the survey evidence support the view that income and happiness go together? As seen previously, the answer depends on whether one looks at cross-sectional or time series data. Support for the hypothesis of a positive association comes from point-of-time regressions, which invariably find a significant positive association between income and happiness, with or without controls for other factors (Argyle 1999; Blanchflower and Oswald 2004; Frey and Stutzer 2002a,b; Graham and Pettinato 2002). Over the life cycle, however, as income increases and then levels off, happiness remains largely unchanged, contradicting the inference that income and well-being go together (Chapters 6, 7).

If one uses education as a proxy for income, then the life cycle data reveal both of these relationships. At any given age those with more education are happier than those with less (Chapter 6). What is even more noteworthy, however, is the life cycle trend in happiness for the more and less educated. If happiness were moving in accordance with the income of each group, then the happiness of both groups would increase, with that of the better educated increasing more, and the happiness differential by educational status widening. In fact, there is no significant trend in happiness for either educational group, or in the happiness differential (see Figure 11.4). Although those fortunate enough to start out with higher income and education remain, on average, happier throughout the life cycle than those of lower socio-economic status, there is no evidence for either group that happiness increases with income.

Figure 11.4

Mean Happiness, Cohort of 1941–50 by Level of Education and Age, Three Year Average Centered at Each Age

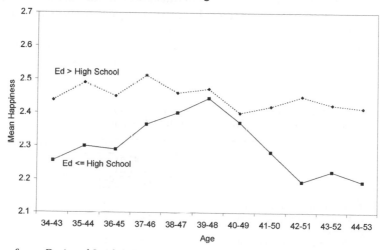

Source: Davis and Smith 2002.

These life cycle patterns clearly contradict the expectation based on economic theory that happiness increases with income. They do, however, support the setpoint model; indeed, findings like these have been cited by psychologists in support of hedonic adaptation. But while there may be fairly complete hedonic adaptation with regard to income, this does not mean that there is as much adaptation with regard to all sources of happiness. As has been seen, the evidence on health and marriage suggests that adaptation in these areas is less than complete, and that changes in these circumstances have a lasting effect on well-being.

11.3. Aspirations and Adaptation

Why should the extent of adaptation differ with regard to the life domain under study? The answer, I suggest, is that people's aspirations in each domain respond differently to changes in their circumstances. Complete adaptation implies that aspirations change to the same extent as one's actual circumstances. This seems to be largely what happens when income changes. Material aspirations increase commensurately with income, and, as a result, one gets no nearer to or farther away from the attainment of one's material goals, and well-being is unchanged. Less than complete adaptation means that aspirations change less than the actual change in one's circumstances. If one's actual circumstances change for the better (a happy marriage), there is greater goal-fulfillment and well-being increases; if for the worse (divorce), there is a greater shortfall from one's goals, and well-being declines. This seems to be what happens in the marriage and health domains.

Table 11.3

Ownership of and Desires for Ten Big-Ticket Consumer Goods Over Three 16-Year Segments of the Adult Life Cycle[a]

	(1)	(2)	(3)
	Stage of life cycle segment		Change over life cycle segment
	Start	End	
A. Early life cycle			
1. Mean number of goods owned	1.7	3.1	1.4
2. Mean number of goods desired	4.4	5.6	1.2
B. Mid life cycle			
1. Mean number of goods owned	2.5	3.2	0.7
2. Mean number of goods desired	4.3	5.4	1.1
C. Late life cycle			
1. Mean number of goods owned	3.0	3.2	0.2
2. Mean number of goods desired	4.4	5.0	0.6
D. Average for all three segments			
1. Change in mean number of goods owned	–	–	0.8
2. Change in mean number of goods desired	–	–	1.0

Note:
[a] Early life cycle is from ages 18–29 in 1978 to 30–44 in 1994. Mid life cycle is from ages 30–44 in 1978 to 45–59 in 1994. Late life cycle is from ages 45–59 in 1978 to 60 and over in 1994.
Source: Roper Starch Organization 1979, 1995.

Is there evidence that the response of aspirations to actual circumstances varies by domain? For the economic and family domains, the answer is yes. Let me start with the ten big-ticket consumer goods that are included on the "good life" list (Chapter 9). Over each stage of the life cycle people typically acquire more of these big-ticket items (Table 11.3, lines A-1, B-1, C-1). But their aspirations for these goods – what they view as part of the good life – also rise (lines A-2, B-2, C-2). Moreover, the increase in the number of goods desired is, on average, roughly equal in magnitude to that in the average number owned (panel D, column 3).

What is happening is that as people acquire those goods for which aspirations were fairly high to start with (a home, a car, a TV) their aspirations increase for goods which were initially much less likely to be viewed as part of the good life. In each segment of the life cycle, travel abroad, a swimming pool, and a vacation home are increasingly named as part of the good life, reaching values of around 40 percent or more of respondents. The proportion that ever actually has any of these items, however, is typically less than 10 percent. This suggests that new material aspirations arise as previous ones are satisfied, and, to judge from the mean number of goods desired, to about the same extent.

This inference of complete adaptation in the economic domain is further supported if we divide the cohort by level of education as in Chapter 6. In each segment of the life cycle the increase in the number of goods owned is greater for those with more education, as one would expect based on their greater income growth, but the increase in number of goods desired is also greater for those with more education. Moreover, for both educational groups, the increase in desires is of the same order of magnitude as the increase in the number of goods owned. Thus, material aspirations are increasing commensurately with material possessions, and the greater the increase in possessions, the greater the increase in desires. It is this differential change in aspirations corresponding to the differential change in income that explains the constancy of happiness over the life cycle for each educational group. The point-of-time happiness differential is also explained by aspirations. At the start of the adult life cycle, material aspirations differ very little between the two education groups; the better-educated, and hence higher income group, comes closer to fulfilling its aspirations, and is happier. Subsequently, aspirations rise more for the better-educated, but at any point in time the dispersion in aspirations relative to that in income continues to be the same, and the happiness differential by education persists.

The responses cited so far are for specific goods. Is there evidence suggesting that income aspirations in general rise in proportion to income? The answer is yes. Consider the answers from a different survey that asks people how much income is needed by a family of four to get along. Over a 36-year period "get along" income increases, on average, to the same degree as actual income (Rainwater 1994).

To turn to the family domain, the desire for a happy marriage is a common one. At every point in the life cycle, three-quarters or more of respondents say that a happy marriage is part of the good life. The proportion that actually has a happy marriage, however, is considerably less, averaging a little over one-half.

If adaptation were complete, then one would expect that persons who are not in a happy marriage would eventually give up their desires for such a marriage. In fact, aspirations for a happy marriage persist among more than half of those respondents who do not actually have one (Table 11.4, column 1). Among never-married persons ages 45 and over, that is, persons who have been single their entire lives, more than four in ten cite a happy marriage as part of the good life as far as they personally are concerned (column 3). Among widows and divorcees 45 years and older, for whom the prospect of remarriage is low, more than half continue to aspire to a happy marriage (column 3). Thus, for around half of unmarried persons who have little prospect of marrying, aspirations have not adjusted to their actual marital circumstances. In contrast to the economic domain, hedonic adaptation seems to be occurring only to a limited extent with regard to marriage circumstances. The substantial persistence of the desire for a happy marriage among those widowed, divorced, and never-married explains, I believe, why these groups are less happy, on average, than married persons, among whom aspirations for a happy marriage are more nearly fulfilled.

Table 11.4

Percent Wanting a Happy Marriage among Persons
Who Do Not Have One, by Marital Status and Age, 1994

Marital status	(1)	(2)	(3)
	Percent wanting happy marriage		
	All ages	Ages 18-44	Ages 45 and over
Married, not in happy marriage	56	8	55
Divorced or separated	63	73	55
Widowed	62	*	62
Never-married	65	68	43

Note: * Sample size less than 20.
Source: Roper Starch Organization 1979, 1995.

In addition to marriage aspirations, the "good life" survey elicits information on aspirations regarding number and "quality" of children, quality being indicated by desires for a college education for one's children. While income growth over the life cycle is accompanied by persistent growth in aspirations for big-ticket consumer goods, income growth is not associated with growth in desires for either the number or quality of children.

I have no cohort data on health aspirations. In 2003, however, "good health" was added to the list of "good life" items. Across the age range the percentage viewing "good health" as part of the good life was much the same – over 80 percent. As seen in Figure 11.1, self-reported health is invariably lower at older than younger ages, so the similarity across the ages in desires for good health implies very little downward adaptation of health aspirations as health deteriorates (cf. Plagnol forthcoming). I think there is evidence of less than complete adaptation to other life circumstances as well, such as friendship and loss of a job (Clark and Oswald 1994; Gallie and Russell 1998; Myers 1999; Oswald 1997; Winkelmann and Winkelmann 1998).

11.4. Explaining Happiness

We can now begin to see the outlines of a better theory of how life events affect happiness. Let us start with the economist's notion that the typical individual has a utility or happiness function such that well-being depends on a variety of pecuniary and nonpecuniary conditions, or domains. The typical person is taken to have certain goals or aspirations and a current state of attainment in each domain. The overall happiness of the individual depends on the shortfall between aspirations and attainments in each domain, and the relative importance of each domain in the individual's utility function.

Economic theory typically assumes that well-being depends only on attainments. However, as previously noted there are two strands of theory – habit formation and interdependent preferences – that recognize the effect on well-being of aspirations. Habit formation stresses that the utility one derives from a given set of goods is affected by comparisons with one's past experience. Interdependent preferences points out that the utility created by one's having a given amount of a good depends partly on the amount of that good that others have. The counterpart in psychology of the economists' concept of habit formation is hedonic adaptation, and of interdependent preferences, social comparison. I use the psychologists' terms in what follows, because these are more common in the literature on subjective well-being.

The central point of the present theory of happiness is that neither hedonic adaptation nor social comparison operate equally across all domains or constituents of domains. Hedonic adaptation, as we have seen, is less complete with regard to family circumstances and health than in the material goods domain. I suggest that social comparison is also less in family life and health than in the material goods domain, because family life and health are less accessible to public scrutiny than material possessions.

Moreover, hedonic adaptation and social comparison may not operate equally with regard to all constituents of a given domain. With regard to the material goods domain, Scitovsky (1976) has argued that cultural goods, such as music, literature, and art, are less subject to hedonic adaptation than "comfort" goods, like homes and cars. Similarly, the distinction drawn between positional and nonpositional goods by Frank (1985b), Hirsch (1976), and Ng (1978) is an example of a classification of goods based on whether or not their utility is affected by social comparison.

Each individual has only a given amount of time to allocate among different domains and their constituents. Clearly, the happiness of an individual can be maximized by allocating his or her time to those domains and constituents of domains in which hedonic adaptation and social comparison are less important.

Do individuals achieve the optimal allocation of time among domains and the constituents thereof? My answer is no; people allocate a disproportionate amount of time to the pursuit of pecuniary rather than nonpecuniary objectives, as well as to "comfort" and positional goods, and shortchange goals that will have a more lasting effect on well-being (cf. also Frank 1997). This misallocation occurs because in making decisions about how to use their time, individuals take their aspirations as fixed at their present levels, and fail to recognize that aspirations may change because of hedonic adaptation and social comparison (Chapter 6). In particular, people make decisions assuming that more income, comfort, and positional goods will make them happier, failing to recognize that hedonic adaptation and social comparison will come into play, raise their aspirations to about the same extent as their actual gains, and leave them feeling no happier than before. As a result, most individuals spend a disproportionate amount of their lives working in order to make money, and sacrifice family life and health, domains in which aspirations remain more nearly constant as actual circumstances change, and where the attainment of one's goals has a more lasting impact on happiness. Hence, a reallocation of time in favor of family life and health would, on average, increase individual happiness.

One may ask if social learning occurs – don't people eventually realize how their material aspirations escalate with economic achievement, and become aware of the self-defeating nature of the pursuit of pecuniary goals? The answer is no, because the change in material aspirations itself works against social learning. As seen in Chapter 6, when asked how happy they were five years ago, people, on average, systematically understate their well-being at that time, because they evaluate their past situation in terms, not of the lower material aspirations they actually had at that time, but on the basis of the new higher level of aspirations they have now acquired. As a result, they tend to think they are better off than they were in the past, rather than realizing that there has been no net improvement.

I have been focusing on the effect on happiness of life circumstances, because these are conditions through which happiness may be especially increased by both individual and social action. Life circumstances other than those discussed here, such as friendships, work, and employment status, affect happiness too, but income, family, and health conditions are typically cited most often by people as sources of happiness. Personality and genetic factors also affect happiness, of course. The interplay between life events and personality in shaping happiness at the individual level is an important subject for research (cf. McCrae and Costa 1990, Chapter 9). So too are the psychological, social, biological, and evolutionary mechanisms underlying the relationships reported here, including the question of why the adjustment of aspirations to actual circumstances differs by domain (cf. Frederick and Loewenstein 1999, p. 314).

Economic policy proposals to improve well-being are typically directed towards altering the socio-economic environment, but not to changing individual preferences. Viewed in terms of the present analysis policies to improve health or facilitate more time with one's family are consistent with greater happiness (cf. Chapter 7). But the present analysis implies that preferences too are an appropriate policy concern. The reason preferences are excluded from policy consideration by mainstream economics is because each individual is assumed to be the best judge of his or her own interests. But if individuals are making decisions in ignorance of the effect that hedonic adaptation and social comparison will have on their aspirations, this assumption no longer holds. Once it is recognized that individuals are unaware of some of the forces shaping their choices, it can no longer be argued that they will successfully maximize their well-being. It is, perhaps, time to recognize that serious attention is needed to devising measures that may contribute to more informed preferences (cf. Scitovsky 1976; Layard 1980).

IV

Epilogue

Happiness is undermined by a bias common to both individual and governmental decision-making, namely to favor income gains and to downplay or disregard other more enduring sources of happiness, such as family, work, and health.

In the public policy arena, an example of this income bias is the 2008 World Bank report of a commission of economic experts, including Nobel Laureates, that hails as "success stories" the exceptional growth rates of GDP per capita achieved in recent decades by countries such as China and South Korea (Commission on Growth and Development 2008, pp. 19–20). Apparently, the higher the growth rate, the better. The evidence presented in Chapters 3 and 5 above, however, gives no indication that higher economic growth is accompanied by a significantly greater advance in subjective well-being. Judgments on desirable growth rates might benefit, one suspects, if serious consideration were given to the impact of economic growth on human lives in domains other than income and material goods.

The bias toward income is evidenced too in the recent flurry of studies acclaiming the benefits of urbanization (see especially the Annual Development Report of the World Bank 2009; also Huang and Bocchi 2009; National Research Council 2003; Spence, Annez and Buckley 2009; UN-Habitat 2004). These benefits are first and foremost income gains, as workers shift from lower-paying rural work to higher-paying urban jobs. Potentially negative effects of urbanization are largely or wholly disregarded. Thus the World Development Report explicitly sets aside social and environmental effects of urbanization under the head "What this Report is not about" (World Bank 2009, p. 34). Despite this unbalanced weighing of costs and benefits, this study concludes with three chapters of detailed policy proposals to promote urbanization in developing countries.

248

In individual decision-making, a vivid illustration of the downplaying of family life is the answers to the following survey question: "Imagine you are 38 years old and are offered a new job in a field you like. The job is more prestigious than your present job. It will also require more work hours and take you far away from your family more often. What is the likelihood you would take the job?"

This query was put to a national sample of 400 adult Americans in 1989 (Glenn 1996, pp. 26–28). There were four response options: the first three – very likely, somewhat likely, somewhat unlikely – each accounted for about one-third of the respondents. The fourth – very unlikely – was chosen by not one person!

The same question was asked of two other equally-sized samples with the added reward of a pay increase (15 percent in once case, 35 percent in the other). In each case, the distribution of answers was much like that in the first sample. The lack of a positive response to the addition of monetary rewards, however, was probably because, in response to a closely preceding question, 85 percent of the sample had agreed that most people today put a higher value on material things than on family. If respondents had not already committed to an anti-materialist view, it is likely that pay increases would have slanted the sample even more in favor of job over family.

The appeal of such survey questions is that they directly elicit respondents' feelings about the allocation of time among different domains, making clear the costs of the choice (more work hours, less family time) versus gains (prestige, perhaps more pay). The answers demonstrate the ease with which family life is sacrificed – this, in a sample in which about half of the respondents acknowledged that they did not currently spend enough time with their families and, as in most national samples, rated "having a happy marriage" as their most important life goal.

The importance for well-being of domains other than income is strikingly evident in the experience of the countries of central and eastern Europe transitioning from socialism to a free market economy (Chapter 4). Both the amount and availability of goods increased dramatically; yet happiness was unchanged. Why? Because higher income was purchased at the cost of job security, family disruption, and diminished child and health care (Table 4.3).

The importance of family life for personal happiness is also demonstrated here by the crossover midway in the adult life cycle in the relative happiness of women and men (Chapters 8 and 9).

This crossover is due to a corresponding shift in the family status of women relative to men. At younger adult ages women are more likely to be in unions and are happier; at older ages men are more likely to be in unions and are happier.

I am not a policy expert, but the general lesson of happiness research such as that presented here – for individuals and government alike – is clear. For happiness, family life is important; job security is important; health is important. In contrast, the happiness gains from more income and material goods – typically accorded top priority in decision-making – may prove to be illusory, because material aspirations rise along with income, and offset the positive effect on happiness of increased income.

How does one get this message across? My suggestion, like that of several other happiness scholars (Layard 1980, 2005; Scitovsky 1976, 1996), is through the development of more informed preferences via education and information. School curricula these days typically incorporate instruction relating to physical health. Why not give attention too to matters affecting psychological health? Some of the most important decisions bearing ultimately on happiness must be made in the early adult years. What kind of job should I take? Should I get married? Young people are woefully unprepared to make such decisions. School curricula that included thoughtful discussion of life goals and the findings of happiness research such as those on aspirations might prepare people to make decisions more in keeping with their desire for greater happiness. We do not have to start with major curriculum changes; a cautious, exploratory approach would seem appropriate.

This is a course of action that should, in time, find reasonably broad support, because the emphasis is on providing more information to individuals, who are free to act as they desire on the basis of better informed preferences – to make "considered judgments", as Sugden (2008, p. 320) would say. This is not to rule out direct governmental policies to improve happiness, such as health programs (Chapter 7). There are already several good scholarly books based on the happiness literature specifically devoted to such proposals (Bok 2010; Diener, Helliwell and Kahneman 2009; Frey 2008; Halpern 2010).

In touching on policy, I have taken the view that happiness is a goal sought by most individuals, and scientific happiness research can contribute to the better attainment of that goal. I am not arguing that happiness *should* be what people want, or that it is the only goal worth pursuing. I am troubled myself by the small part played in individual happiness by civil and political liberties, which in my judgment are of fundamental importance to the "good society". I do believe, however, that happiness is a better goal than income, which is so often given operative priority in individual and governmental decisions.

Notes

Introduction by the Editors

1 See http://worlddatabaseofhappiness.eur.nl
2 See Stiglitz, Sen, Fitoussi et al. (2009) and www.stiglitz-sen-fitoussi.fr for details on this influential expert commission. Chaired by Economics Nobel laureate Joseph E. Stiglitz, the commission engages in a broad range of topical discussions. 2006 IZA Prize Laureate Alan B. Krueger coordinates the commission's working group on "Quality of Life." The first report of the commission is available online at www.stiglitz-sen-fitoussi.fr/documents/rapport_anglais.pdf and provides many insights on the political implementation of the economics of happiness.
3 Stiglitz, Sen, Fitoussi et al. (2009), p. 12.
4 Easterlin (2004), p. 20.

Chapter 1

1 A differing conclusion, perhaps more representative of the economics profession at large, is reached by Nordhaus and Tobin (1972): "Is growth obsolete? We think not. Although GNP and other national income aggregates are imperfect measures of welfare, the broad picture of secular progress which they convey remains after correction of their most obvious deficiencies" (p. 24).
2 Abramovitz (1959), pp. 21–22.
3 It is used, for example, in welfare economics by Mishan (1968): "If, for instance, welfare is used as a synonym for happiness ..." (p. 504). Similarly, Little (1950) comments: "And, according to our present definition of 'welfare' (='happiness') ..." (p. 30). In a recent economics text, Eckaus (1972) writes: "What is the economic system supposed to do? The answer that it should contribute to human happiness is as good a start as any" (p. 7).
4 Cf. Edwards (1957). Recent work by Block (1965) and Rorer (1965) suggests that the importance of this factor in biasing survey results has been exaggerated.
5 This statement is based on a comparison of the 1963 AIPO data, shown here in part in Table 1.10, with the NORC data (from a somewhat more restricted population) in the work of Bradburn (1969, p. 45). I am grateful to William H. Kruskal for suggesting this comparison.
6 In interpreting the association between mental health and socioeconomic status, Davis (1965, pp. 74–77) leans in this direction also. The point that for some countries some of the status designations are essentially hereditary also indicates that we are dealing here in substantial part with "permanent income" differences, and that the results cannot be dismissed on the grounds that they are dominated by transitory influences.

7 Actually Cantril (1965, pp. 193–194) uses a somewhat different measure of socioeconomic development, of which the GNP data shown here are one component.

8 The comparability of the Cuban data is further qualified by the fact that the survey was confined to the urban population. For Egypt, the coverage of the rural population was quite limited, and the survey is labeled by Cantril (1965, pp. 346–347) as a "preliminary pilot investigation".

9 The Gallup article on the 1970 survey reported that there was an upward trend over the last quarter century, apparently because a comparison was made only between the first and last surveys shown in Table 1.8.

10 As quoted by Lipset (1960, p. 63). I am grateful to Leonard Berkowitz for bringing this to my attention.

11 My colleagues, Stefano Fenoaltea and John C. Lambelet, have contributed importantly to the development of the argument in this section.

12 The present view of taste formation, while not precluding the mechanism stressed by Galbraith, is different and broader. This is shown clearly by the height analogy, where the norm is seen to change as a function simply of the social experience of individuals, without any overt attempt at manipulation by persons or organizations in the society.

13 In a five-country study of attitudes toward ways of life, Morris found much greater differences among countries than among economic classes within countries. The study, however, was confined to college students, and economic status referred to the income group of parents (Morris 1956, Chapter 4).

14 An exception is Hagen's work (1962), based on McClelland's n-achievement motive (McClelland 1961). It should be noted that achievement motivation, which relates to goal-striving, differs from level of aspiration, the concern here, which refers to goal-setting.

15 As quoted by Ekirch (1944, p. 120). I am grateful to Joseph S. Davis for bringing this to my attention.

Chapter 2

1 Similar theoretical reasoning is found in studies of relative deprivation and reference groups (cf. Hyman 1968).

2 The habit formation model accords closely with Helson's (1964) adaptation level theory in psychology of how judgments are formed. Put succinctly: "The most general principle of adaptation level theory is that people's judgments of current levels of stimulation depend on whether this stimulation exceeds or falls short of the level of stimulation to which their previous history has accustomed them" (Brickman and Coates 1978, p. 918). A number of ingenious experimental studies in social psychology have provided empirical support for this proposition (Brickman and Campbell 1971; Diener 1984).

3 See Cantril (1965); the "aspiration-adjustment model" in Inglehart and Rabier (1986), and Inkeles (1993, p. 10).

4 An interesting study by Morawetz (1977) of two Israeli settlements concludes that the distribution of income may influence self-rated happiness. However, this does not appear to be true of the seventeen countries in Figure 2.4 for which income distribution data are available (World Bank 1990). Happiness and income distribution are not significantly related in either a bivariate regression or a multivariate regression with GNP per capita.

5 Some evidence from international comparisons suggests that cultural influences may also operate in a way observed in United States data. An analysis of survey responses for blacks and whites in the United States indicates that blacks have a tendency to choose more extreme response categories (Bachman and O'Malley 1984). This is not a matter of blacks being consistently more positive or more

negative, but simply of their preferring a more extreme response (or alternatively, of whites preferring a less extreme one). A possible illustration of this response pattern appears in Inkeles 1993, p. 11. On each of six indicators of positive subjective circumstances ("generally very happy," "very satisfied with standard of living," etc.), Brazil is highest or close to highest of the eight geographic areas compared. On four indicators relating to negative circumstances ("worry a lot," "not able to meet expenses,") Brazil is the worst on every one. How could Brazilians be so happy, and at the same time, so anxious and financially insecure? The answer may be that when asked about their feelings, Brazilians tend to put things in more extreme fashion than those in the other areas studied.

Chapter 3

1   Analysts sometimes try to infer time series change by comparing the responses to "ladder-of-life" questions of the type asked in the recent Gallup World Poll to Hadley Cantril's (1965) results. To assume the recent responses are comparable to Cantril's is questionable. Before presenting respondents with the ladder-of-life question, Cantril's interviewers conducted a lengthy in-depth interview probing the respondents' concerns about the best and worst of all possible worlds (see Chapter 1 and Cantril 1965, pp. 22–24). The recent ladder-of-life questions have no counterpart to this lengthy preamble.

2   Special thanks go to Professor Valerie Møller of Rhodes University, Grahamstown, South Africa for providing tabulations of these data (that are not in the public domain) and valuable help regarding the comparability over time of the survey questions. Professor Møller has published extensively on quality of life in South Africa (see, e.g. Møller 1998, 2001, 2007).

3   The Kusago series is used here in Appendix B as a check on the "Life in Nation" series.

4   In the Latinobarometer the questions preceding the family economic situation question in 2005 and 2006 were:
2005. In the following twelve months, do you think that, in general, the economic situation of the country will be much better, a little better, the same, a little worse, or much worse than now?
2006. Do you think you have a job much better, a little better, the same as, a little worse, or much worse than your father did?
The response categories are identical for the two questions, so we computed for each country the mean response to each of the questions on a scale from 5 (much better) to 1 (much worse). We hypothesize that the shift to the 2006 question invoking a comparison of one's personal economic situation (one's job) with one's father's situation would put the respondent in a more favorable context to respond to the next question on one's current family economic situation than the 2005 question about the country's general economic outlook. The evidence confirms this. In every one of 17 Latinobarometer countries the 2006 question requiring comparison with one's father elicited a mean response much higher than the 2005 question on the country's economic outlook, the answer averaging 0.9 points higher on the 1–5 scale. Moreover, the more favorable context invoked by the 2006 comparison with one's father resulted in more favorable responses to the subsequent question on one's family's economic situation. In 14 of the 17 countries there was an increase from 2005 to 2006 in the assessment of one's own economic situation, the average increment being about 0.1 points on a 1–5 scale. If one compares the 17 countries, one finds that the magnitude of the 2005–2006 increase in one's family's economic situation was significantly positively correlated with the magnitude of the 2005–2006 increase between the immediately preceding questions. We are grateful to Malgorzata Switek for carrying out this analysis.

Chapter 4

1　The parallel to the Great Depression has not escaped the notice of transition analysts, most notably Branko Milanovic (1997).

2　In transition countries, however, the effect of the shift to democracy is not significant, ibid., p. 514.

3　Cf. Haisken-DeNew and Frick (2005). The German data were made available by the German Socio-Economic Panel Study of the German Institute for Economic Research (DIW Berlin).

4　GDP data here are from Economic Commission for Europe (2003), except those for 1986–1988, which are from Philipov and Dorbritz (2003).

5　The value for 1990 is based chiefly on the urban population; however, the 1995 data reveal no significant difference between the urban and rural population's life satisfaction. The series is given in Inglehart et al. (2008, p. 283).

6　For those who find it hard to believe that life satisfaction did not improve in a poor country like China experiencing such enormous improvement in real income, it is worth noting that China's neighbor, Japan, life satisfaction has not increased in the last half century, despite an over five-fold rise in GDP per capita from initially low levels (Chapter 3; Kusago 2007).

7　It is likely that some ethnic minorities are also among the losers, but this has not been explored here.

8　There are no controls for life circumstances because the impact of the transition operates via life circumstances. If, say, deteriorating employment conditions differentially affect those with more and less education, one wants to see the effect of this on the relative life satisfaction of the more and less educated, and a control for employment status would eliminate this effect.

9　The exception to the rise in life satisfaction inequality is the former GDR, where massive income transfers from West to East Germany buttressed especially the income of the poorer segments of the East German population. See Busch (1999); Headey, Andorka and Krause (1995); Schwarze (1996).

10　A good overview of economic coping strategies, with empirical evidence for Latvia is Gassmann and deNeubourg (2000, 2002); cf. also Górniak (2001). A forerunner of this type of analysis of coping strategies is Modigliani (1949), who argued that during the Great Depression households sought to maintain their habitual consumption in the face of falling income by reducing their savings rates.

11　Cf. Brown et al. (2005); Tammaru, Kulu and Kask (2004). On the rise of subsistence agriculture see Alber and Kohler (2008); Mickiewicz (2005), p. 86. In the WVS data, in 5 countries for which comparison is possible, between the beginning and end of the 1990s the population living in places with less than 2,000 population rises noticeably – by an average of 7 percentage points – a redistribution of population that contrasts markedly with increasing urbanization invariably observed during long term economic growth.

12　The paper also gives life satisfaction estimates for four other transition countries included here. The Eurobarometer survey data were chosen instead because ten countries are covered including these four and the ten countries share the same survey date. In October 2008, after the present article was completed, Wave 5 data for about 50 countries, including the five transition countries in Inglehart et al. (2008), were placed in the public domain (World Values Survey 2005 Official Data File V. 20081015, 2008).

13　For five countries the period spanned by the question is the same as that for the WVS happiness question; for the other countries the period covered by the question differs by one year from that to which the happiness question refers.

14　Some psychologists are, in fact, advocating the adoption by government policy makers of a variety of measures of subjective well-being (Diener and Seligman 2004), and there is some evidence of a movement in this direction in Europe (cf. Donovan and Halpern 2002).

Chapter 5

1   The time span analyzed here for Japan is 1958–1991. By the latter date Japan had risen to 80 percent of the 2000 U.S. value. We omit the ensuing period of economic stagnation in Japan.

2   The following surveys were biased due to the financial satisfaction question: October–November 1985, 1986, 1987, and 1990. We also deleted the survey conducted in November–December 2004 due to a different question format.

3   In re-doing the Stevenson and Wolfers' analysis we have converted both variables to a per year basis, because the interval between two given waves sometimes differs among countries. The effect on the results is negligible.

Chapter 6

1   Household income in Figure 6.1 has been converted to a per capita basis to give a better idea of the change in material living level over the life cycle; for a more refined adjustment see Easterlin and Schaeffer (1999).

2   For further analysis of the relation of the cross-sectional happiness-age patterns to the life cycle patterns in the United States, see Easterlin and Schaeffer (1999), pp. 289 ff.

3   Loewenstein and Schkade (1999, p. 90) report other instances in which future changes in well-being are systematically projected to be greater than past.

4   See March and Simon's (1968) 'general model of adaptive motivated behaviour'. De la Croix (1998), building on Ramsey (1928), presents a formal economic model of well-being, using this approach. For similar models in psychology, see Michalos (1986, 1991).

5   For a review of studies of the relation between education and income, see Ashenfelter and Rouse (1999). The authors' survey concludes that education has an important causal impact on income independently of ability and family background.

6   For the cohort of 1941-50, the total sample size for the 3-year moving average is around 900 or more and the percentage of the cohort with a high school education or less fluctuates within a few percentage points of 44. For the cohort of 1931-40, the corresponding figures are 600 or more and 65; for that of 1921-30, 600 or more and 71.

7   The approach here is to follow a 'synthetic cohort' as in the happiness analysis described in Section 6.2.2. The analysis is more approximate, however, because the Roper 'good life' question has been asked only intermittently, the sample size is smaller, and the age reporting in the data is usually for groups of five years or more. For the analysis reported in Tables 6.4 and 6.5, I have paired the 1978 data for ages 18-29 with the 1994 data for ages 30-44 (roughly the birth cohort of 1950-64) and the 1978 data for ages 30-44 with the 1994 data for ages 45-59 (roughly the birth cohort of 1935-49).

8   Hirsch (1976, p. 61) discusses how the 'fulfillment of given wants generates new and higher order wants.' Cf. also Durkheim ([1930] 1952, p. 248); Leibenstein (1976, p. 197). Rainwater (1994) finds that in the United States the income perceived as necessary to get along rose between 1950 and 1986 in the same proportion as actual per capita income.

9   Kahneman (1999a) points out that adaptation level and aspiration level are two different concepts. It seems likely, however, that they change in tandem. As one adapts to improved performance at the ring toss, aspirations correspondingly increase.

Chapter 7

1 Economists sometimes describe their U-shaped finding as describing the ceteris paribus impact of aging on well-being. But the references above by economists to possible life cycle changes in aspirations make clear that the ceteris paribus characterization of their result is inappropriate, because aspirations are not held constant in their studies.

2 Headey and Wearing were among the first to reject the strong setpoint model, arguing from their longitudinal data that "life events influence SWB over and above the effects of personality" (1989, p. 731; cf. also Headey, Holmström, and Wearing 1994; Diener 1996). However, life events in the Headey-Wearing empirical analysis are not specific circumstances but an aggregate measure that combines numerous favorable and/or unfavorable experiences, each experience being assumed to have equal weight in determining satisfaction.

3 In the media this view has found expression as the "futile pursuit of happiness" (Gertner 2003).

4 This approach is sometimes termed multiple discrepancy theory (Michalos 1986, 1991; cf. also Diener et al. 1999; Solberg et al. 2002). The issue sometimes raised of a common bias due to personality or genetic factors in self-reports of happiness and domain satisfaction is discussed in Chapter 10.

5 More specifically, this estimation procedure yields probabilities for each response category – in the case of happiness, for example, the probabilities that happiness equals 1, 2, or 3 respectively. The adjusted mean value is obtained by multiplying the category value (1, 2, or 3) by the probability for that category, and summing the products.

6 Survival rates are from the 2001 United States life table available at http://www.ssa.gov/OACT/STATS/table4c6.html.

7 In discussing psychological strategies that might increase SWB, Parducci (1995, p. 161) describes another possible type of adaptation. People might "tune out" less happy domains and place more emphasis on happier ones – what would be equivalent in the present statistical analysis to shifting the relative weights of the domains in the regression in Table 7.1, column 4. But statistical tests give no evidence that this "across-domain" adaptation actually takes place. Indeed, in later life the tendency, on average, is to place greater weight on the less happy domain of health, and less weight on the more happy domain of finances.

Chapter 8

1 Some surveys give a slight edge to women (Frey and Stutzer 2002a, p. 54; Nolen-Hoeksema and Rusting 1999, p. 333).

2 As discussed in Chapter 7, Mroczek and Spiro estimate separate life cycle trajectories for males who died and those who remained alive, an analysis possible only with data following the same individuals as they age. Assuming Mroczek-Spiro estimates are applicable here, then the upward bias in male happiness in Figure 8.1 is probably small for males up to, say, their mid-seventies.

No comparable estimate of the mortality bias is available for females. Their lower mortality implies a smaller upward bias than for males. However, it is likely that the females lost through mortality are less likely to be in unions than their male counterparts, and the shortfall in their happiness relative to surviving females, greater than the 8 percent figure for males. If so, this would make for a greater upward bias in happiness than for males. Our tentative conclusion is that differential bias due to mortality probably has little impact on the X-pattern through the mid-seventies; thereafter male happiness may be somewhat elevated relative to females, because of ever-widening differential mortality.

3   The scales for family and health satisfaction in the figure are one-third as large as for happiness and financial satisfaction because the range in the number of their response categories is three times greater.

4   We are grateful to John Helliwell and Haifang Huang for providing us with tabulations from the Eurobarometer data 1970–1999 of mean life satisfaction by age and cohort. The number of female respondents is 419,441; of male respondents, 393,991. Eastern Europe is not included in the survey.

Chapter 9

1   We are grateful to John Strauss for suggesting this procedure.

Chapter 10

1   An exception is the article by Blanchflower and Oswald (2000), which focuses on the trend of happiness among younger persons since 1972. However, their analysis controls for differences among cohorts in life circumstances, whereas the present analysis does not. If one wants to know, say, how the "baby bust" cohort compares with its predecessors, one needs to take account of such factors as its distinctive employment and family circumstances (Easterlin 1987).

References

1. Introduction by the Editors

Easterlin, R. A. (2004). The Reluctant Economist: Perspectives on Economics, Economic History, and Demography, Cambridge: Cambridge University Press.

Macunovich, D. J. (1997). A Conversation with Richard Easterlin, in: Journal of Population Economics, 10(2): 119-36.

Sokoloff, K. (2008). Richard A. Easterlin, in: Lyons, J. S., Cain, L. P., Williamson, S. H. (Eds.), Reflections on the Cliometrics Revolution: Conversations with Economic Historians, Milton Park: Routledge, 309-21.

Stiglitz, J. E., Sen, A., Fitoussi, J. P. et al. (2009), Report by the Commission on the Measurement of Economic Performance and Social Progress.
www.stiglitz-senfitoussi.fr/documents/rapport_anglais.pdf

2. Bibliography Sections II-IV

Abramovitz, M. (1959). The Welfare Interpretation of Secular Trends in National Income and Product, in: Abramovitz, M., Alchian, A., Arrow, K. J., Baran, P., A., Cartwright, P. W., Chenery, H. B., Hilton, G. W., Houthakker, H. S., Lindblom, C. E., Reder, M. W., Scitovsky, T., Shaw, E. S., Tarshis, L., The Allocation of Economic Resources: Essays in Honor of Bernard Francis Haley, Stanford, CA: Stanford University Press, 1-22.

Abramovitz, M. (1979). Economic Growth and its Discontents, in: Boskin, M. J. (Ed.), Economics and Human Welfare: Essays in Honour of Tibor Scitovsky, New York, NY: Academic Press, 3-22.

AIPO Poll (1970). Reported in San Francisco Chronicle, January 14, 1971.

Alber, J., Kohler, U. (2008). Informal Food Production in the Enlarged European Union, in: Social Indicators Research, 89(1): 113-27.

Alesina, A., Fuchs-Schündeln, N. (2007). Goodbye Lenin (or not)? The Effect of Communism on People, in: American Economic Review, 97(4): 1507-28.

Anand, S., Ravallion, M. (1993). Human Development in Poor Countries: On the Role of Private Incomes and Public Services, in: Journal of Economic Perspectives, 7(1): 133-50.

Andorka, R., Kolosi, T., Rose, R., Vukovich, G. (Eds.) (1999). A Society Transformed: Hungary in Time – Space Perspective, Budapest: Central European University Press.

Andrews, F. M. (Ed.) (1986). Research on the Quality of Life, Ann Arbor, MI: Survey Research Center, Institute for Social Research, University of Michigan.

Andrews, F. M., Withey, S. B. (1976a). Developing Measures of Perceived Life Quality: Results from Several National Surveys, in: Social Indicator Research, 1(1): 1-26.

References

Andrews, F. M., Withey, S. B. (1976b). Social Indicators of Well-Being: Americans' Perceptions of Life Quality, New York, NY: Plenum Press.

Argyle, M. (1999). Causes and Correlates of Happiness, in: Kahneman, D., Diener, E. Schwarz, N. (Eds.), Well-Being: The Foundations of Hedonic Psychology, New York, NY: Russell Sage, 353–73.

Argyle, M. (2001). The Psychology of Happiness, New York, NY: Routledge.

Ashenfelter, O., Rouse, C. (1999). Schooling, Intelligence, and Income in America: Cracks in the Bell Curve, NBER Working Paper No. 6902.

Bachman, J. G., Johnston, L. D., O'Malley, P. M. (1980). Monitoring the Future: Questionnaire Responses from the Nation's High School Seniors, Ann Arbor, MI: Survey Research Center, Institute for Social Research, University of Michigan.

Bachman, J. G., O'Malley P. M. (1984). Yea-Saying, Nay-Saying, and Going to Extremes: Are Black-White Differences in Survey Results Due to Response Styles?, in: Public Opinion Quarterly, 48(2): 409–27.

Barr, N. (2005). Labor Markets and Social Policy in Central and Eastern Europe: The Accession and Beyond, Washington, DC: The World Bank.

Bell, D. (1970). Unstable America, in: Encounter, 34(June): 11–26.

Belson, W. A. (1966). The Effects of Reversing the Presentation Order of Verbal Rating Scales, in: Journal of Advertising Research, 6(4): 30–37.

Berkowitz, L. (1971). Frustrations, Comparisons, and Other Sources of Emotion Arousal as Contributors to Social Unrest, in: Journal of Social Issues, 28(1): 77–91.

Bertrand, M., Mullainathan, S. (2001). Do People Mean What They Say? Implications for Subjective Survey Data, in: American Economic Review, 91(2): 67–72.

Blanchflower, D. G., (2009). International Evidence on Well-Being, in: Krueger, A. B. (Ed.), Measuring the Subjective Well-Being of Nations: National Accounts of Time Use and Well-Being, Chicago, IL: University of Chicago Press, 155-226.

Blanchflower, D. G., Oswald, A. (2000). The Rising Well-Being of the Young, in: Blanchflower, D. G., Freeman, R. B. (Eds.), Youth Employment and Joblessness in Advanced Countries, Chicago, IL: University of Chicago Press and NBER

Blanchflower, D. G., Oswald, A. (2004). Well-Being over Time in Britain and the USA, in: Journal of Public Economics, 88(7-8): 1359–86.

Blanchflower, D. G., Oswald, A. (2007). Is Well-Being U-Shaped over the Life Cycle?, IZA Discussion Paper 3075, Bonn: IZA.

Block, J. (1965). The Challenge of Response Sets, New York, NY: Appleton.

Blundell, R., Preston, I., Walker, I. (Eds.) (1994). The Measurement of Household Welfare, Cambridge: Cambridge University Press.

Boguszak, M., Gabal, I., Rak, V. (1990). Czechoslovakia – January 1990 (Survey Report), Prague: Association for Independent Social Analysis.

Bok, D. (2010). The Politics of Happiness: What Government Can Learn from the New Research on Well-Being, Princeton, NJ: Princeton University Press.

Bradburn, N. M. (1969). The Structure of Psychological Well-Being, Chicago, IL: Aldine.

Brady, D. S., Friedman, R. (1947). Savings and the Income Distribution, in: NBER (Ed.), Studies in Income and Wealth, Vol. 10, New York, NY: NBER, 247–65.

Brainerd, E. (1998). Winners and Losers in Russia's Economic Transition, in: American Economic Review, 88(5): 1094–116.

Brainerd, E., Cutler, D. M. (2005). Autopsy on an Empire: Understanding Mortality in Russia and the Former Soviet Union, in: Journal of Economic Perspectives, 19(1): 107–30.

Brickman, P., Campbell, D. T. (1971). Hedonic Relativism and Planning the Good Society, in: Appley, M. H. (Ed.), Adaptation Level Theory: A Symposium, New York, NY: Academic Press, 287–302.

Brickman, P., Coates, D. (1978). Lottery Winners and Accident Victims: Is Happiness Relative?, in: Journal of Personality and Social Psychology, 36(8): 917–27.

Brown, D. L., Kulcsár, L. J., Kulcsár, L., Obádovics, C. (2005). Post-Socialist Restructuring and Population Redistribution in Hungary, in: Rural Sociology, 70(3): 336–59.

Bruni, L., Pier L. P. (2005). Economics and Happiness: Framing the Analysis, Oxford: Oxford University Press.

Busch, U. (1999). Sozialtransfers für Ostdeutschland – Eine Kritische Bilanz, in: Utopie Kreativ, 105: 12-24.

Campbell, A. (1972). Aspirations, Satisfaction, and Fulfillment: in: Campbell, A., Converse, P. E. (Eds.), The Human Meaning of Social Change, New York, NY: Russell Sage, 441–66.

Campbell, A. (1981). The Sense of Well-Being in America, New York, NY: McGraw-Hill.

Campbell, A., Converse, P. E., Rodgers, W. L. (1976). The Quality of American Life: Perceptions, Evaluations, and Satisfactions, New York, NY: Russell Sage.

Campos, N. F., Coricelli, F. (2002). Growth in Transition: What We Know, What We Don't, and What We Should, in: Journal of Economic Literature, 40(3): 793–836.

Cantril, H. (1951). Public Opinion, 1935–1946, Princeton, NJ: Princeton University Press.

Cantril, H. (1965). The Pattern of Human Concerns, New Brunswick, NJ: Rutgers University Press.

Casper, L. M., Cohen, P. N. (2000). How Does POSSLQ Measure Up? Historical Estimates of Cohabitation, in: Demography, 37(2): 237–45.

Chan, J. C. (1991). Response-Order Effects in Likert-type Scales, in: Educational and Psychological Measurement, 51(3): 531–40.

Charles, S. T., Reynolds, C. A, Gatz, M. (2001). Age-Related Differences and Change in Positive and Negative Affect over 23 Years, in: Journal of Personality and Social Psychology, 80(1): 136–51.

Clark, A. E. (2005). What Makes a Good Job? Evidence from OECD Countries, in: Bazen, S., Lucifora, C., Salverda, W. (Eds.), Job Quality and Employer Behaviour, Basingstoke: Palgrave MacMillan, 11–30.

Clark, A. E., Frijters, P., Shields, M. A. (2008). Relative Income, Happiness, and Utility: An Explanation for the Easterlin Paradox and Other Puzzles, in: Journal of Economic Literature, 46(1): 95–144.

Clark, A. E., Oswald, A. J. (1994). Unhappiness and Unemployment, in: Economic Journal, 104(424): 648–59.

Commission on Growth and Development (2008). The Growth Report: Strategies for Sustained Growth and Inclusive Development, Washington, DC: The World Bank.

Costa Jr., P. T., Zonderman, A. B., McCrae, R. R., Cornoni-Huntley, J., Locke, B. Z., Barbano, H E. (1987). Longitudinal Analyses of Psychological Well-Being in a National Sample: Stability of Mean Levels, in: Journal of Gerontology, 42(1): 50–5.

Coyle, D. (2007). The Soulful Science, Princeton, NJ: Princeton University Press.

Csikszentmihalyi, M., Hunter, J. (2003). Happiness in Everyday Life: The Uses of Experience Sampling, in: Journal of Happiness Studies, 4(2): 185–99.

Cummins, R. A. (1996). The Domains of Life Satisfaction: An Attempt to Order Chaos, in: Social Indicators Research, 38(3): 303–28.

Cutler, D., Angus D., Lleras-Muney, A. (2006). The Determinants of Mortality, in: Journal of Economic Perspectives, 20(3): 97–120.

Davies, J. C. (1962). Toward a Theory of Revolution, in: American Sociological Review, 27(1): 5–19.

Davis, J. A. (1965). Education for Positive Mental Health, Chicago, IL: Aldine.

Davis, J. A., Smith, T. W. (2002). General Social Surveys, 1972–2002, Chicago: National Opinion Research Center.

Davis, L. E., Easterlin, R. A., Parker, W. N. (1972). American Economic Growth: An Economist's History of the United States, New York, NY: Harper.

Day, R. H. (1986). On Endogenous Preferences and Adaptive Economizing, in: Day, R. H., Eliasson, G. (Eds.), The Dynamics of Market Economies, Amsterdam: North Holland, 153–70.

De la Croix, D. (1998). Growth and the Relativity of Satisfaction, in: Mathematical Social Sciences, 100(36): 105–25.

Deaton, A. (2008). Income, Health, and Well-Being around the World: Evidence from the Gallup World Poll, in: Journal of Economic Perspectives, 22(2): 53–72.

Delbes, C., Gaymu, J. (2002). The Shock of Widowhood on the Eve of Old Age: Male and Female Experiences, in: Population, 57(6): 885–914.

Di Tella, R., MacCulloch, R. (2008). Gross National Happiness as an Answer to the Easterlin Paradox?, in : Journal of Development Economics, 86(1): 22–42.

References

Di Tella, R., MacCulloch, R. J., Oswald, A. J. (2001). Preferences over Inflation and Unemployment: Evidence from Surveys of Happiness, in: American Economic Review, 91(1): 335–41.

Diaz-Serrano, L. (2006). Housing Satisfaction, Homeownership and Housing Mobility: A Panel Data Analysis for Twelve EU Countries, IZA Discussion Paper No. 2318.

Diener, E. (1984). Subjective Well-Being, in: Psychological Bulletin, 95(3): 542–75.

Diener, E. (1996). Traits Can Be Powerful, but Are not Enough: Lessons from Subjective Well-Being, in: Journal of Research in Personality, 30(3): 389–399.

Diener, E. (2000). Subjective Well-Being: The Science of Happiness and a Proposal for a National Index, in: American Psychologist, 55(1): 34–44.

Diener, E., Lucas, R. E (1999). Personality and Subjective Well-Being, in: Kahneman, D. Diener, E., Schwarz, N. (Eds.), Well-Being: The Foundations of Hedonic Psychology, New York, NY: Russell Sage, 213–29.

Diener, E., Lucas R. E., Schimmack, U., Helliwell, J. F. (2009). Well-Being for Public Policy, New York, NY: Oxford University Press.

Diener, E., Lucas, R. E., Scollon, C. N. (2006). Beyond the Hedonic Treadmill: Revising the Adaptation Theory of Well-Being, in: American Psychologist, 61(4): 305–14.

Diener, E., Oishi, S. (2000). Money and Happiness: Income and Subjective Well-Being across Nations, in: Diener, E., Suh, E. M. (Eds.), Culture and Subjective Well-Being, Cambridge, MA: MIT Press, 185–218.

Diener, E., Seligman, M. E. P. (2004). Beyond Money: Toward an Economy of Well-Being, in: Psychological Science in the Public Interest, 5(1): 1–31.

Diener, E., Suh, E. M., Lucas, R. E., Smith, H.L. (1999). Subjective Well-Being: Three Decades of Progress, in: Psychological Bulletin, 125(2): 276–302.

Directorate of General Research, European Commission (2005). Eurobarometer 63.1: Social Values, Science and Technology, downloaded from: http://www.gesis.org/en/data service/eurobarometer/

Donovan, N., Halpern, D. (2002). Life Satisfaction: The State of Knowledge and Implications for Government, UK Long Term Strategy Unit.

Dorn, D., Fischer, J. A. V., Kirchgassner, G., Sousa-Poza, A. (2007). Is it Culture or Democracy? The Impact of Democracy and Culture on Happiness, in: Social Indicators Research, 82(3): 505–26.

Dubnoff, S. (1985). How Much Income is Enough? Measuring Public Judgements, in: Public Opinion Quarterly, 49(3): 285–99.

Duesenberry, J. S. (1949). Income, Savings, and the Theory of Consumer Behaviour, Cambridge, MA: Harvard University Press.

Duncan, O. D. (1975). Does Money Buy Satisfaction?, in: Social Indicators Research, 2(3): 267–74.

Durkheim, E. (1996). Suicide: A Study in Sociology, New York, NY: Free Press.

Easterlin, R. A. (1969). Towards a Socio-Economic Theory of Fertility: a Survey of Recent Research on Economic Factors in American Fertility, in: Behrman, S.J., Corsa, Jr., L., Freedman, R. (Eds.), Fertility and Family Planning: A World View, Ann Arbor, MI: University of Michigan Press, 127–56.

Easterlin, R. A. (1973). Does Money Buy Happiness?, in: The Public Interest, 30: 3–10.

Easterlin, R. A. (1973). Relative Economic Status and the American Fertility Swing, in: Sheldon, E. B. (Ed.), Family Economic Behavior: Problems and Prospects, Philadelphia, PA: L. B. Lippincott, 170–223.

Easterlin, R. A. (1974). Does Economic Growth Improve the Human Lot?, in: David, P. A., Reder, M. S. (Eds.), Nations and Households in Economic Growth: Essays in Honour of Moses Abramovitz, New York, NY: Academic Press, 89-125. [Chapter 1 in this volume]

Easterlin, R. A. (1987). Birth and Fortune: The Impact of Numbers on Personal Welfare, Chicago, IL: University of Chicago Press.

Easterlin, R. A. (1995). Will Raising the Incomes of all Increase the Happiness of All?, in: Journal of Economic Behavior and Organization, 27(1), 35–47. [Chapter 2 in this volume]

Easterlin, R. A. (2000). The Worldwide Standard of Living Since 1800, in: Journal of Economic Perspectives, 14(1): 7–26.

References

Easterlin, R. A. (2001a). Income and Happiness: Towards a Unified Theory, in: Economic Journal, 111(473), 465–84. [Chapter 6 in this volume]

Easterlin, R. A. (2001b). Life Cycle Welfare: Trends and Differences, in: Journal of Happiness Studies, 2(1): 1–12.

Easterlin, R. A. (2003a). Happiness of Women and Men in Later Life: Nature, Determinants, and Prospects, in: Sirgy, M. J., Rahtz, D., Coskun Samli, A. (Eds.), Advances in Quality-of-Life Theory and Research, Dordrecht: Kluwer Academic Publishers, 13–26.

Easterlin, R. A. (2003b). Explaining Happiness, in: Proceedings of the National Academy of Sciences, 100(19): 11176–83. [Chapter 11 in this volume]

Easterlin, R. A. (2004). The Reluctant Economist: Perspectives on Economics, Economic History, and Demography, Cambridge: Cambridge University Press.

Easterlin, R. A. (2005a). Diminishing Marginal Utility of Income? Caveat Emptor, in: Social Indicators Research, 70(3): 243–55.

Easterlin, R. A. (2005b). Feeding the Illusion of Growth and Happiness: A Reply to Hagerty and Veenhoven, in: Social Indicators Research, 74(3): 429–43.

Easterlin, R. A. (2006). Life Cycle Happiness and Its Sources: Intersections of Psychology, Economics and Demography, in: Journal of Economic Psychology, 27(4): 463–82. [Chapter 7 in this volume]

Easterlin, R. A. (2009). Lost in Transition: Life Satisfaction on the Road to Capitalism, in: Journal of Economic Behavior and Organization, 71(2): 130–45. [Chapter 4 in this volume]

Easterlin, R. A., Angelescu, L. (2009). Happiness and Growth the World Over: Time Series Evidence on the Happiness-Income Paradox, IZA Discussion Paper No. 4060. [Chapter 5 in this volume]

Easterlin, R. A., Crimmins, E. A. (1991). Private Materialism, Personal Self-Fulfillment, Family Life, and Public Interest, in: Public Opinion Quarterly, 55(4): 499–533.

Easterlin, R. A., Plagnol, A. (2008). Life Satisfaction and Economic Conditions in East and West Germany Pre- and Post-Unification, in: Journal of Economic Behavior & Organization, 68(3): 433–44.

Easterlin, R. A., Schaeffer, C. M. (1999). Income and Subjective Well-Being over the Life Cycle, in: Ryff, C. D., Marshall, V. W. (Eds.), The Self and Society in Aging Processes, New York, NY: Springer, 279–301.

Easterlin, R. A., Sawangfa, O. (2009). Happiness and Domain Satisfaction: New Directions for the Economics of Happiness, in: Dutt, A. K., Radcliff, B. (Eds.), Happiness, Economics, and Politics: Towards a Multi-Disciplinary Approach, Cheltenham: Edward Elgar, 70–96. [Chapter 10 in this volume]

Easterlin, R. A., Sawangfa, O. (2010). Happiness and Economic Growth: Does the Cross-Section Predict Time Trends? Evidence from Developing Countries, in: Diener, E., Helliwell, J. F., Kahneman, D. (Eds.), International Differences in Well-Being, New York, NY: Oxford University Press, 166–216. [Chapter 3 in this volume]

Easterly, W. (1999). Life during Growth, in: Journal of Economic Growth, 4(3): 239–75.

Eckaus, R. S. (1972). Basic Economics, Boston, MA: Little, Brown.

Economic Commission for Europe (2003). Economic Survey of Europe, No. 1, New York and Geneva: United Nations.

Economic Report of the President (1993). Washington, DC: U.S. Government Printing Office.

Edwards, A. L. (1957). The Social Desirability Variable in Personality Assessment and Research, New York, NY: Holt.

Ekirch, A. A. (1944). The Idea of Progress in America, 1815–1860, New York: NY, Columbia University Press.

Emerson, R. W. (1860). Wealth, in: Emerson, R. W., The Conduct of Life, Boston, MA: Ticknor and Fields.

European Bank for Reconstruction and Development (2007). Transition Report 2007: People in Transition, London: European Bank for Reconstruction and Development.

Fox, L. (2003). Safety Nets in Transition Economies: A Primer. Social Safety Net Primer Series, Washington, DC: The World Bank.

References

Frank, R. H. (1985a). Choosing the Right Pond, New York, NY: Oxford University Press.

Frank, R. H. (1985b). The Demand for Unobservable and Other Nonpositional Goods, in: American Economic Review, 75(1): 101–16.

Frank, R. H. (1997). The Frame of Reference as a Public Good, in: Economic Journal, 107(445): 1832–47.

Frederick, S., Loewenstein, G. (1999). Hedonic Adaption, in: Kahneman, D., Diener, E., Schwarz, N. (Eds.), Well-Being: The Foundations of Hedonic Psychology, New York, NY: Russell Sage, 302–29.

Freedman, D. S. (1963). The Relation of Economic Status to Fertility, in: American Economic Review, 53(3): 412-26.

Freedman, D. S. (1975). Consumption of Modern Goods and Services and Its Relation to Fertility: A Study in Taiwan, in: Journal of Development Studies, 12(1): 95–117.

Frey, B. S. (2008). Happiness: A Revolution in Economics, Cambridge, MA: The MIT Press.

Frey, B. S., Stutzer, A. (1999). Measuring Preferences by Subjective Well-Being, in: Journal of Institutional and Theoretical Economics, 155(4): 755–78.

Frey, B. S., Stutzer, A. (2000). Happiness, Economy, and Institutions, in: Economic Journal, 110(466): 918–38.

Frey, B. S., Stutzer, A. (2002a). Happiness and Economics: How The Economy and Institutions Affect Well-Being, Princeton, NJ: Princeton University Press.

Frey, B. S., Stutzer, A., (2002b). What Can Economists Learn From Happiness Research?, in: Journal of Economic Literature, 40(2): 402–35.

Frijters P., Haisken-DeNew, J. P., Shields, M. A. (2004). Money Does Matter! Evidence from Increasing Real Income and Life Satisfaction in East Germany Following Reunification, in: American Economic Review, 94(3): 730–40.

Frijters, P., Geishecker, I., Haisken-DeNew, J. P., Shields, M. A. (2006). Can the Large Swings in Russian Life Satisfaction be Explained by Ups and Downs in Real Incomes?, in: Scandinavian Journal of Economics, 108(3): 433–58.

Frijters, P., Shields, M. A., Haisken-DeNew, J. P. (2004). Investigating the Patterns and Determinants of Life Satisfaction in Germany Following Reunification, in: Journal of Human Resources, 39(3): 649–74.

Fuchs, V. (1983). How We Live, Cambridge, MA: Harvard University Press.

Fuchs, V. R. (1967). Redefining Poverty and Redistributing Income, in: The Public Interest, 8: 88–95.

Fujita, F., Diener, E. (2005). Life Satisfaction Setpoint: Stability and Change, in: Journal of Personality and Social Psychology, 88(1): 158–64.

Galbraith, J. K. (1958). The Affluent Society, Boston, MA: Houghton.

Galbraith, J. K. (1967). Review of a Review, in: The Public Interest, 9: 109–18.

Gallie, D., Russell, H. (1998). Unemployment and Life Satisfaction: a Cross-Cultural Comparison, in: Archives Européennes de Sociologie, 39(2), 248–80.

Gallup, G. H. (1976). Human Needs and Satisfactions: A Global Survey, in: Public Opinion Quarterly, 40(4): 459–67.

Gassmann, F., de Neubourg, C. (2000). Coping with Little Means in Latvia, Quantitative Analysis of Qualitative Statements, Social Policy Research Series, Riga: Ministry of Welfare of the Republic of Latvia.

Gassmann, F., de Neubourg, C. (2002). Not only for the Poor: The Relevance of Coping Strategies to Make Ends Meet, Maastricht University, Mimeo.

George, L. K. (1992). Economic Status and Subjective Well-Being: A Review of the Literature and an Agenda for Future Research, in: Cutler, N. R., Gregg, D. W., Lawton, M. P. (Eds.), Aging, Money, and Life Satisfaction: Aspects of Financial Gerontology, New York, NY: Springer, 69–99.

Gertner, J. (2003). The Futile Pursuit of Happiness, The New York Times Magazine, September 7: 44–7, 86, 90–1.

Gilbert, M. et al. (1958). Comparative National Products and Price Levels, Paris: OEEC.

Glatzer, W., Bös, M. (1998). Subjective Attendants of Unification and Transformation in Germany, in: Social Indicators Research, 43(1-2): 171–96.

Glenn, N. D. (1996). Values, Attitudes, and the State of American Marriage, in Popenoe, D. Elshtain, J. B., Blankenhorn, D. (Eds.), Promises to Keep: Decline and Renewal of Marriage in America, Lanhman, MD: Rowman and Littlefield, 15–33.

Górniak, J. (2001). Poverty in Transition: Lessons from Eastern Europe and Central Asia, in: Grinspun, A. (Ed.), Choices for the Poor: Lessons from National Poverty Strategies, New York, NY: United Nations, 145–72.

Graham, C. (2005). Insights on Development from the Economics of Happiness, World Bank Research Observer, 20(2): 201–31.

Graham, C. (2008). The Economics of Happiness: New Lenses for Old Policy Puzzles, in: Durlauf, S., Blume L. (Eds.), The New Palgrave Dictionary of Economics, Basingstoke: Palgrave-MacMillan.

Graham, C., Pettinato, S. (2002). Happiness and Hardship: Opportunity and Insecurity in New Market Economies, Washington, DC: The Brookings Institution.

Guriev, S., Zhuravskaya, E. (2009). (Un)happiness in Transition, in: Journal of Economic Perspectives, 22(2): 143–68.

Gurin, G., Veroff, J., Feld, S. (1960). Americans View their Mental Health, New York, NY: Basic Books.

Gurr, T. R. (1970). Why Men Rebel, Princeton, NJ: Princeton University Press.

Hagen, E. E. (1962). On the Theory of Social Change: How Economic Growth Begins, Homewood, IL: Dorsey Press.

Hagerty, M. R., Veenhoven, R. (2003). Wealth and Happiness Revisited – Growing National Income Does Go with Greater Happiness, in: Social Indicators Research, 64(1): 1–27.

Hagerty, M. R., Veenhoven, R. (2006). Rising Happiness in Nations 1946-2004: A Reply to Easterlin, in: Social Indicators Research, 79(3): 421–436.

Hahnel, R., Albert, M. (1990). Quiet Revolution in Welfare Economics, Princeton, NJ: Princeton University Press.

Haisken-DeNew, J. P., Frick, J. R. (Eds.) (2005). Desktop Companion to the German Socio-Economic Panel (GSOEP), Version 8.0, Berlin: DIW (German Institute for Economic Research).

Halpern, D. (2010). The Hidden Wealth of Nations, Cambridge: Polity Press.

Hansen, T., Slagsvold, B., Moum, T. (2008). Financial Satisfaction in Old Age: A Satisfaction Paradox or a Result of Accumulated Wealth?, in: Social Indicators Research, 89(2): 323–47.

Hausman, D., McPherson, M. S. (1993). Taking Ethics Seriously: Economics and Contemporary Moral Philosophy, in: Journal of Economic Literature, 31(2): 671–731.

Havrylyshyn, O. (2006). Divergent Paths in Post-Communist Transformation, Basingstoke: Palgrave Macmillan.

Hayo, B., Seifert, W. (2003). Subjective Economic Well-Being in Eastern Europe, in: Journal of Economic Psychology, 24(3): 329–48.

Headey, B., Andorka, R., Krause, P. (1995). Political Legitimacy versus Economic Imperatives in System Transformation: Hungary and East Germany 1990-93, in: Social Indicators Research, 36(3): 247–273.

Headey, B., Holmström, E., Wearing, A. (1984). The Impact of Life Events and Changes in Domain Satisfaction on Well-being, in: Social Indicators Research, 15(3): 203–27.

Headey, B., Veenhoven, R., Wearing, A. (1991). Top-down versus Bottom-up Theories of Subjective Well-being, in: Social Indicators Research, 24(1): 81–100.

Headey, B., Wearing, A. (1989). Personality, Life Events, and Subjective Well-Being: Toward a Dynamic Equilibrium Model, in: Journal of Personality and Social Psychology, 57(4): 731–9.

Helliwell, J. F., Putnam, R. D. (2004). The Social Context of Well-Being, in: Articles from Philosophical Transactions of the Royal Society B, Biological Sciences, 359(1449): 1435–46.

Helson, H. (1964). Adaptation-Level Theory, New York, NY: Harper and Row.

Herzog, A. R., Rodgers, W. L., Woodworth, J. (1982). Subjective Well-Being among Different Age Groups, Ann Arbor, MI: University of Michigan, Institute for Social Research.

Heston, A., Summers, R., Aten, B. (2006). Penn World Table Version 6.2, University of Pennsylvania: Center for International Comparisons of Production, Income and Prices.

Hirata, J. (2001). Happiness and Economics: Enriching Economic Theory with Empirical Psychology, Unpublished Master Thesis, Maastricht: Maastricht University.

Hirsch, F. (1976). Social Limits to Growth, Cambridge, MA: Harvard University Press.

References

Hollander, H. (2001). On the Validity of Utility Statements: Standard Theory versus Duesenberry's?, in: Journal of Economic Behavior and Organization, 45(3): 227-49.

Hornans, G. C. (1961). Social Behavior: Its Elementary Forms, New York, NY: Harcourt.

Houthakker, H. S., Pollak, R. A. (forthcoming). The Theory of Consumer's Choice. San Francisco, CA: Holden-Day.

Hsieh, C.M. (2003). Income, Age and Financial Satisfaction, in: International Journal of Aging & Human Development, 56(2): 89-112.

Huang, Y., Bocchi, A. M. (Eds.) (2009). Reshaping Economic Geography in East Asia, Washington DC: The World Bank.

Hyman, H. H. (1968). Reference Groups, in: Sills, D. L. (Ed.), International Encyclopedia of the Social Sciences, Vol. XIII, New York, NY: Macmillan, 353-61.

Idler, E. L., Benyamini, Y. (1997). Self-Rated Health and Mortality: A Review of Twenty-Seven Community Studies, in: Journal of Health and Social Behavior, 38(1): 21-37.

Inglehart, R. (1988). The Renaissance of Political Culture, in: American Political Science Review, 82(4): 1203-30.

Inglehart, R., Foa, R., Peterson, C., Wetzel, C. (2008). Development, Freedom, and Rising Happiness: A Global Perspective (1981-2007), in: Perspectives on Psychological Science, 3(4): 264-85.

Inglehart, R., Klingemann, H.-D. (2000). Genes, Culture, Democracy, and Happiness, in: Diener, E. Suh, E. M. (Eds), Culture and Subjective Well-being, Cambridge, MA: MIT Press, 165-84.

Inglehart, R., Rabier, J. (1986). Aspirations Adapt to Situations – But Why are the Belgians So Much Happier Than the French?, in: Andrews, F. M. (Ed.), Research on the Quality of Life, Ann Arbour, MI: Survey Research Centre, Institute for Social Research, University of Michigan, 1-56.

Inglehart, R., Reif, K. (1992). European Communities Studies, 1970-1989: Cumulative File, Ann Arbour, MI: Inter-University Consortium for Political and Social Research.

Inkeles, A. (1960). Industrial Man: The Relation of Status to Experience, Perception, and Value, in: American Journal of Sociology, 66(1): 1-31.

Inkeles, A. (1993). Industrialization, Modernization and the Quality of Life, in: International Journal of Comparative Sociology, 34(1-2): 1-23.

Inkeles, A., Diamond, L. (1980). Personal Development and National Development: A Cross-National Perspective, in: Szalai, A., Andrews, F. M. (Eds.), The Quality of Life: Comparative Studies, London: Sage, 73-109.

Johnson, D. R., Wu, J. (2002). An Empirical Test of Crisis, Social Selection, and Role Explanations of the Relationship between Marital Disruption and Psychological Distress: A Pooled Time-Series Analysis of Four-Wave Panel Data, in: Journal of Marriage and Family, 64(1), 211-24.

Johnson, H. G. (1967). Money, Trade, and Economic Growth, Cambridge, MA: Harvard University Press.

Kahneman, D. (1999). Objective Happiness, in: Kahneman, D., Diener, E., Schwarz, N. (Eds.), Well-Being: The Foundations of Hedonic Psychology, New York, NY: Russell Sage, 3-27.

Kahneman, D. (2003). A Psychological Perspective on Economics, in: American Economic Association Papers and Proceedings, 93(2): 162-68.

Kahneman, D. (2008). The Sad Tale of the Aspiration Treadmill, Edge World Question Center at http://www.edge.org/q2008/q08_17.html#kahneman

Kahneman, D., Diener, E., Schwarz N. (Eds.) (1999). Well-Being: The Foundations of Hedonic Psychology, New York, NY: Russell Sage.

Kahneman, D., Knetsch, J. L., Thaler, R. H. (1991). Anomalies: The Endowment Effect, Loss Aversion, and Status Quo Bias, in: Journal of Economic Perspectives, 5(1): 193-206.

Kahneman, D., Krueger, A. B. (2006). Developments in the Measurement of Subjective Well-being, in: Journal of Economic Perspectives, 20(1): 3-24.

Kahneman, D., Krueger, A. B., Schkade, D. A., Schwarz, N., Stone, A. A. (2004). A Survey Method for Characterizing Daily Life Experience: The Day Reconstruction Method (DRM), in: Science, 306(5702): 1776-80.

Kahneman, D., Snell, J. (1992). Predicting Taste Change: Do People Know What They Will Like?, in: Journal of Behavioral Decision-Making, 5(3): 187-200.

Kahneman, D., Wakker, P. P., Sarin, R. (1997). Back to Bentham? Explorations of Experienced Utility, in: Quarterly Journal of Economics, 112(2): 375–405.

Kammann, R. (1983). Objective Circumstances, Life Satisfactions, and Sense of Well-being: Consistencies across Time and Place, in: New Zealand Journal of Psychology, 12(1): 14–22.

Katona, G. (1951). Psychological Analysis of Economic Behavior, New York, NY: McGraw-Hill.

Katona, G., Strumpel, B., Zahn, E. (1971). Aspirations and Affluence, New York, NY: McGraw-Hill.

Knight, J. R., Gunatilaka, R. (2009). Does Economic Growth in China Raise Happiness?, Paper presented to the Conference on Finance and Economic Performance in China, China Economic Research Center, Stockholm School of Economics.

Knight, J. R., Gunatilaka, R. (2010). Great Expectations? The Subjective Well-Being of Rural Urban Migrants, in: World Development, 38(1): 113-24.

Kuran, T., (1991). Now Out of Never: The Element of Surprise in the East European Revolution of 1989, in: World Politics, 44: 7–48.

Kusago, T. (2007). Rethinking of Economic Growth and Life Satisfaction in Post-WWII Japan – A Fresh Approach, in: Social Indicators Research, 81(1): 79–102.

Kuznets, S. (1948). National Income: A New Version, in: The Review of Economics and Statistics, 30(3): 151-79.

Kuznets, S., Epstein, L., Jenks, E. (1941). National Income and Its Composition, 1919–1938, Volume I, New York, NY: NBER.

Lane, R. E. (1993). Does Money Buy Happiness?, in: The Public Interest, 113, 56–65.

Layard, R. (1980). Human Satisfactions and Public Policy, in: Economic Journal, 90(363): 737–50.

Layard, R. (2005). Happiness: Lessons from a New Science, New York, NY: Penguin Press.

Leibenstein, H. (1976). Beyond Economic Man, New York, NY: Harvard University Press.

Lelkes, O. (2006). Tasting Freedom: Happiness, Religion and Economic Transition, in: Journal of Economic Behavior and Organization, 59(2): 173–94.

Lewin, K., Dembo, T., Festinger, L., Sears, P. S. (1944). Level of Aspiration, in: Hunt, J. McV. (Ed.), Personality and the Behavior Disorders, New York, NY: Ronald Press.

Lewin, S. (1996). Economics and Psychology: Lessons for Our Own Day from the Early Twentieth Century, in: Journal of Economic Literature, 34(3): 1293–323.

Lipset, S. M. (1960). Political Man: The Social Bases of Politics, Garden City, NY: Doubleday.

Lipset, S. M., Schneider, W. (1987). The Confidence Gap: Business, Labor, and Government in the Public Mind, Baltimore, MD: Johns Hopkins University Press.

Little, I. M. D. (1950). A Critique of Welfare Economics, London and New York, NY: Oxford University Press.

Loewenstein, G., Schkade, D. (1999). Wouldn't It Be Nice? Predicting Future Feelings, in: Kahneman, D., Diener, E, Schwarz, N. (Eds.), Well-Being: The Foundations of Hedonic Psychology, New York: Russell Sage, 87–105.

Lucas, R. E., Clark, A. E., Georgellis, Y., Diener, E. (2003). Reexamining Adaptation and the Set Point Model of Happiness: Reactions to Changes in Marital Status, in: Journal of Personality and Social Psychology, 84(3): 527–39.

Lucas, R. E., Clark, A. E., Georgellis, Y., Diener, E. (2004). Unemployment Alters the Set Point for Life Satisfaction, in: Psychological Science, 15(1): 8–13.

Lykken, D. (1999). Happiness: What Studies on Twins Show Us about Nature, Nurture, and the Happiness Set-Point, New York, NY: Golden Books.

Lykken, D., Tellegen, A. (1996). Happiness is a Stochastic Phenomenon, in: Psychological Science, 7(3): 180–9.

Lyubomirsky, S. (2001). Why Are some People Happier than Others? The Role of Cognitive and Motivational Processes on Well-Being, in: American Psychologist, 56(3): 239–49.

Mack, R. P. (1956). Trends in American Consumption and the Aspiration to Consume, in: American Economic Review, 46(1): 55–68.

Macunovich, D. J. (1997). A Conversation with Richard Easterlin, in: Journal of Population Economics, 10(2): 119-36.

References

Maddison, A. (1991). Dynamic Forces in Capitalist Development, Oxford: Oxford University Press.

Maddison, A. (2003). The World Economy: Historical Statistics (CD-ROM), Paris: OECD.

March, J. G., Simon, H. A. (1958). Organizations, New York, NY: John Wiley.

Markus, C. B. (1986). Stability and Change in Political Attitudes: Observed, Recalled, and Explained, in: Political Behavior, 8(1): 21–44.

McClelland, D. C. (1961). The Achieving Society, Princeton, NJ: Van Nostrand Reinhold.

McCrae, R. R., Costa Jr., P. T., (1990). Personality in Adulthood, New York, NY: Guilford.

McLanahan, S., Sorensen, A. B. (1985). Life Events and Psychological Well-Being over the Life Course, in: Elder Jr., C. H. (Ed), Life Course Dynamics: Trajectories and Transitions, 1968–1980, Ithaca, NY: Cornell University Press, 217–38.

Mehnert, T., Krauss, H. H., Nadler, R., Boyd, M. (1990). Correlates of Life Satisfaction in Those with Disabling Conditions, in: Rehabilitation Psychology, 35(1): 3–17.

Merton, R. K. (1968). Social Theory and Social Structure, New York, NY: Free Press.

Michalos, A. C. (1986). Job Satisfaction, Marital Satisfaction and the Quality of Life, in: Andrews F. M. (Ed.), Research on the Quality of Life, Ann Arbor, MI: University of Michigan, Survey Research Center, Institute for Social Research, 57–83.

Michalos, A. C. (1991). Global Report on Student Well-Being: Vol. I, Life Satisfactions and Happiness, New York, NY: Springer.

Michalos, A. C., Zumbo, B. D., Hubley, A. (2000). Health and the Quality of Life, in: Social Indicators Research, 51(3): 245–86.

Mickiewicz, T. (2005). Economic Transition in Central Europe and the Commonwealth of Independent States, Basingstoke: Palgrave Macmillan.

Milanovic, B. (1997). Income, Inequality, and Poverty during the Transition from Planned to Market Economy, Washington, DC: The World Bank.

Milanovic, B. (1999). Explaining the Increase in Inequality during the Transition, in: Economics of Transition, 7(2): 299–341.

Mishan, E. J. (1968). Welfare Economics, in: International Encyclopedia of the Social Sciences, Vol. 16, New York, NY: Macmillan, 504–12.

Mishan, E. J. (1969). Welfare Economics: Ten Introductory Essays, New York, NY: Random House.

Modigliani, F. (1949). Fluctuations in the Saving-Income Ratio: A Problem in Economic Forecasting, in: Conference on Research in Income and Wealth, Studies in Income and Wealth, Vol. XI, New York, NY: NBER, 371–443.

Møller, V. (1998). Quality of Life in South Africa: Post-Apartheid Trends, in: Social Indicators Research, 43(1-2): 27–68.

Møller, V. (2001). Happiness Trends under Democracy: Where will the New South African Set-level Come to Rest?, in: Journal of Happiness Studies, 2(1): 33–53.

Møller, V. (2007). Researching Quality of Life in A Developing Country: Lessons from the South Africa Case, in: Gough, I., McGregor, J. A. (Eds.), Wellbeing in Developing Countries: From Theory to Research. Cambridge: Cambridge University Press, 242–58.

Morawetz, D., Atia, E., Bin-Nun, G., Felous, L., Gariplerden, Y., Harris, E., Soustiel, S., Tombros, G., Zarfaty, Y. (1977). Income Distribution and Self-Rated Happiness: Some Empirical Evidence, in: The Economic Journal, 87(347): 511–22.

Morgan, J. N. (1968). The Supply of Effort, the Measurement of Well-Being, and the Dynamics of Improvement, in: American Economic Review, 58(3): 1–39.

Morris, C. (1956). Varieties of Human Value, Chicago, IL: University of Chicago Press.

Mroczek, D. K., Kolarz, C. M. (1998). The Effect of Age on Positive and Negative Affect: a Developmental Perspective on Happiness, in: Journal of Personality and Social Psychology, 75(5), 1333–49.

Mroczek, D. K., Spiro III, A., (2005). Changes in Life Satisfaction during Adulthood: Findings from the Veterans Affairs Normative Aging Study, in: Journal of Personality and Social Psychology, 88(1): 189–202.

Murrell, P. (1996). How Far has the Transition Progressed?, in: Journal of Economic Perspectives, 10(2): 25–44.

Myers, D. G. (1992). The Pursuit of Happiness: Who is Happy and Why, New York, NY: William Morrow.

Myers, D. G. (1999) Close Relationships and Quality of Life, in: Kahneman, D., Diener, E, Schwarz, N. (Eds.), Well-Being: The Foundations of Hedonic Psychology, New York, NY: Russell Sage, 374-91.

Myers D. G. (2000). The Funds, Friends, and Faith of Happy People, in: American Psychologist, 55(1): 56-67.

National Opinion Research Centre, (1991) General Social Surveys, 1972-1991: Cumulative Codebook, Chicago, IL: National Opinion Research Centre.

National Opinion Research Center (1999). General Social Surveys, 1972-1998: Cumulative Codebook, Chicago, IL: National Opinion Research Center.

National Research Council (2003). Cities Transformed: Demographic Change and Its Implications in the Developing World, Washington, DC: National Academies Press.

Ng, Y. K. (1978). Economic Growth and Social Welfare: The Need for a Complete Study of Happiness, in: Kyklos, 31(4): 575-87.

Ng, Y. K (1997). A Case for Happiness, Cardinalism, and Interpersonal Comparability, in: Economic Journal, 107(445): 1848-58.

Noelle-Neumann, E. (1991). The German Revolution: The Historic Experiment of the Division and Unification of Germany as Reflected in Survey Research Findings, in: International Journal of Public Opinion Research, 3(3): 238-59.

Nolen-Hoeksema, S., Rusting, C. L. (1999). Gender Differences in Well-Being, in: Kahneman, D., Diener, E., Schwarz , N. (Eds.), Well-Being: the Foundations of Hedonic Psychology, New York, NY: Russell Sage, 330-50.

Nordhaus, W., Tobin, J. (1972). Is Growth Obsolete?, in: NBER, Economic Growth, 5th Anniversary Series, New York. NY: Columbia University Press, 1-80.

Nussbaum, M. C., Sen, A. (Eds.) (1993). The Quality of Life, Oxford: Clarendon Press.

OECD (1970). National Accounts Statistics: 1950-1968, Paris: OECD.

OECD (1992). Historical Statistics 1960-1990, Paris: OECD.

Offer, A. (Ed.) (1996). In Pursuit of the Quality of Life, New York, NY: Oxford University Press.

Olson, J. M., Herman, C. P., Zanna, M. P. (Eds.) (1986). Relative Deprivation and Social Comparison, The Ontario Symposium, Vol. 4, Hillsdale, NJ: Erlbaum.

Orenstein, M. A., Haas, M. R. (2005). Globalization and the Development of Welfare States in Central and Eastern Europe, in: Glatzer, M., Rueschemeyer, D. (Eds), Globalization and the Future of the Welfare State, Pittsburgh, PA: University of Pittsburgh Press, 130-52.

Oswald, A. J. (1997). Happiness and Economic Performance, in: Economic Journal, 107(445): 1815-31.

Parducci, A. (1995). Happiness, Pleasure, and Judgment: The Contextual Theory and Its Applications, Mahwah, NJ: Erlbaum.

Pascall, G., Manning, N. (2000). Gender and Social Policy: Comparing Welfare States in Central and Eastern Europe and the Former Soviet Union, in: Journal of European Social Policy, 10(3): 240-66.

Pettigrew, T. F. (1967). Social Evaluation Theory: Convergences and Applications, in: Levine, D. (Ed.), Nebraska Symposium on Motivation, Lincoln, NE: Nebraska University Press, 241-311.

Pfaff, M. (1973). Economic Life Styles, Values, and Subjective Welfare – an Empirical Approach: a Response, in: Sheldon, E. B. (Ed.), Family Economic Behavior: Problems and Prospects, Philadelphia, PA: J. B. Lippincott, 126-38.

Philipov, D. (2002). Fertility in Times of Discontinuous Societal Change: The Case of Central and Eastern Europe, MPIDR Working Paper 2002-024, Max Planck Institute for Demographic Research.

Philipov, D., Dorbritz, J. (2003). Demographic Consequences of Economic Transition in Countries of Central and Eastern Europe, Population Studies No. 39, Strasbourg: Council of Europe Publishing.

Pigou, A. C. (1932). The Economics of Welfare, London: Macmillan.

Plagnol, A. (forthcoming). Chasing the 'Good Life': Gender Differences in Work Aspirations of American Men and Women, in: Eckermann, E. (Ed.), Gender, Lifespan and Quality of Life: International Perspectives, New York, NY: Springer.

References

Plagnol, A., Easterlin, R. A. (2008). Aspirations, Attainments and Satisfaction: Life Cycle Differences between American Women and Men, in: Journal of Happiness Studies, 9(4): 601–19. [Chapter 9 in this volume]

Pollak, R. A. (1970). Habit Formation and Dynamic Demand Functions, in: Journal of Political Economy, 78(4): 745–63.

Pollak, R. A. (1976). Interdependent Preferences, in: American Economic Review, 66(3): 309–20.

Prescott, E. (2007). Review of Alessina (Alberto) and Gianazzi (Francesco) 'The Future of Europe: Reform or Decline', in: Economic Journal, 117(524): F648–F650.

Rabin, M. (1998). Psychology and Economics, in: Journal of Economic Literature, 36(1): 11–46.

Rainwater, L. (1974). What Money Buys, New York, NY: Basic Books.

Rainwater, L. (1990). Poverty and Equivalence as Social Constructions, paper presented at the Seminar on Families and Levels of Living: Observations and Analysis. European Association for Population Studies, Barcelona, October 29–31 (Luxembourg Income Study Working Paper No: 55).

Rainwater. L. (1994). Family Equivalence as a Social Construction, in: Ekert-Jaffe, O. (Ed.), Standards of Living and Families: Observation and Analysis, Montrouge: John Libbey Eurotext, 23–39.

Ramsey, F. (1928). A Mathematical Theory of Savings, Economic Journal, 38(152): 543–59.

Reynolds, S. L., Crimmins, E. M., Saito, Y. (1998). Cohort Differences in Disability and Disease, in: The Gerontologist, 38(5): 576–90.

Robinson, J. P., Shaver, P. R. (1969). Measures of Social Psychological Attitudes, Appendix B to Measures of Political Attitudes, Ann Arbor, MI: Survey Research Center, Institute for Social Research.

Robinson, J. P., Godbey, G. (1997). Time for Life: The Surprising Ways Americans Use their Time, University Park, PA: Pennsylvania State University Press.

Rojas, M. (2007). The Complexity of Well-Being: A Life Satisfaction Conception and Domains-of-Life Approach, in: Gough, I., McGregor, J.A. (Eds.), Well-Being in Developing Countries: From Theory to Research, New York, NY: Cambridge University Press, 259–80.

Roper-Starch Organization (1979). Roper Reports 79-1, Storrs, CT: University of Connecticut, The Roper Center.

Roper-Starch Organization (1995). Roper Reports 95-1, Storrs, CT: University of Connecticut, The Roper Center.

Rorer, L. G. (1965). The Great Response-Style Myth, in: Psychological Bulletin, 63(3): 129–56.

Rosenstein-Rodan, P. N. (1961). International Aid for Underdeveloped Countries, in: Review of Economics and Statistics, 43(2): 107–38.

Rostow, W. W. (1960). The Stages of Economic Growth, London and New York, NY: Cambridge University Press.

Salvatore N., Muñoz Sastre, M. T. (2001). Appraisal of Life: "Area" Versus "Dimension" Conceptualizations, in: Social Indicators Research, 53(3): 229–55.

Samuelson, P.A. (1947). Foundations of Economic Analysis, Cambridge, MA: Harvard University Press.

Sanfey, P., Teksoz, U. (2007). Does Transition Make you Happy?, in: Economics of Transition, 15(4): 707–31.

Saris, W. E. (2001). What Influences Subjective Well-Being in Russia?, in: Journal of Happiness Studies, 2(2): 137–46.

Saris, W. E., Andreenkova, A. (2001). Following Changes in Living Conditions and Happiness in Post Communist Russia: The Russet Panel, in: Journal of Happiness Studies, 2(2): 95–109.

Saris, W. E., Veenhoven, R., Scherpenzeel, A. C., Bunting, B. (Eds.) (1996). A Comparative Study of Satisfaction with Life in Europe, Budapest: Eötvös University Press.

Schmidt, L., Sevak, P. (2006). Gender, Marriage, and Asset Accumulation in the United States, in: Feminist Economics, 12(1–2): 139–66.

Schuman, H., Presser, S. (1981). Questions and Answers in Attitude Surveys: Experiments on Question Form, Wording and Context, New York, NY: Academic Press, 56–77.

Schwarz, N., Strack, F. (1999). Reports of Subjective Well-Being: Judgmental Processes and their Methodological Implications, in: Kahneman, D., Diener, E., Schwarz , N. (Eds.), Well-Being: the Foundations of Hedonic Psychology, New York, NY: Russell Sage, 61-84.

Schwarze, J. (1996). How Income Inequality Changed in Germany Following Reunification: An Empirical Analysis Using Decomposable Inequality Measures, in: Review of Income and Wealth, 42(1): 1-11.

Scitovsky, T. v.(1976). The Joyless Economy, Oxford: Oxford University Press.

Scitovsky, T. v. (1986). Human Desire and Economic Satisfaction, New York, NY: New York University Press.

Scitovsky, T. v.(1996). My Own Criticism of the Joyless Economy, in: Critical Review: A Journal of Politics and Society, 10(4): 595-605.

Seligman, M. E. P. (2002). Authentic Happiness: Using the New Positive Psychology to Realize Your Potential for Lasting Fulfillment, New York, NY: Free Press.

Siegel, S. (1964). Level of Aspiration and Decision Making, in: Brayfield, A. H., Messick, S. (Eds.), Decision and Choice. Contributions of Sidney Siegel, New York, NY: McGraw-Hill, 111-26.

Silver, M. (1980). Money and Happiness?: Towards 'Eudaimonology', in: Kyklos, 33(1): 157-60.

Simai, M. (2006). Poverty and Inequality in Eastern Europe and the CIS Transition Countries, Working Paper No. 17, New York: United Nations, Department of Economic and Social Affairs.

Smelser, N. J. (1962). Theory of Collective Behavior, New York, NY: Free Press.

Smith, T. W. (1979). Happiness: Time Trends, Seasonal Variations, Intersurvey Differences, and Other Mysteries, in: Social Psychology Quarterly, 42(1): 18-30.

Smith, V. K., Taylor Jr., D. H., Sloan, F. A. (2001). Longevity Expectations and Death: Can People Predict Their Own Demise?, in: American Economic Review, 91(4): 1126-34.

Smolensky, E. (1965). The Past and Present Poor, in: Chamber of Commerce of the United States Task Force on Economic Growth and Opportunity (Ed.), The Concept of Poverty, Washington, DC: Chamber of Commerce of the United States, 35-67.

Sobotka, T. (2002). Ten Years of Rapid Fertility Changes in the European Post-communist Countries: Evidence and Interpretation, Population Research Centre, University of Groningen, Working Paper Series 02-1, 1-86.

Sobotka, T. (2003). Re-emerging Diversity: Rapid Fertility Changes in Central and Eastern Europe after the Collapse of the Communist Regimes, in: Population, 58(4-5): 451-85.

Sokoloff, K. (2008). Richard A. Easterlin, in: Lyons, J. S., Cain, L. P., Williamson, S. H. (Eds.), Reflections on the Cliometrics Revolution: Conversations with Economic Historians: Routledge.

Solberg, E. C., Diener, E., Wirtz, D., Lucas, R. E., Oishi, S. (2002). Wanting, Having, and Satisfaction: Examining the Role of Desire Discrepancies in Satisfaction with Income, in: Journal of Personality and Social Psychology, 83(3): 725-34.

Spéder, Z., Paksi B., Elekes, Z. (1999). Anomie and Satisfaction at the Beginning of the Nineties, in: Kolosi, T., György Tóth, I., Vukovich, G. (Eds), Social Reporter 1998, Budapest: Social Research Informatics Center, 483-505.

Spence, M., Annez, P.C., Buckley, R.M. (Eds.) (2009). Urbanization and Growth. Washington, DC: The World Bank.

Stevenson, B., Wolfers, J. (2008). Economic Growth and Subjective Well-Being: Reassessing the Easterlin Paradox, in: Brookings Papers on Economic Activity, 2008(Spring): 1-87.

Stouffer, S. A., Suchman, E. A., De Vinney, L. C., Star, S. A., Williams jr., R. M. (1949). Studies in Social Psychology in World War II, Vol. I, The American Soldier: Adjustment During Army Life, Princeton, NJ: Princeton University Press.

Strumpel, B. (1973). Economic Life Styles, Values, and Subjective Welfare – An Empirical Approach, in: Sheldon, E.B. (Ed.) Family Economic Behavior: Problems and Prospects, Philadelphia, PA: J. B. Lippincott, 69-125.

Stutzer, A. (2004). The Role of Income Aspirations in Individual Happiness, in: Journal of Economic Behavior & Organization, 54(1): 89-109.

References

Sugden, R. (1993). Welfare, Resources, and Capabilities: A Review of 'Inequality Reexamined' by Amartya Sen, in: Journal of Economic Literature, 31(4): 1947–62.

Sugden, R. (2008). Capability, Happiness, and Opportunity, in: Bruni, L., Comim, F., Pugno, M. (Eds.), Capabilities and Happiness, New York, NY: Oxford University Press, 299–322.

Summers, R., Heston, A. (1991). The Penn World Table (Mark 5): An Expanded Set of International Comparisons, 1950–1988, in: Quarterly Journal of Economics, 106(2): 327–68.

Svejnar, J. (2002). Transition Economies: Performance and Challenges, in: Journal of Economic Perspectives, 16(1): 3–28.

Szivós, P., Giudici, C. (2004). Demographic Implications of Social Exclusion in Central and Eastern Europe, Population Studies No.46, Strasbourg: Council of Europe Publishing.

Tabbarah, R. B. (1972). The Adequacy of Income, A Social View of Economic Development, in: Journal of Development Studies, 8(3): 57–76.

Tammaru, T., Kulu, H., Kask, I. (2004). Urbanization, Suburbanization, and Counterurbanization in Estonia, in: Eurasian Geography and Economics, 45(3): 212–29.

Tomes, N. (1986). Income Distribution, Happiness, and Satisfaction: a Direct Test of the Interdependent Preferences Model, in: Journal of Economic Psychology, 7(4): 425–46.

TransMONEE Database, 2008. UNICEF Innocenti Research Centre, Florence. Available at http://www.unicef-irc.org/databases/transmonee/.

Tversky, A., Griffin, D. (1991). Endowment and Contrast in Judgments of Well-Being, in: Strack, F., Argyle M., Schwarz, N. (Eds.), Subjective Well-Being: An Interdisciplinary Perspective, Oxford: Pergamon Press, 101–18.

Tversky, A., Kahneman, D. (1991). Loss Aversion in Riskless Choice: A Reference-Dependent Model, in: Quarterly Journal of Economics, 106(4): 1039–61.

U.S. Bureau of the Census (1992). Measuring the Effect of Benefits and Taxes on Income and Poverty: 1979 to 1991, Current Population Reports: Consumer Income Series P–60, No. 182–RD.

UN-Habitat (United Nations Human Settlement Programme) (2004). The State of the World's Cities 2004/2005: Globalization and Urban Culture, London: Earthscan.

UNICEF (2001). A Decade of Transition, The MONEE Project: CEE/CIS/Baltics. Regional Monitoring Report No. 8, Florence: UNICEF.

UNICEF, (1999). Women in Transition, The MONEE Project: CEE/CIS/Baltics. Regional Monitoring Report No. 6. Florence: UNICEF.

Van Praag, B., Ferrer-i-Carbonell, A. (2004). Happiness Quantified: A Satisfaction Calculus Approach, Oxford: Oxford University Press, Chapter 3.

Van Praag, B., Frijters, P. (1999). The Measurement of Welfare and Well-Being: The Leyden Approach, in: Kahneman, D., Diener, E., Schwarz, N. (Eds.), Well-Being: The Foundations of Hedonic Psychology, New York, NY: Russell Sage, 413–33.

Van Praag, B., Frijters P., Ferrer-i-Carbonell, A. (2003). The Anatomy of Subjective Well-Being, in: Journal of Economic Behavior and Organization, 51(1): 29–49.

Van Praag, B., Kapteyn, A. (1973). Further Evidence on the Individual Welfare Function of Income, in: European Economic Review, 4(1): 33–62.

Varian, H.R. (1987). Intermediate Economics: A Modern Approach, New York, NY: Norton.

Veenhoven, R. (1991). Is Happiness Relative?, in: Social Indicators Research, 24(1): 1–34.

Veenhoven, R. (1993). Happiness in Nations, Subjective Appreciation of Life in 56 Nations 1946-1992, Rotterdam: Erasmus University.

Veenhoven, R. (2001). Are the Russians as Unhappy as they say they are?, in: Journal of Happiness Studies, 2(2): 111–36.

Veenhoven, R. (2005). World Database of Happiness. Available at: worlddatabaseofhappiness.eur.nl.

Vera-Toscano E., Ateca-Amestoy V., Serrano-del-Rosal R. (2006). Building Financial Satisfaction, in: Social Indicators Research, 77(2): 211–43.

Veroff, J., Douvan, E., Kulka, R. A. (1981). The Inner American: A Self-Portrait from 1957 to 1976, New York, NY: Basic Books.

Wachter, M.L. (1971a). A Labor Supply Model for Secondary Workers. Discussion Paper No. 226, Wharton School of Finance and Commerce, University of Pennsylvania.

Wachter, M. L. (1971b). A New Approach to the Equilibrium Labor Force, Wharton School of Finance and Commerce Discussion Paper No. 226.

Waite, L. J. (1995). Does Marriage Matter?, in: Demography, 32(4): 483–507.

Waite, L. J., Browning, D., Doherty, W. J., Gallagher, M., Luo, Y., Stanley, S. M. (2002). Does Divorce Make People Happy? Findings from a Study of Unhappy Marriages, New York, NY: Institute for American Values.

Waite, L. J., Luo Y. (2009). Marital Happiness and Marital Stability: Consequences for Psychological Well-Being, in: Social Science Research, 38(1): 201–12.

Warr, P. (1999). Well-Being and the Workplace, in: Kahneman, D., Diener, E., Schwarz, N. (Eds.), Well-Being: The Foundations of Hedonic Psychology, New York, NY: Russell Sage, 392–412.

Wessman, A. E. (1956). A Psychological Inquiry into Satisfactions and Happiness. Ph.D. Dissertation in Psychology, Princeton, NJ: Princeton University.

Wilson, W. (1967). Correlates of Avowed Happiness, Psychological Bulletin, 67(4): 294–306.

Winkelmann, L., Winkelmann, R. (1998). Why are the Unemployed so Unhappy? Evidence from Panel Data, in: Economica, 65(257): 1–15.

World and European Values Surveys Four Wave Integrated File, 1981–2004, v.20060423, 2006. World Value Survey Association (www.worldvaluessurvey.org) and European Values Study Foundation (www.europeanvalues.nl).

World Bank (1990). World Development Report 1990, Oxford: Oxford University Press.

World Bank (2000a). Balancing Protection and Opportunity: A Strategy for Social Protection in Transition Economies, Washington, DC: World Bank.

World Bank (2000b). Making Transition Work for Everyone: Poverty and Inequality in Europe and Central Asia, Washington, DC: World Bank.

World Bank (2002). Transition: The First Ten Years. Analysis and Lessons for Eastern Europe and the Former Soviet Union, Washington, DC: World Bank.

World Bank (2009). World Development Report 2009: Reshaping Economic Geography, Washington, DC: World Bank.

World Development Indicators. World Bank. Retrieved from February 26, 2008 to June 11, 2008 from http://go.worldbank.org/IW6ZUUHUZ0.

World Survey 111 (1965). International Data Library and Reference Service, University of California, Berkeley: Survey Research Center.

World Values Survey 2005 Official Data File, v.20081015, 2008. World Values Survey Association (www.worldvaluessurvey.org). Aggregate File Producer: ASEP/JDS, Madrid.

Wortman, C. B., Silver, R. C., Kessler, R. C. (1993). The Meaning of Loss and Adjustment to Bereavement, in: Stroebe, M. S., Stroebe, W., Hansson, R. O. (Eds.), Handbook of Bereavement: Theory, Research, and Intervention, New York, NY: Cambridge University Press, 349–66.

Yasuba, Y. (1991). Japan's Post-War Growth in Historical Perspective, Japan Forum, 57-70.

Zimmermann, A. C. (2007). Adaptation, Assets, and Aspirations, Three Essays on the Economics of Subjective Well-Being, Los Angeles, CA: University of Southern California.

Zimmermann, A. C., Easterlin, R. A. (2006). Happily Ever After? Cohabitation, Marriage, Divorce and Happiness in Germany, in: Population Development Review, 32(3): 511–28.

Index

Index

Index

278

Index

Y

Z

About the Author...

 **Richard A. Easterlin** received his education at the University of Pennsylvania and the Stevens Institute of Technology. He is currently University Professor and Professor of Economics at the University of Southern California. He is a past president of the Population Association of America and the Economic History Association, a Distinguished Fellow of the American Economic Association, a Fellow of the American Academy of Arts and Sciences and the Econometric Society, and a former Guggenheim Fellow. He joined IZA as Research Fellow in November 1999 and is a member of the National Academy of Sciences and holder of the Mellon Award for Excellence in Mentoring from the Center for Excellence in Teaching. From 2008 through 2009, Easterlin served as Vice President of the Western Economic Association International, and since 2004 he has been Vice President of the International Society for Quality of Life Studies, on whose Board of Directors he has been since 2003. In 2009 he received the IZA Prize in Labor Economics.

...and the Editors

__Holger Hinte__ received his Master's degree in Modern History, Political Science and Business Administration from Bonn University in 1991. Since 1989 he has worked for various members of the German Federal Parliament. From 1992 to 1998 he was Personal Assistant and Public Relations Consultant to the Federal Government Commissioner for Foreigners'
Issues. In October 1998 he joined IZA where he first served as Head of Public Relation and is currently acting as Head of Publications. He is also involved in various IZA research and policy advice activities. Holger Hinte is co-publisher of several books dealing with current changes in German society.

__Klaus F. Zimmermann__ has been Full Professor of Economics at Bonn University and Director of the Institute for the Study of Labor (IZA Bonn) since 1998. He is also President of the German Institute for Economic Research (DIW Berlin, since 2000), Honorary Professor of Economics at the Free University of Berlin (since 2001), and Honorary Professor at the Ren-
min University of Peking (since December 2006). He serves as Chairman of the Society of the German Economic Research Institutes (ARGE) (since 2005), advisor to the President of the EU Commission (2001–2003 and since 2005), economic advisor to the Prime Minister of North Rhine-Westphalia (since 2008), and is a member of the World Economic Forum's Global Agenda Council on Migration.

Printed in the USA/Agawam, MA
August 12, 2020

759669.042